THE DODGER

The Extraordinary Story of
Churchill's Cousin and
the Great Escape

Tim Carroll

WINDSOR
PARAGON

First published 2012
by Mainstream Publishing Company
This Large Print edition published 2012
by AudioGO Ltd
by arrangement with
Mainstream Publishing Company (Edinburgh) Ltd

Hardcover   ISBN: 978 1 4713 0118 6
Softcover   ISBN: 978 1 4713 0119 3

British Library Cataloguing in Publication Data available

Printed and bound in Great Britain by
MPG Books Group Limited

He was an incredible man: intelligent, fearless
. . . he never had anger or hatred for anyone,
not even the Germans. To me, he was like
a nineteenth-century man in the twentieth
century. I was impressed with his generosity of
spirit. He turned his back on a life of privilege
and put himself in dangerous situations.

*Christopher Reeve, actor, famous for his role in
the 1978 film* Superman, *who starred as Johnny
Dodge in the 1988 NBC television mini-series*
The Great Escape II: The Untold Story

He was one of the kindest and happiest men I
have ever met and was always ready to help
anybody in trouble.

*Jimmy James, Great Escaper,
and great friend of Johnny Dodge*

To Patrick Owen Carroll
Be like Johnny

AUTHOR'S NOTE

Throughout this narrative I refer to Johnny Dodge as 'Johnny'. This might imply a lack of objectivity, but it should not do so. I have been critical or wryly mocking of my subject on several occasions, not least because his wealth and lofty connections made Johnny's war a far more comfortable one than that endured by millions of the less fortunate. However, a central feature of Johnny's appeal is the uncommon affection he aroused in others of vastly different social backgrounds and political temperaments. They usually called him Johnny, and it would seem odd to refer to him as anything else.

ACKNOWLEDGEMENTS

I must begin with a posthumous thank you to the late Phyllis Boushall Dodge, whose tireless work on a prospective biography of Johnny did not come to fruition, but whose notes and indices form the bedrock upon which this book rests. Phyllis spent several years travelling the United States and Europe compiling an intricate card index of Johnny's life and times, and making voluminous notes. The result was a short unpublished biography entitled, 'John Bigelow Dodge, 1894–1960: A Précis of his Life', which she wrote in 1990. Without this material my job would have been very much harder. It was provided to me by Phyllis's daughter, Alice Berkeley, whom I must also thank, not least for her patience and good humour while I took far too long to write the book. Alice also supplied me with dozens of photographs belonging to Johnny, many of them taken in the prison camps he was incarcerated in during the war, and some of which appear in these pages. They are an invaluable treasure trove of material, much of which has never been seen before.

This book would not have been possible without the help of Jane Aitken, Johnny's former daughter-in-law, the ex-wife of his second son, Tony, and niece of Lord Beaverbrook, Johnny's great friend. Jane saved hundreds of Johnny's letters, diaries and other papers, and also some family photographs, another valuable material resource that, again, has formed the basis for much of this work. Jane's archive is remarkable in that it charts Johnny's life from his very first letters to his mother Flora when he was a boy of five at the Fay School in Massachusetts, through his adventures in the Far East and Caucasus, to almost every single letter he sent from prison camps during the Second World War. Jane was kind enough to allow me to copy much of this material, and patient enough to endure my presence in her condominium one snowy Toronto week in early 2010. I am most grateful to her for her patience and good nature.

I must also thank Camilla Dodge, Tony's second wife and widow, for an entertaining lunch and afternoon at her Hampshire home. (She told me that when Tony was asked about his father he would sometimes say, 'I don't really know much about him: he was in prison for most of my life.') Equally, thanks to Johnny's elder son, David, and his wife, Elizabeth, who live in Devon, for their recollections and memories of Johnny. I am inordinately grateful to Johnny's stepson, Peter Sherman, in Tampa, Florida, for giving me carte blanche to use segments of his extremely entertaining memoir of his own remarkable life, 'Memoirs of Another Time', much of which concerns Johnny. 'Memoirs of Another Time' has thus far failed to find a publisher, which is sad given the quality of its content, so I hope this book might encourage a publisher to consider Peter's fine manuscript.

Thanks also to June Bowerman, the daughter of 'Wings' Day, Johnny's great friend, for her memories of 'a noble man'. The late Sydney Dowse and the late 'Jimmy' James, who endured captivity with Johnny in many camps and escaped with him in the most famous escapades, were generous with their memories over the years, before they both died within weeks of each other in 2008. Other former inmates of Stalag Luft III were also helpful, not least Alan Bryett and Bill Ash in London, and the late Albert Patton Clark, Senior American Officer at Stalag Luft III, whom I interviewed on several occasions at the United States Air Force Academy in Colorado Springs for a television series about the 'Great Escape'.

David Saunders of the Gallipoli Association, who, like so many others, has long hoped that a biography of Johnny Dodge would be written, was particularly helpful, as was Leonard Sellers, author of *The Hood Battalion* (1995), who provided me with photographs of Johnny during the First World War, and Valerian Freyberg, the current Lord Freyberg, grandson of Johnny's First World War commanding officer, who granted me permission to use them. I have used excerpts from *The Hood Battalion* for my chapters dealing with the First World War, with grateful thanks to Leonard. Thanks to Peter Elliott, Head of the Department for Research and Information Service at the Royal Air Force Museum, Hendon, the staff at the British Library, the British Newspaper Library, the German Historical Institute, the Imperial War Museum and the National Archives, who were, as ever, generous with their time and patient with my queries.

I am indebted to my fellow author David Garnett, who was kind enough to give me a leisurely summer tour around Ferring, the Sussex seaside home and resting place of Johnny and his wife, Minerva. David guided me to their tombstones in St Andrew's Church and showed me 'Florida', the quaint home where they enjoyed so many happy days, and the site of 'Wookyi-Tipi', where Johnny's mother, Flora, lived with her husband, Lionel Guest. He was also good enough to introduce me to Ed Miller, who provided me with valuable historical background to the Guests' and Dodges' life and times in this beautiful seaside haven.

At Mainstream Publishing I am grateful to my friend Bill Campbell, publisher and joint managing director, for commissioning this book, and to Ailsa Bathgate, Graeme Blaikie and Claire Rose in the editorial department; I also thank Eleanor Collins, my editor, for her patience and assistance in scrutinising the manuscript and bringing it up to scratch. Any errors are entirely my own. I apologise in advance for any that might occur and, if they are brought to my attention, will do my utmost to correct them in future editions.

Finally, but not least, I would like to thank Ian Sayer for providing me with letters, which I draw upon in the following pages, written to Second World War camp commandants by various prisoners, such as Johnny and Wings Day. Ian has been unstinting in his generosity with advice and material in a wide variety of areas relating to the war over the years that we have known each other. I would further like to thank him for allowing me to stay at his home in Spain in order to finish this book. Thanks also to his beautiful partner, Marielle, who overindulged me throughout my stay, and his charming son, Jamie.

Casa Acuarios, Bel-Air, Estepona

CONTENTS

PREFACE

The name Johnny Dodge crops up repeatedly in almost every book written about 'the Great Escape', that 'Boys' Own' escapade of World War II immortalised by the eponymous 1963 Hollywood movie starring Dick Attenborough and Steve McQueen. That is how I came to know about 'Johnny' when, several years ago, I began researching my own book about this fascinating episode of wartime folklore. Johnny Dodge, and the myths and legends around him, were forever present. His story cannot help but grab the imagination. Johnny's heroism at Gallipoli and on the Western Front in the Great War, his epic 1,700-mile horseback ride across Asia in between the wars and his imprisonment at the hands of the Russian secret police as a suspected spy made him seem like a swashbuckling adventurer of a bygone era.

His record during the Second World War was no less compelling. That he was a central figure in the Great Escape is well documented. But his subsequent time behind enemy lines is even more interesting. Johnny was thrown into a 'special' compound for potential hostage prisoners at Sachsenhausen concentration camp, no doubt because he was related by marriage to Winston Churchill. He was threatened with death if he ever tried to escape again. But he did escape, in a tunnel break that the Germans judged was far more audacious than that of the Great Escape. Johnny was recaptured, but the SS thought his political connections were valuable enough not to have him shot. It's no wonder that Johnny earned the sobriquet, 'the Dodger'. The SS took him to Berlin instead, for a meeting with Paul Schmidt, Hitler's one-time personal interpreter. Schmidt, possibly at the behest of SS intelligence chief Brigadeführer Walther Schellenberg, dispatched Johnny to Britain to persuade his 'cousin' in Downing Street of the merits of an Anglo-German anti-Bolshevik pact. Johnny's quixotic travels through the dying embers of the Third Reich in the company of a former Nazi newspaper correspondent is one of the great untold tales of the war.

Perhaps American-born Johnny was no different from many of his wealthy contemporaries, not least his great buccaneering friends Kermit Roosevelt, the president's son, and Fred Dalziel, the big game hunter. The privileged classes of the early part of the twentieth century belonged to a gilded generation, which produced many titanic figures to fuel the popular imagination. Johnny's membership of The Ends of the Earth Club testifies to his position in this international fellowship of indomitable Anglo-Saxon adventurers. When Johnny was incarcerated in Hermann Göring's 'escape proof' camp in German-occupied Poland, he found himself among scores of larger-than-life personalities from Britain and its Commonwealth, many of them intriguing characters in their own right.

There was always something about John Bigelow Dodge, however, that set him apart from the many other great men of his life and times. Perhaps it was

2

the benevolent innocence he displayed throughout his life, and his extraordinarily amiable nature. Nobody seemed to dislike Johnny, and almost everybody appeared to look up to him as a brotherly figure who could be trusted and relied upon. His first German prison camp commandant liked Johnny so much that he 'transferred' him from the British Army, in which he was a major, to the RAF, so that he could be a prisoner of the Luftwaffe. Even those who were radically opposed to Johnny's hopelessly antediluvian conservative views were inclined to treat him affectionately. Another POW, John Casson, was a left-winger who at the outset of the war had considered becoming a conscientious objector. 'My dear chap,' Johnny once said to him, 'I agree with you entirely.' Exasperated, Casson protested, 'But you *don't* agree with me.'

What Johnny had probably meant was that they were both friends, and that was all that mattered, for comradeship was everything to him; his life was a celebration of human fellowship. When he stood as a Conservative candidate in Mile End, he lost the election but won the hearts and minds of hundreds of constituents in the poverty-stricken borough of east London. When, in the 'Khaki Election' of 1945, he stood for Gillingham only to lose to the Labour candidate Joseph Binns, Johnny told his disappointed followers, 'We must all pull together behind him.' Fair play, honesty and civic-minded decency were other cornerstones of Johnny's simple philosophy.

Simple, in fact, was a word often used in connection with Johnny, but never in the pejorative. 'Inquisitive and simple hearted,' wrote the poet

3

Rupert Brooke. Johnny's great friend Jimmy James, the greatest of the Great Escapers, once wrote that he would not call Johnny 'simple'—though that had been the immediate word to cross his mind—but would say that he possessed a childlike innocence that was enchanting. 'He was one of the kindest and happiest men I have ever met and was always ready to help anybody in trouble.'

It was this childlike faith in the power of goodness that gave Johnny his appealing aura, I think. He believed that so long as he was decent and honest and good towards other men, then they would reciprocate in kindness. He was rarely wrong. When he and four officers escaped through a daring tunnel out of Sachsenhausen concentration camp, none of the others wanted to partner him. While they all had worked out cover stories and had detailed plans for their escape routes, Johnny was simply going to head vaguely west in the hope of bumping into the Western allies, or vaguely east in the hope of bumping into the Red Army. In the end he found himself vaguely travelling north and lodging in a pigsty. But while his friends were all recaptured quickly, Johnny was on the run for a month. He would have been caught much sooner, but the policeman who knew of his hiding place didn't want to arrest him—because everybody said what a thoroughly good chap he was.

Johnny survived the war but did not live long enough to enjoy the peace he had fought so valiantly for over so many years. He died suddenly on 2 November 1960 at the age of 66. At his memorial service in London's elegant Chester Square, some of the most eminent people of post-war Britain were among the congregation, including

4

Lord Longford (or Frank Pakenham, as he was then) and Enoch Powell, as well as Group Captain Douglas Bader and fellow Great Escapers. Giving the address was Johnny's old Gallipoli commander, the redoubtable Lieutenant General Bernard Freyberg, who said:

> Johnny was built on heroic scale both in physique and character. Tall and splendid looking, he had a selflessness, a simplicity and a generosity of nature that made him loved by all who had the good fortune to call him their friend . . . So on this day we say 'goodbye' to a fighting soldier with great sorrow, but with pride and thanksgiving, for it is through the example and inspiration of such men that the British tradition endures.

Several people have tried to tell the story of John Bigelow Dodge and his remarkable life. The first was the author of *The Great Escape*, Paul Brickhill, who was researching Johnny's biography when he died. The *Superman* film actor Christopher Reeve played Johnny in a made-for-television movie based on the Great Escape but which was purely fiction. Reeve was so enthralled by Johnny's character that he embarked upon producing his own film about him. Unfortunately Reeve, as is well known, suffered a terrible riding accident and tragically became incapacitated. He too died before his pet project could be realised. Finally, Johnny's namesake Phyllis Dodge also passed away before she could put pen to paper on her proposed book about Johnny. This book, then, represents the aspirations of many people who think a life well led

is a life worth writing about. It is the first biography
of Johnny 'the Dodger' Dodge.

WOOKYI-TIPI

John Bigelow Dodge was born in Manhattan on 15 May 1894. 'Johnny', as he was almost invariably known from childhood onwards, was the second child and only son of Flora Bigelow and Charles Stuart Dodge. His parents both came from old New York families, descended from the early settlers of the Massachusetts Bay Colony who had come out from England in the first half of the seventeenth century. The Dodges were the wealthier; the Bigelow side of the family was more intellectually accomplished.

Johnny's paternal grandfather, General Charles Cleveland Dodge, had been one of the youngest brigadier-generals on the Union side during the Civil War. In peacetime he became a successful, if obscure, businessman. Johnny's grandfather on his mother's side was a towering figure of his time. John Bigelow was a Renaissance man of the modern age, one of the foremost United States diplomats of the time, a renowned newspaperman, author and historian. Bigelow was a co-owner and editor of the *New York Evening Post*, a liberal democratic newspaper strongly in favour of humanitarian reform. Bigelow broke with the Democratic Party when it supported the expansion of slavery, and instead gave his endorsement to the Republican Party, which was opposed to slavery expansion. In the years before the Civil War, Bigelow used his influence to staunchly oppose slavery. When he became an American envoy and minister to the court of Napoleon III in France, Bigelow helped block the Confederacy's efforts to acquire ships in Europe.

Johnny's parents were never to achieve quite such conspicuous distinction as his grandparents. His father Charles has been described in family legend as 'worthy but dull' or, more crushingly, 'just plain boring'. The most adventurous endeavour Charles Stuart Dodge undertook, it seems, was to spend a year in Europe after he graduated from Yale. It is difficult to know whether this is true or not as there is, sadly, little record remaining of Charles to paint a fuller, and perhaps more fulsome, picture of him. It would be unfair to malign a man on such slender authority. It is clear, however, that Charles played a distinctly distant role in his son Johnny's life.

The same could not be said of Johnny's mother, Flora Bigelow, who was one of John Bigelow and his wife Jane Tunis Poultney's nine children. The Bigelows were a boisterous and colourful clan. One of Flora's brothers, Poultney Bigelow, followed in his father's footsteps to become a celebrated man of letters, an inveterate explorer, travel writer, journalist and the author of 11 books. A childhood friend of the future Kaiser, Poultney Bigelow was an enthusiast about everything German and penned several books about his pet subject. Poultney would have a great deal of influence on his nephew Johnny. Flora's early years were spent between the Bigelows' substantial homes, a large house in Gramercy Park, the genteel oasis of stately town houses and apartment buildings above the Lower East Side of Manhattan, and an upstate New York estate at Highland Falls called 'The Squirrels' (which is now listed on the National Register of Historic Places).

Described variously as 'vibrant', 'flamboyant', 'melodramatic' and 'gushing', Johnny's mother was felt to be a domineering figure by everyone she encountered. Flora was to be the dominant person in her son's life, even, in later years when he was married, in comparison to his wife. The bond between mother and son was an extraordinarily strong one. Whichever part of the world Johnny found himself in over the forthcoming decades of his adventurous life, and in whatever circumstances—no matter how oppressive—he rarely missed an opportunity to write home to the woman whom he invariably addressed as 'My Precious Mother'.

Johnny had one sibling, his older sister Lucy, who had been born in 1890. The first nine years of Johnny's life were spent in happy harmony with Lucy in their parents' New York home, a handsome brownstone on East 37th Street in the Murray Hill district of mid-Manhattan. They grew up surrounded by the retinue of nannies and servants that was usual in those days for children of their class. But in other ways their upbringing was not quite so conventional. Flora was not the distant figure that many mothers of her elevated status so often were. At night she would sit by her children's bedsides and sing them to sleep, accompanying herself on the guitar. Under her patient tutelage, Lucy and Johnny learnt to play several instruments.

When Lucy and Johnny were older, Flora took them to Sing Sing Correctional Facility, the infamous jail on the banks of the Hudson River, some 30 miles north of New York City. Her father John Bigelow was a volunteer inspector at Sing Sing. There, his boisterous daughter and her two children entertained the captive audience with mandolin, trumpet, guitar and popular songs. Philanthropy has long played a prominent part in American society, but Flora's efforts on behalf of some of the most hardened criminals in New York State were an unusual display of charity that must have required a great degree of commitment and personal sacrifice.

It was this commendable social consciousness, and Flora's belief in the affirmative and nurturing force of song and music that were, perhaps, her greatest gifts to Lucy and Johnny. Lucy became a proficient guitarist and violinist. Later in her life, as the chatelaine of a beautiful Westchester estate, she began the Caramoor International Music Festival, which is dedicated to fostering musical talent and continues to thrive to this day. Music and singing were to sustain Johnny's soul during the many dark days he was compelled to endure the misery of incarceration at the hands of both the Soviet and Nazi regimes. Like his mother, his life was one of unstinting service. When he stood for election in London's impoverished Mile End, Johnny purposely moved into a house in the borough to be amid the destitute people he sought to represent.

Unfortunately, Flora and Charles' relationship was not quite such a melodious affair. The union began to founder soon after the children were born, though the reason remains a mystery. It might simply have been because of the manifest difference in their personalities. 'Flora was a vibrant, one might even say flamboyant person,

10

whilst Charles Stuart was worthy but dull,' observed Johnny's would-be biographer, Phyllis B. Dodge, in her 'John Bigelow Dodge, 1894–1960: A Précis of his Life'.

Around about 1900, when Johnny was six years old, his parents separated. Then, in the autumn of 1903, Flora went to South Dakota, which was one of the few states where it was possible to get a divorce on grounds other than adultery. In Sioux Falls Flora bought a handsome cottage and gave it the Indian name 'Wookyi-Tipi', which means 'peaceful teepee'. It was the beginning of her lifelong fascination with Indian customs. Flora became particularly interested in Indian methods of healing, and throughout her life would surprise friends with her insistence that she had learnt their ways of curing medical conditions. As the years unfolded Flora attempted to try her methods on the likes of the English poet Rupert Brooke and Herbert Asquith, son of the British prime minister.

Flora lived at Wookyi-Tipi with Lucy and their faithful maid, Delia, but Johnny was sent to school on the East Coast. For a boy with such an attachment to his mother it must have been a dreadful blow to be separated from her. Nevertheless, he dutifully enrolled in the elite Fay School in Southborough, Massachusetts, and began his first formal education away from home. Fay School was established in 1866 to cater for the rapidly growing number of wealthy families in America's North East. The school's simple philosophy was to educate the whole child to his fullest potential in preparation for a productive and fulfilled life. Its stated core values—'Academic excellence, earnest effort, honorable conduct,

11

dedicated service, wellness of mind and body . . . '—
were ideals Johnny would maintain for the rest of
his life.

Johnny might have hoped that he would be able
to spend the Christmas vacation of 1903 with Flora
and Lucy at Wookyi-Tipi, but he was to be sorely
disappointed. Instead he spent it with Jane and
John Bigelow, his grandparents, at their Manhattan
home in Gramercy Park. Johnny no doubt enjoyed
the love and adoration of his grandparents, but
there are hints he was beginning to feel the strain of
separation from Flora. At about this time he wrote
to his mother somewhat plaintively, 'I do want to
see you before I am 10 years old. Life is so short.'

He appeared less concerned about the absence
of his father in his life. In his many letters to Flora,
Johnny mentioned Charles Dodge infrequently. In
early 1904, Dodge had evidently proposed to visit
his son over the Washington Birthday holiday
(sometimes called Presidents' Day), which is
celebrated on the third Monday of February. For
one reason or another, however, the visit did not
take place. The impression is left of a disorganised
man, insensitive to his son's feelings. To be fair to
Charles, that was not an unusual trait among men
of his generation and social position. Johnny was to
spend much of his life among men who came from
fractured families and who hardly knew their
fathers.

Thankfully for Johnny, Flora bowed to his wish
that he see her before his tenth birthday. A few
weeks after Charles' putative visit, Flora invited
Johnny to Wookyi-Tipi. He had a wonderful time
indulging his passion for rural life, riding his
mother's bucking bronco (named Dakota) and

shooting a gopher. Shortly after his return to Fay, Flora's divorce was granted, and she was awarded custody of the children. From school in April 1904, Johnny wrote to his mother to say he was 'so glad to get your letter saying your Div [divorce] was over'. On his tenth birthday Johnny pleaded with Flora, 'Will you please tell me if father can come and see me this month?' Her reply is not known. But two weeks later Johnny wrote that 'Papa sent me 20 dollars for a birthday present'. It is the last mention of his father in any of his letters.

At Fay Johnny was not academically brilliant, but he threw himself enthusiastically into physical pursuits. On Founder's Day he came third in the 100-yard dash. He was elected captain of the football team, played tennis and sailed. He liked boxing, baseball and running. He also took up the mandolin, a pleasure he would indulge in for the rest of his life. He was fascinated by motorcars and wrote home about rides he had had in the Packard of Mrs Fay (presumably the wife of the owner of the school) and the Peerless of Mrs Mitchell (possibly a wife of one of the masters). Johnny's letters from school reveal the innocent and enthusiastic soul that was to beguile so many people throughout his life. They were littered with appalling spelling mistakes, which fortunately did not persist into manhood, when his handwriting became neat and accurate.

While Johnny was at Fay, his sister Lucy enrolled in Montreal's Royal Victoria College, a female-only arm of McGill University. By then Lucy was a tall, handsome girl of slim build with light-brown hair and blue eyes, and she was developing firm ideas about the way she wanted to live her life. Unlike

13

her brother, Lucy did not relish the idea of her life being dominated by the overbearing Flora. But Lucy's growing independence from her mother was but one small development amid far more dramatic changes in the world that would alter their family circumstances.

As Lucy and Johnny were growing up, the tectonic plates of world power were shifting decisively. While Britain still boasted an empire that held sway over a quarter of the world's population, she could no longer presume that her superiority in international affairs could be sustained as effortlessly in the future as it had been in the past. Old rivals like France and Spain and rising nations such as Germany resented Britain's power and were rapidly developing their industries. It was plainly obvious that the United States, with its vast landmass and natural resources, and seemingly limitless capacity to absorb immigrants, was poised to overtake the United Kingdom as the world's dominant industrial, and perhaps military, power.

The landed aristocracy of England were particularly irked by these changing circumstances. Their fabulous power had reached its peak in the late 1870s when 80 per cent of Britain's land was owned by 7,000 families, the greatest of whom were the 400 or so that had hereditary peers in the House of Lords: the famed barons, dukes, earls and viscounts of the United Kingdom. Their staggering worldwide clout was based almost entirely upon wealth generated by agriculture.

But as the iron grip of industrialisation took hold, the source of their immense wealth began to weaken. Agricultural rents would be the same in the 1930s as they had been in 1800. What had been the lifeblood of the great estates for hundreds of years was rapidly being cut off. To add to the aristocracy's misery, taxation began rising punitively as socially progressive governments adopted more egalitarian policies. Death duties were introduced in 1894—the year of Johnny's birth—at 8 per cent. It was a fiscal innovation that would have had the dukes of England rolling in their faux-Grecian mausoleums, if only their descendants could still afford to maintain them. It was the dawn of the age of meritocracy, and the 'undeserving rich' faced their pending doom with trepidation—but not without ingenuity.

In response to these dire economic straits, many of the great landed families of England sought marital alliances of convenience on the other side of the Atlantic. Where the Americans could bring cash to the table, and mountains of it, the British could supply the sort of social elan and centuries-long pedigree that their nouveau riche 'cousins' were hopelessly in awe of. As early as 1892, Sir Arthur Conan Doyle had noted in *The Adventures of Sherlock Holmes* that: 'One by one the management of the noble houses of Great Britain is passing into the hands of our fair cousins from across the Atlantic.' Typical of this unseemly trend was Consuelo Vanderbilt who brought a $2.5 million dowry ($66 million in today's money) when she (reluctantly) married the Duke of Marlborough. In 1895, nine American heiresses married titled British aristocrats. In between 1870 and the Great War, 100 aristocratic marriages were contracted with Americans. The United States advanced into English society on a variety of fronts.

Nancy Astor, a divorcee from Virginia, competed with the flamboyant, gay Henry 'Chips' Channon, a native of Chicago, and Elsa Maxwell, author, songwriter and professional hostess from Iowa, to be the leading lights of London society. Elsa Maxwell was the first person to be nicknamed 'the hostess with the mostess'. 'Chips' Channon became a Conservative MP and was strongly anti-American in his views, feeling that American cultural and economic imperatives threatened traditional European and British civilisation. And Nancy Astor became the first woman Member of Parliament to sit in the House of Commons.

The most controversial and famous—if not infamous—imported American wife was to be Baltimore's Wallis Simpson, the double divorcee who would fall in love with Edward VIII of Britain. But before Wallis appeared in British society, Flora Bigelow made her own bid to join the two-way marital trade of convenience between the New World and the Old—with dramatic consequences for the future of her son, Johnny.

2

AGE QUOD AGIS

It was thanks to one of Flora's best friends, Marguerite Hyde Leiter, that she found herself migrating from America to Britain. Marguerite Leiter, better known as Daisy, was a member of a fabulously wealthy nouveau clan that part-owned the nascent Marshall Field retail empire and huge chunks of Chicago real estate. Levi Ziegler Leiter was Marshall Field's business partner. He and his family lived in grand style on DuPont Circle in Washington, D.C. Daisy's sister Mary Victoria had become Lady Curzon thanks to her marriage to the Viceroy of India, Lord Curzon. It was when Daisy Leiter followed in her sister's footsteps and married Henry Molyneaux Paget Howard, the 19th Earl of Suffolk, that her friend Flora Bigelow met his best man, the quiet and self-effacing Englishman she would marry.

The Honourable Lionel Guest was the fourth son of Ivor Guest, the Earl of Wimborne. Lionel's mother, Lady Cornelia Spencer-Churchill, was the daughter of the 7th Duke of Marlborough and sister of Lord Randolph Churchill, father of the thrusting political enfant terrible and swashbuckling adventurer, Winston. Thus Lionel Guest was a nephew of Randolph and first cousin of the future wartime prime minister. Lionel Guest's family was one of the wealthiest in Britain, having made its fortune in the eighteenth and nineteenth centuries in the iron and steel

17

industries. Lionel's eldest brother Frederick was said to be the richest man in Britain. Lionel, for his own part, had built up a successful business in electrical and hydraulic engineering in Canada. There he became aide-de-camp to the Governor General. Lionel owned a pied-à-terre near Montreal: a farm on an island in the St Lawrence River called the Île St Gilles, where he kept a herd of pedigree cows and liked to devote his private hours to rustic pursuits.

Guest was some ten or so years younger than Flora, but the difference in ages did not present an obstacle to their admiration for each other. They both enjoyed their idiosyncrasies. As Flora was drawn to the mystical practices of ancient Indian tradition, so Lionel was attracted to the boundless possibilities of the stars and galaxies of outer space. It was an interest he would pursue with some distinction to the end of his life, becoming one of the foremost amateur astronomers of his age. While Flora was forcible and often overbearing, Lionel was modest and scrupulously polite and could appear to be painfully shy. But despite their divergent personalities, Flora and Lionel immediately struck up a friendship and embarked upon a brief courtship.

On 6 July 1905, a year after Flora's divorce from Charles came through, Flora and Lionel were married. Flora was 35, and Lionel was 24. The ceremony took place in Wookyi-Tipi but the married couple would not spend much time in the isolated idyll of Flora's South Dakota home. Immediately after the wedding Flora signed the deeds of Wookyi-Tipi over to a friend from New York. The transaction complete, she and her new husband set off on a grand tour of a honeymoon to Montreal via Minneapolis and Duluth by way of the Great Lakes. From then on, the little island of the Île St Gilles would be Flora's main residence. It became a much-loved refuge for Johnny, too, who from then on spent all his school holidays on the island and came to appreciate it in all the seasons of the year. Many a happy week was spent working with Lionel repairing the buildings of the farm and tending to the animals.

Flora's marriage to Lionel also seemed to spell the beginning of the final break in her children's relationship with their father's side of the family. Lucy felt this first when, at the age of 17, she asked for permission to visit her grandfather, General Charles Cleveland Dodge. Flora insisted that she could only go to the distinguished old general's home if she were accompanied by a Bigelow relative, namely her unmarried aunt, Grace. Lucy complained vigorously against this ruling.

> Aunt Grace says she could very well send me with her maid Eugenie who could wait outside while I was there and could take me home . . . I should not like to limit my one visit in every few years to half an hour in a very constrained atmosphere, such as the chaperone of one of my aunts would occasion.

This was the first indication of the fractious relationship that was developing between mother and daughter.

Johnny, on the other hand, was to become closer to his mother as the years passed. He finished at Fay in June 1906 and that autumn moved to St

Mark's in Southborough, the bigger school in the same town, for which Fay was a 'feeder'. St Mark's motto was *'Age Quod Agis'*—literally translated as 'do what you are doing' but intended as an aphorism for 'put your heart and soul into everything you do'. St Mark's was (and is) one of the most prestigious schools in the United States. A flavour of it is given in a wonderfully evocative passage from the 1937 memoir of John Franklin Carter, a near-contemporary of Johnny's at St Mark's in the earlier part of the century:

St Mark's was then pretty much a school for snobs, in the sense that its numbers were limited and that its prestige and fees were high. You had to be entered at birth for membership. On the whole it was a good school for snobs. The living accommodations were simple, the food was not calculated to satisfy an epicure, the discipline was strict . . . The day began with prayers after breakfast in the school-room, chapel in the evenings, church on Sunday morning and chapel on Sunday afternoon, with grace before every meal. And the work was hard. The school's motto—*'Age Quod Agis'*—was designed to glorify thoroughness and thoroughness was what they taught . . . Before the Church school is condemned as a mere hot-bed for wealthy snobs, these things are to be set to its credit: that it made the boys live hard and simply, that smoking and drinking were punished by immediate expulsion, that money gave no one the slightest material advantage at the school, that the scholastic standards were extremely

20

high and tolerated no cribbing or faking, and that scandals of any sort were few and far between. There is granite there, too, underneath the thin soil of privilege.

Whenever Johnny travelled back and forth from Boston to Montreal, if he had time between stops for the local train to Southborough, he would visit Keith's Vaudeville Theatre. He once saw Houdini there: 'the person that can get out of everything. It was great.' The big event of the winter at St Mark's was the sixth-form dance to which sophisticated young ladies from as far afield as New York flocked. The dining room was decorated with college banners and the new boys had to slide on the floor to make it slippery enough for dancing. Johnny continued to play the mandolin, and that winter joined the school choir. He was a keen boxer, in the featherweight class, though not actually a featherweight, and came fourth in the first year's 100-yard swimming race. That year St Mark's beat Groton, its greatest rival, 9–1 in the annual baseball match. 'The boys,' wrote Johnny, 'had a great parade till 10.30pm all around. There was a band. Lots of speeches. A Huge bonfire. Torches and lots of cheering. A grand roughhouse.' It was not all joy however. On the second occasion one boy 'slugged' him during a football match, Johnny uttered the profanity 'damn', earning him a serious reprimand from the headmaster, Mr Thayer. And at one stage it appeared Johnny suffered from some sort of heart defect. His mother was so concerned she thought he should drop out of school for the 1908–09 year. Johnny pleaded to stay, warning her that there were so many boys on the waiting list he might not ever get back in.

21

During this time, Flora attempted to follow in the literary footsteps of her father, John, and her brother, Poultney, both of whom had forged iron-cast reputations as prolific writers. She wrote a novelette entitled *The Jewelled Ball*, which was published in 1908. Set between London, New York and Paris, the narrative spans half a generation or more and tells the story of a humble girl who becomes an actress and promises to marry a man of distinguished descent. Unfortunately, the subject of her affection has a mother who is not inclined to see her son marry an actress of lowly origins. The mother persuades the actress to disappear. The plot has been described as 'strikingly clever' but it is not clear where this plaudit came from. A review in the *New York Times* was less flattering:

> Mrs. Guest shows that she has some faculty of penetration into character and motive and some skill in setting forth the more obvious traits of her people. But her knowledge of life is such 'as sheltered women know' and her method of telling her story is deplorably crude.

Flora was not put off: she went on to write more novels and many factual books, mainly advising about animal rearing and diet or containing home-spun philosophy. None received plaudits of any great resound, but all were avidly devoured by her doting son.

As for Johnny, after a summer at Île St Gilles and a sailing trip to Ottawa with a Montreal friend, he was passed fit to play in the football team as a half-back. He began singing tenor in the choir ('I

22

think it fits my voice better'), took one mandolin lesson a week and nurtured his soul with Sacred Studies. He studied mathematics and Roman history, and he tried to learn Greek, English and Latin, though he never had an ear for languages and failed to master anything other than a smattering of French. As his fifteenth birthday approached he went to confirmation lessons given by the headmaster, but told his mother he did not intend to be confirmed. He did not plan to stay any longer at St Mark's either, hoping to complete his education through private tutoring and go to McGill University in Montreal. The headmaster pleaded with him to stay, but Johnny suspected he was only interested in him for his athletic abilities or, as he wrote, 'atheletics'. Eventually Johnny got his way and began private tuition with a lady called Mrs Davis in Montreal.

Around about this time, Johnny began one of the most enduring friendships of his lifetime. He met Kermit Roosevelt, son of Theodore, at a football match where they happened to be seated next to each other. Kermit, though some five years Johnny's senior, shared the same open good nature and adventurous spirit. They were both aficionados of the natural world and outdoor pursuits. When his father left office, Kermit accompanied the ex-President on a safari in Africa, and the two would embark upon many more father-and-son expeditions in the future. Johnny was tremendously fond of Kermit. The two boys' lives would run in parallel courses up until Kermit's untimely death during the Second World War when, overcome by a lifelong struggle with depression and alcoholism, he committed suicide.

In the spring of 1910, Lionel and his family crossed the Atlantic to visit their relatives-in-law in Great Britain. When they returned to Canada, Johnny began the first real adventure of his life. He went out to Saskatchewan to take a job on the Grand Trunk Pacific Railway with a view to learning all he could about engineering. It was late May by the time he got to Saskatchewan, but the weather was still cold and the snow was heavy. He and two other men were assigned to a 'ballasting gang' of some ninety-four navvies with the job of making sure the workmen set the track straight and even. Conditions were primitive. They lived in a freight car with three bunks and a hole in the roof for a stovepipe, 'but as yet no stove'. There were also holes in the sides and floor of the sleeping car wide enough to see through. Despite the abundant snow there was a shortage of water, so the men tended not to waste this valuable resource on washing themselves.

Much of the next two years were spent in a whirl of social activity, with Johnny apparently staying in the homes of America's great and good. He sent his mother letters full of witty observations about their mansions, manners and social mores. At one stage during this time he seems to have suffered from a mild dose of tuberculosis and spent some weeks recuperating.

It appeared increasingly likely, however, that the family's future would be in England rather than North America. In 1912 Lionel wound up his farming interests on the Île St Gilles. Though the farm remained his property, the pedigree cows were sold, and in October of that year the family moved to London. They took up residence at

44 Seymour Street in Bayswater, a road of elegant houses close to Hyde Park. They instantly became a fixture of Edwardian London's social whirl. Johnny adapted well to the change in milieu and would become increasingly fond of life in England and of everything English in general. He went to work for the Dominion Bond Company in the City and began a career as a stockbroker. His sister, Lucy, however, did not enjoy life in London, which she found stifling.

Lucy had, around about this time, endured something of a nervous breakdown, possibly caused by her stressful relationship with Flora, or possibly because of some less-than-innocent advances that Lionel made upon his step-daughter. In early April 1913, Lucy ran away from home. She was 22. Her disappearance caused something of a sensation on both sides of the Atlantic, with the newspapers in London and New York devoting several days' coverage to the scandal. 'She said she wanted to earn her own living,' Flora told the *New York Times*, 'we had several spirited interviews on the subject, for I don't think the child quite knows what she really wants to do . . . She has American ideas about women working.' Another report said Lucy 'was tired of living on her relatives and of the eternal succession of social engagements'.

Her stepfather hired a private eye to track her down. (Another version of events, from a family member, is that it was Flora who hired the gumshoe, not to find Lucy, but to establish whether it was true that Lionel had illicit intentions towards her daughter.) Whatever the truth, Lucy was traced to a boarding house in Shaftesbury Avenue in the theatre district, leading to speculation that she hoped for a career on the stage—a shocking ambition then for a putative member of the aristocracy. Perhaps Lucy's motivations were more prosaic. It was the time of the suffragettes and young women everywhere were beginning to display more independence than they had dared to in the past. Lucy considered herself more American than English, and intensely disliked the pretensions of London society, complaining about the 'silly emptiness of her life'. The final straw appears to have been when Flora attempted to arrange Lucy's debut at court and marry her into the British aristocracy. Lucy agreed to return to Seymour Street only if she were allowed to leave England immediately. Ten days later the newspapers announced that she was on board the steamship *Oceanic* on the way to New York in the company of her aunt Grace, her mother's long-suffering unmarried sister. The newspaper announced that Lucy was to take up residence in the old Bigelow home in Gramercy Park.

In November of that year Johnny followed Lucy across the Atlantic with three tasks on his mind. He was to visit Lucy at Gramercy Park and put his mother's mind at rest as to the state of her daughter's mental health. He was to explore the prospects for selling the farm on Île St Gilles. And he was to make his mind up as to which country he wanted to live and forge a career in. He was already exploring the possibility of becoming a naturalised Englishman. But when he arrived back in London for the Christmas of 1913, he had no conclusive answer to any of the three problems.

In the new year he sailed back to New York once more, this time to take up a position with a Wall

Street stockbroking firm. The plan was for him to stay in North America until the autumn, when he would return to join the London City firm of Williams de Broë. He spent the early spring and summer months of 1914 in the United States setting up business opportunities. Most of the work was conducted over luncheons and dinners in town and at weekends away in the country with friends of friends. In the meantime Flora took Lucy to the Île St Gilles and they re-opened the house.

It was from there that the strong-willed Lucy made headlines once more. She told her mother she had fallen in love with a German-born banker who lived in Manhattan. Walter Tower Rosen, a Harvard graduate of the class of 1894, was considerably older than Lucy. Surprisingly, Flora was delighted with the match and announced her daughter's engagement in July, news which came as a shock to Lucy's friends and relatives in New York. John Bigelow and his wife had never heard of Rosen even though Lucy had been staying with them at their houses in Gramercy Park and Highland Falls. They told reporters that there must be some mistake. But it was true, and preparations began for the wedding, which was due to take place on 11 August, on the Île St Gilles. Unfortunately, a slightly more momentous event intervened when, on 4 August, war broke out between England and Germany. The wedding was brought forward a week, and Lucy and Walter cancelled their planned honeymoon in Paris. They married on 6 August. Shortly afterwards, Johnny joined Flora and Lionel for the ocean voyage back to wartime England.

ESPRIT DE CORPS

They arrived back in a country where the national mood of jingoistic excitement was barely tempered by the prospect of the mortal sacrifices that inevitably lay ahead. Once home in Seymour Street, one of Flora's first acts was to write to Lionel's cousin Winston Churchill, then the First Lord of the Admiralty. Flora appears to have asked Churchill if it were possible to find a commission for her son. Fortunately Britain's supreme naval commander was in a position to oblige, as he was in the midst of organising a new and slightly unusual fighting division to which Johnny was ideally suited.

The Royal Naval Division (R.N.D.) owed its origin to a pre-war plan to provide the Admiralty with a land force to safeguard naval and air bases in any chosen theatre of war. It was originally called the Advanced Base Force. In the event of war with Germany, the 'advanced bases' most likely to require defending were the Belgian ports of Antwerp and Ostend, and the Channel ports of France. The R.N.D. would be a hybrid outfit made up of the many thousands of naval reservists available to the War Office, and the many new army and navy recruits eager to enlist for service. An amphibious marine force, it would fight as soldiers under Admiralty direction. There would be two naval brigades of four battalions each, and one marine brigade, the last of which had already been formed, was fully equipped, trained and ready for action.

The slightly unusual composition of the R.N.D. was to produce one of the most quixotic fighting units the British armed forces have known. The officers were allowed to grow beards, as in the navy, and remain seated during the loyal toast to the King (standing up in ships could produce a nasty bump on the head). They went into battle flying the White Ensign, and their battalions were named after eight famous admirals: Anson, Benbow, Collingwood, Drake, Hawke, Hood, Howe and Nelson.

So many of the officer recruits to the R.N.D. were friends or relatives of the First Lord of the Admiralty that Herbert Asquith, the Prime Minister, dubbed it 'Winston's Little Army'. It gained something of a reputation for the quality and glamour of its officer cadre, who were among the *jeunesse dorée* of the time. The Prime Minister's own son Arthur 'Oc' Asquith was one of them. Among others from the beau monde of the pre-war Empire who served in this elite armed force were Denis Browne, one of England's finest young musicians; Frederick Septimus 'Cleg' Kelly, an extraordinary Australian composer, pianist and Olympic athlete; and Patrick Shaw-Stewart, a brilliant scholar.

The most famous and romantic of their number was the boyishly good-looking poet Rupert Brooke, dubbed by W.B. Yeats 'the handsomest young man in England'. A member of the Bloomsbury group of writers, Brooke was the pin-up boy of his generation and destined, as fate would have it, to become the symbol of Gallipoli, one of the most controversial campaigns in which the R.N.D. fought. Many of the first members of the R.N.D.

29

were recruited by Churchill's private secretary, the polymath 'Eddie' Marsh, intellectual and classical scholar, translator and patron of the arts, and sponsor of the 'Georgian school' of poets. Marsh was a great friend of Brooke and Siegfried Sassoon. Johnny Dodge would become one of the most popular members of this band of dazzling young men.

In his history of this eccentric and illustrious military outfit, Douglas Jerrold wrote: 'if ever there was a military formation with a *carrière ouvert* [*sic*] *au talent* it was the Naval Division'. There were in each battalion, Jerrold observed, experienced officers who had undergone regular military training and had some experience of battle. 'But, broadly, the junior officers had to teach themselves anything they wanted to know about the art of war, and to learn from experience the habit of command.' The Naval Division was initially divided between two locations near the rural settlements of Walmer and Betteshanger in Kent, two camps which Jerrold described as:

> vast experimental stations containing all the material for successful improvisation, unhampered by any limiting conditions prescribing the line of development. Under these conditions audacity and initiative were at a premium, and the more conventional qualities of junior subalterns less in request . . . Discipline there was, but it was the discipline which bowed to superior judgement or ability more than to superior rank . . .

Churchill was grateful to have Johnny for this new

and noble fighting endeavour. In a handwritten note to Flora, the First Lord of the Admiralty wrote: 'My dear Mrs Lionel. He is splendid. Quite one of the best I have ever seen. We are grateful to you for giving him to England . . .' By 10 September 1914, Johnny was a sub-Lieutenant in the Hood Battalion of the 2nd Royal Naval Brigade. His new home was a sprawling camp in the grounds of Lord Northbourne's country estate near Betteshanger. His mother was keen to visit him in his new setting, and Johnny wrote to Flora on 19 September from the camp. 'My darling Mother . . . you had better stop at the Royal Hotel, Deal, which is about 6 miles from here overlooking the sea.' He described what appeared to be a relaxed regime at the camp, told her that he was keeping the French prismatic glasses, which she had sent him, and would like to pay for them out of the 'about 10' shillings a day he was receiving in pay.

Johnny had been assigned to A Company of Hood Battalion. He found himself sharing a tent with the company commander, a remarkable character who was to become a friend for life. Bernard Freyberg was a brilliant and brave soldier who had been born in Britain but grew up in New Zealand. He had studied dentistry in England and practised it in San Francisco but, finding his chosen profession dull, Freyberg crossed the Rio Grande to fight in the Mexican revolutionary war with General Francisco 'Pancho' Villa. As soon as he heard the news of European hostilities breaking out, he walked 300 miles to catch the first ship he could find destined for Britain. After a chance meeting with Churchill in Horse Guards Parade, he persuaded the First Lord to give him a commission

31

in the R.N.D. and was posted to the Hood Battalion.

The countryside surrounding Lord Northbourne's land was ideally suited for the sham battles and night 'schemes' necessary to turn this newly recruited and diverse group of men into an effective fighting force. For their comfort and pleasure there were two enormous YMCA marquees where they could read, write letters home or hold concerts. The local rector made his bathroom available for officers to bathe, and his two nieces provided a canteen for the men. On Sunday, officers and men paraded at the picturesque village church, a spectacle that Lord Northbourne and the locals would gather to watch with pride.

In his history of the Hood Battalion, Leonard Sellers eloquently evokes the mood of the moment 'when hopes were high, hearts were young, expectations soared, romantic ideals held sway, and blood flowed through youthful veins in the certain knowledge of early and righteous victory'. One of the battalion's temporary chaplains reported enthusiastically:

Lord Northbourne and his friends in the vicinity of the camp always took a kindly interest in the men's welfare, and he was frequently a spectator at the numerous boxing and football contests which were held in the camp. I remember very well a speech that he made at the conclusion of a vigorous boxing match between two rival battalions. He concluded by saying that the men had proved themselves excellent fighters with the gloves, and he had no doubt that when by and by they were called on to take part in a sterner fight they would acquit themselves equally as well . . .

The R.N.D. was an admirable example of the British knack for improvising combined with boundless indomitability. But the division was woefully unprepared for its task, as so many such enterprises often are. It was raised in barely a few weeks and was plagued with the sort of organisational difficulties inevitable in such a hurried mobilisation. Few of the men were equipped with basic equipment such as packs, cooking tins and water bottles or even khaki. There was no ancillary support in the form of heavy artillery or field ambulances, and the weapons most of the men were issued with were ancient charger-loading rifles. Consisting, as it did, of retired ratings, and commanded by young men with little or no battle experience, it was, in the words of Sir Conan Doyle, a 'strange force, one-third veterans and two thirds practically civilians'. It was almost a recipe for disaster.

DEBACLE

Thus when, in the first few days of October, the Royal Naval Division heard that it was being sent into battle on the Continent immediately, thoughts of catastrophe loomed in many wise heads. The desperate decision had been prompted by imminent threat to the strategically important fortress city of Antwerp. While the R.N.D. had been enjoying its exertions in the countryside of Kent, the military outlook in Europe had gone from bad to worse. The retreat from Mons, followed by the battles of the Aisne and Marne had at least saved Paris from German occupation. But then began what was called 'the race for the sea' in which German forces tried to outflank Allied armies in a bid to capture the Channel ports, a coup that would have undoubtedly assured their domination of the Continent.

In this race for the sea Antwerp was the first important city to come under threat. The Flemish city was heavily defended, surrounded by three lines of fortifications. When the Germans broke through the outer line of these fortifications on 2 October, the resolve of the Belgian Field Army began to waver. Its surrender would have opened the way for the Germans to descend on the critically important Channel ports, so Churchill acted decisively. Within hours he was in Antwerp reassuring the Belgians that British reinforcements were on the way. These would consist primarily of the three R.N.D. brigades, followed by further, unspecified, troops. The battle-hardened marine brigade, already fighting on the Continent under the command of Sir Archibald Paris, was on its way within hours of this pledge. The two volunteer naval brigades were shortly to follow suit. Throwing these young men, unprepared and ill-equipped, into the heat of battle was later the subject of much controversy. But the brutal truth was there were no other trained forces available.

Few such concerns were in the minds of the officers and men when they heard the news of their impending engagement with the enemy. Such was the mood of brotherly camaraderie and *esprit de corps* that they all broke out into enthusiastic cheers. Johnny, no doubt, was among those who relished the prospect of battle. But not all of the officers joined in the mood of buoyant optimism. The commanding officer of D Company, Anson Battalion, in which Rupert Brooke was serving, told his officers that they would be best advised to spend their remaining hours in camp writing what would undoubtedly be their last letters home. To a woman friend Brooke wrote: '. . . so we all sat under lights writing last letters: a very tragic and amusing affair'.

Johnny and his happy gang of poets and aesthetes set off for battle on 4 October, marching from their camp at Betteshanger to Dover, where they paraded along the pier for the pleasure of the flag-waving townsfolk. They were crammed so tightly on cross-Channel steamers that some of the men had to stand for the entire journey. It was a grey October morning and the days to follow were to become grislier with each passing hour. Once the transports got into Dunkirk harbour the disembarkation was chaotic. It was 12 noon on 5 October and the officers and men had had only one meal since the day before. That evening, nevertheless, exhausted and hungry, they entrained for Antwerp where the military situation was even more desperate. Their vastly more experienced comrades in the marine brigade had been valiantly propping up the deflated Belgian forces, but they were fighting a losing battle.

This would not have been immediately apparent to the men of the naval brigades when they began arriving in the city the next morning, 6 October. They were greeted enthusiastically—if not ecstatically—in the eastern suburbs of the fortress city by the civic guard and numerous smiling officials. Once they had received their marching orders, the whole town seemed to turn out to cheer them on. Historian of the R.N.D. Douglas Jerrold observes:

> The whole city was astir, and the scene was one of poignant humour, of romantic excitement, of that unintelligible optimism which comes to men in any brief respite from an incalculable menace.

Rupert Brooke wrote: 'Everyone cheered and flung themselves on us, and gave us apples and chocolate and kisses, and cried *"Vivent les Anglais"* and *"Heep! Heep! Heep!"*' Jerrold, again:

> The enthusiasm was infectious. The doubts of the evening dusk had given way to the resilient optimism of midday, and so these raw

battalions, without any orders, without equipment, with but few senior officers skilled in the control of troops in the field, and few junior officers who had been taught anything save to be controlled with a good grace, marched through Antwerp without more, perhaps, than a subconscious repudiation of the cheers which acclaimed them as seasoned troops, possessing in their bayonets the veritable means of deliverance to a great city.

Only when the men arrived at their front-line positions were they given their first food in two days. While they hungrily devoured their long overdue repast, Winston Churchill, who had remained in the theatre of war, began addressing General Paris and his senior commanders. The fate of Antwerp was no longer in doubt. The German attack was strong and insistent. The lines of defence were gradually crumbling. Churchill had to admit there were no reinforcements on the way. The plan now was one of orderly retreat while the strongest Allied forces held the attacking Germans off. The bulk of the Belgian Army would retreat westwards possibly as far as Ostend, leaving some elements to support the two naval brigades and Paris's marine brigade, and a suitable force to protect the crossings over the River Scheldt. Johnny and his 2nd Naval Brigade would entrench on Antwerp's second line of defence, which consisted of eight forts and eighteen smaller redoubts spread around the south-east of the city.

By now the mood of ecstatic enthusiasm had evaporated. Once more Jerrold captures the scene:

The two brigades of British troops filled the square, yet, through the ranks, came endless Belgian troops returning from the trenches. Excited staff officers shouted indiscriminately to everybody to keep cool, guns galloped in all directions, motor cyclists rushed through with apparently endless dispatches, and, threading their way in humble, pitiful groups, by by-streets and on the edges of crowds, the refugees from the outlying villages fled from the certain, to the uncertain, disaster. Here, too, the brigades had their first sight of war-weary troops. Later, the division came to know well enough that look, which marks out men exhausted by desperate and long-continued exposure to the risks of imminent and horrifying death. The sight of the Belgian troops in Vieux Dieu was their first introduction to the realities of war.

Through a lifetime of fighting wars, Johnny would come to know well this rapid transformation of mood from buoyant optimism to grim desperation. He would come to know, too, how, in war, moments of horror and apparent impending doom can quickly disappear to be replaced by periods of quiet and serenity, as if the enemy had gone home. Thus was the situation on the morning of 7 October, when the men were greeted by the incongruous sight of red London motorbuses, which arrived on the line to distribute rations. It was so quiet that some officers commandeered abandoned carts to go into town and buy food and drink for their company messes. Only the occasional shell whistling above their heads reminded them of the enemy's continued presence.

But the young men of the naval brigades were already demonstrating their hopeless inexperience. Instead of allowing their men to sleep—a cardinal rule for soldiers who are not actively fighting—they wore them out by ordering them to strengthen the trenches, thus expending vital physical energy, which needed to be preserved for the enemy. Perhaps it was all academic anyway: General Paris had already decided the game was up, and had ordered officers to reconnoitre routes of retreat over the Scheldt. Boats were being secured to take men across in the event of the bridges being destroyed. And a pontoon bridge to the south of the city was standing by under heavy guard, awaiting the expected military evacuation.

It was during these moments that the magnificent figure of Bernard Freyberg displayed the battlefield mettle that was to earn him so many medals over his lifetime in arms. While surveying a possible route of retreat, Freyberg placed his hand on an electrified barbed wire. As the current shot through his body, his hand became 'glued' to the fence. It was some time before the switch to turn the power off could be found and Freyberg's hand remained attached to the wire throughout. His palm and fingers were lacerated and the scars remained with him for the rest of his life.

In the early evening of 8 October, General Paris issued the order to retreat. All the brigades and supporting Belgian troops were to immediately evacuate the city, cross the Scheldt and march westwards. In the meantime, the order went out to destroy any war resources, the dozens of vast vats of oil that were in the area and 30 to 40 merchantmen in the harbour. When Johnny and the 2nd Brigade set out at 7.30 p.m., their progress was illuminated by spectacular pyrotechnics: enormous flashes of fire and light as the vats were sabotaged and flames leapt hundreds of feet into the sky. In the harbour, more fire, smoke and red-hot flame billowed from the vessels that had been put to the torch. Nevertheless, the men reached the pontoon bridge across the Scheldt without incident.

On the other side of the river, however, they encountered a pitiful scene, which, again, would become a familiar one to Johnny in his life of struggle. Jerrold observed:

> It seemed as if the whole population of Antwerp, women and children, priests and nuns, the sick, the aged and the infirm, had fled from their homes, and yet, momentarily indifferent to the consequences, they must halt ever and again to look back at the burning ruin of their hopes and their aspirations . . . Mixed up with the procession of fugitives were men driving cattle, and mules and peasants' carts, fleeing in an interminable procession along the same road; and each man in his haste impeding the progress of the others.

Marching under these onerous conditions, many of the men without water, it was fortunate they reached their rendezvous point at 11.30 p.m. They would soon be on the ships that would take them back to England. Their comrades in the 1st Brigade were not so fortunate. Due to an initial misunderstanding and subsequent mix-ups they did not obey the order to retreat immediately. They left it so late that at one stage, fearing they were about to fall into German hands, their commanding officers made the decision to cross into neutral Holland. Some 1,500 of them were to spend the rest of the war interned.

The 1915 defence of Antwerp aroused mixed emotions. Conan Doyle said Winston Churchill's decision to send them was a resolution 'as bold to the verge of rashness and so chivalrous as to be almost quixotic'. To some it was an ignominious episode. Herbert Asquith wrote in his diary, 'They should never have been sent.'

THE SOLDIER

Once back at Betteshanger the division was given a week's leave. Johnny went up to London with Bernard Freyberg and they stayed at Seymour Street with Flora and Lionel. The Guests' town house near Hyde Park was to become a home from home for Freyberg throughout the war. On this particular occasion he met the Duchess of Marlborough, the erstwhile Consuelo Vanderbilt, who was unhappily married to Lionel Guest's cousin, the 9th Duke. Consuelo was so taken by Freyberg that she presented him with a Jaeger sleeping bag. On their last night of leave at Seymour Street, Flora entertained Eddie Marsh and Rupert Brooke to dinner with Johnny and Freyberg. When they had returned to camp, Johnny wrote to his mother that Freyberg was so pleased with the 'flea bag' that he'd christened it 'Consuelo'.

The view that the loss of Antwerp was an unequivocal debacle was not one shared by the military establishment. Heaping praise on the Royal Naval Division, Churchill declared, 'Officers of all ranks and ratings have acquitted themselves admirably, and have thoroughly justified the confidence reposed in them.' He attached no blame to the loss of a portion of the 1st Brigade. He stated with typical bravado:

The Belgian people will never forget that the men of the Royal Navy and Royal Marines were with them in their darkest hour of misery, as, please God, they may also be with them when Belgium is restored to her own by the Armies of the Allies.

Military wisdom had it that the action had considerably slowed the enemy advance, and destroyed valuable war resources.

Nevertheless, it was evident that the R.N.D. needed to complete its training if it were to be an effective fighting force in the future. The decision had been made to move its main training centre to a camp at Blandford, in Devon, which was already under construction. In the meantime, the battalions were dispersed to temporary accommodation around the south of England. When Johnny finally arrived at Blandford in the first few days of December, he found a vast camp of wooden huts arranged in tidy rows, though unfortunately the beautiful green pastures in which it was situated soon became a muddy quagmire. By then his company had acquired some interesting new officers in the reorganisation that followed Antwerp. Rupert Brooke and Denis Browne, irritated by the defeatism of their own commanding officer, persuaded Eddie Marsh to arrange their transfer to the Hood Battalion. Johnny wrote to Flora on 1 December, 'Yesterday Rupert Brooke joined our company as a platoon officer. I am delighted as, besides being very nice personally, he is good at his job.' They were joined by Arthur 'Oc' Asquith, Patrick Shaw-Stewart and Lord Ribblesdale's son Charles Lister. And in February they would all be joined by multi-talented Australian Frederick 'Cleg' Kelly.

They were among the brightest men of their generation. Brooke, writing to a friend in New York, praised his new comrades, glorying at how they had swiftly changed from intellectuals to fighting men. Of Johnny Dodge, Brooke wrote that he was a 'young and charming American' who had come to fight 'for the right'. Johnny was certainly young and charming but he was not going to be an American for much longer. Already he was contemplating becoming a British subject and before many weeks had passed he completed the formal paperwork required to facilitate the transformation. But much as he admired the British, and much as he wanted to become one of them, Johnny was not seduced by the joys of Britain's West Country weather in the bleak mid-winter. In a letter to Flora, Johnny mused, somewhat optimistically, on the possibility of transferring training to the South of France. He thought that Flora might raise the suggestion with the assistant divisional commander. If she did make any representations on his behalf, nothing came of it: the R.N.D. remained in cold and soggy Blandford, and time began to hang heavily on the young and impatient men, whose only experience of action had been so short and frustrating. Johnny wrote: 'The ground surrounding the huts was mud and slush . . . fumes from the coke stoves had given everyone a sore throat . . . Day followed day, and there was no news of a move.'

That Christmas the Allies were contemplating a far from satisfactory situation. The German advance in the west had been bold and implacable and the Western Front threatened to become a stalemate. In the east the Russians were equally hard pressed by the obdurate forces of the Germans and their Austro-Hungarian brothers in arms. Since 31 October their difficult situation had become even more unenviable with the entry into the fray of the Ottoman Empire on the side of the Central Powers. Allied supply lines to Russia were now sorely challenged on all fronts.

The overriding fear was that Turkey would turn her formidable army on the Russian flank, drawing valuable men and resources away from the fight with Austro-Hungary and Germany. Added to this was the possibility that Bulgaria and Romania would join the German cause. If they did, Italy, which was actively considering joining the Allies, might be intimidated into staying out of the war. It was against this unfolding scenario that the Allies contemplated opening a second front in the east.

Ignorant of these plans being made in higher places, Johnny took part in endless toughening-up exercises, which were invariably dominated by route marches. Two days before Christmas, Rupert Brooke scribbled down a single portentous line: 'If I should die, think only this of me.' He finished what would become his most famous epitaph in the late hours of Christmas Day itself.

The Soldier (1915)
If I should die, think only this of me:
That there's some corner of a foreign field
That is for ever England. There shall be
In that rich earth a richer dust concealed;
A dust whom England bore, shaped, made
    aware,
Gave, once, her flowers to love, her ways to
    roam,

A body of England's, breathing English air,
Washed by the rivers, blest by suns of home.
And think, this heart, all evil shed away,
A pulse in the eternal mind, no less
Gives somewhere back the thoughts by
    England given;
Her sights and sounds; dreams happy as her
    day;
And laughter, learnt of friends; and
    gentleness,
In hearts at peace, under an English heaven.

MEDITERRANEAN ADVENTURE

During leave over the Christmas period, Rupert Brooke dined with Churchill at the Admiralty. During the encounter, the First Lord could not resist dropping indiscreet hints about an imminent action in which the Royal Naval Division might play a central part. Brooke would undoubtedly have passed his comments on to Johnny and his fellow officers at Blandford. But it was only during the last days of January 1915 that they first learnt of the putative plan to launch an assault on the Dardanelles Straits, the narrow channel of water at the crossroads of the world, which links the Aegean and Europe to the Black Sea and Asia.

Gathering his senior commanders together, General Paris explained the principle of the attack. A powerful British and French naval force would begin by launching a bombardment on the lines of forts that stood on the cliffs at either side of the Straits. When they had been reduced to rubble, a military force would land on the Gallipoli Peninsula, the chain of rugged uplands and mountain peaks running down from the Thracian mainland between the Aegean and the Sea of Marmora. Moving swiftly inland, the invading force would seize Constantinople while the navy stormed through the Dardanelles to the Black Sea. The marine brigade would leave immediately as the spearhead of what would become known as the Mediterranean Expeditionary Force; the naval brigades would leave as soon as expedient. The action would be over within six weeks.

General Paris's precis of the Dardanelles expedition was, sadly, somewhat imprecise and also hopelessly optimistic. At that early stage there was no definite plan for significant military landings. It was hoped that the Straits could be forced by the shock and awe of sea power alone. The existence of fighting troops close to the theatre of operations was intended to leave the War Office with the option to pursue other expeditions in the region. The General did not hint at the severe misgivings about the operation that were expressed at every level of government and the military high command. It is unlikely, however, that these misgivings would have been greeted with anything other than customary good cheer and enthusiasm by Johnny and his friends. They began to prepare for their task by redoubling their already rigorous training regime, including route marches of up to 20 miles a day.

Two weeks later Churchill turned up at Blandford to carry out an inspection. It poured with rain all day long but the First Lord was impressed by what he witnessed of his 'Little Army'. The next day, orders came through for two naval brigades to join the marines in the Mediterranean theatre. Two days later, the first naval attack on the Dardanelles began with the Anglo-French force bombarding two forts at the entrance to the Straits. This initial assault, on the fort of Sedd-el-Bahr on the European side and that of Kum Kale on the Asiatic side, proved inconclusive, but a second action produced more satisfactory results, the forts having clearly sustained considerable damage. Marines were sent ashore to complete the demolishment.

Before Johnny and the others joined them, the R.N.D. were paraded once more, this time for the benefit of the King. Churchill came again, this time with his wife Clementine, who in turn brought her friend Violet Asquith, sister of Arthur 'Oc'. The party had come to wish the men—so many of them family friends—a fond goodbye and good luck. On this occasion there was not a hint of drizzle in the firmament: the day dawned cold but clear, the first breath of spring was in the air and high spirits reigned. The men presented a splendid sight drawn up on the Downs, their officers standing ramrod straight before them. Clementine and Violet on horseback cantered between their ranks. It was a scene of almost medieval pageantry.

In her diary, Violet recorded: 'they all looked splendid sweeping past in battalion formation—& I had a great thrill when the Hood came on proceeded [*sic*] by its silver band . . .' The formalities over, the officers enjoyed a convivial lunch of grapefruit, marrons glacés, foie gras and champagne. But the bubbly was not quite sparkling enough to stifle an underlying current of unease that Violet might have been recalling when she wrote: 'It somehow wasn't quite the fun it ought to have been. I had a tightening of the heart throughout.' As well she might, for events were not going to unfold quite as the military planners had hoped.

In the last days of February at Avonmouth the brigades boarded dozens of civilian vessels requisitioned to transport R.N.D. battalions of the Mediterranean Expeditionary Force. The Hood Battalion occupied the Union Star liner *Grantully Castle*, and Johnny found himself sharing a cabin with Rupert Brooke. (Brooke wrote to Eddie Marsh that he found the young American 'inquisitive and simple hearted'.) When the ships finally slipped their moorings and cleared the harbour mouth, the decks were lined with smiling faces, the men and officers singing happily. The impressive flotilla was accompanied by destroyer escorts down the Bristol Channel and out to the sea far beyond. It would be a gruelling journey to the eastern Mediterranean. The *Grantully Castle* passed through Gibraltar Strait in the first days of March and hugged the shore of North Africa on the way to her destination.

There is no finer illustration of the inequities of the British class system than a British troop ship, as so many of those soldiers who have endured one have observed. The conditions for the Other Ranks below decks were squalid, particularly as the temperature rose. They slept on hammocks two or three upon one another in the stagnant holds below. The mainstay of their diet was porridge and weak tea. Above decks the officers attempted to observe, with some success, the more elevated standards to which they were accustomed. They were quartered in cabins and entertained themselves by inviting one another around for afternoon tea and evening drinks. They were served much higher quality food. Johnny, along with Brooke, Asquith, Browne, Freyberg, Kelly and Shaw-Stewart, was part of a small cadre of 'frighteningly brilliant young officers' famous for their high spirits and *joie de vivre*. Their erudition and intellectual refinement was such that when they dined together, they were known as 'the Latin table' (though Johnny must have felt a little left out in this respect, considering he could barely muster a few words of French). Writing home, one officer reported Rupert Brooke as 'splendid'; young Asquith 'a calculated and measured delight' and Freyberg 'a fine big jolly thing'. He called Johnny 'a dear unconscious funny'.

The first port of call was the British naval island base of Malta. After brief leave ashore in Valletta, the convoy set sail once more and headed for the Aegean Archipelago. The officers maintained a spirit of noble adventure and no jarring note was allowed to intrude into proceedings, though some of them must surely have had their doubts about the enterprise ahead. Finally, on the evening of 11 March, the tranquil shores of the island of Lemnos drew into view. When the convoy slipped into the harbour of Mudros Bay, the weather-worn ships found themselves among a vast maritime armada.

Every conceivable vessel, from modern battleships to humble tramp steamers, crowded into the small bay. The scene was dominated by the sleek lines of the most modern in the flotilla. HMS *Queen Elizabeth*—known universally among the men as 'the Lizzie'—was the flagship of Admiral de Roebeck, commander of naval operations in the Dardanelles. The *Grantully Castle* moored alongside the somewhat less modern battleships HMS *Triumph* and HMS *Swiftsure*.

For the next few days, the men practised naval landing exercises, which consisted of repeatedly rowing boats between ships and shore. But they were also given leave to go ashore for relaxation, when they would lie on the beaches. The hectic but sometimes leisurely and almost playful atmosphere came to an end on the afternoon of 17 March when

51

the order to stand at battle stations was issued. The Expeditionary Force was going to go into action in the early hours of the following morning. That night, presuming they were embarking upon what could be the last hours of their lives, officers and men hastily scribbled letters of farewell to their loved ones.

In the darkness of the following morning their convoys slipped out of Mudros Bay and they left the dark shadows of Lemnos behind. When the sun rose they saw that they were only a mile or two off the western shore of Turkey. There, at the entrance of the Straits, a phalanx of British and French warships led by the *Queen Elizabeth* began a desultory bombardment of the Turkish forts. It appeared, to the untrained eyes of the officers and men in the R.N.D., that the Allied naval force had rapidly achieved superiority over the defenders. The Turkish infantry could be seen lining the cliffs around the forts, no doubt in expectation of a ferocious battle to come.

But there was no easy superiority. The movement of the transport ships carrying the officers and men had been a classic naval feint: an effort to distract enemy eyes from the true focal point of the Allied attack, an assault elsewhere that was intended to be overwhelming in firepower. Unfortunately, it was not overwhelming, and the presence of the ships was no longer required. Within two hours of setting eyes on the enemy for the first time, the R.N.D. received orders to return to Lemnos. The engagement they had just witnessed was critical in the Gallipoli campaign because on that day naval command decided that the Straits could not be taken by sea power alone and that the Allies could only progress with the assistance of military units. The question that now arose was when, and exactly where, the joint attack would be launched.

Some in the high command, fearing that the element of surprise would be lost unless the Allies acted straight away, demanded an immediate landing. But the Secretary of State for War, Lord Kitchener, had made it clear that no military operations should be undertaken until the arrival of the battle-hardened 29th Division, known as the 'Incomparable Division' for their prowess and experience in battle. Kitchener deemed it inconceivable to start military operations without them. But the Incomparables, late in embarking, were at least two weeks' sailing distance away. The mistake had been to start naval operations without having the 29th waiting in the wings. Thus most of the Expeditionary Force decamped to Egypt to await their arrival and make more detailed preparations.

Arriving at the cheerless Port Said, the men disembarked to establish temporary accommodation in tents next to the docks on a scrubby piece of land near the Arab quarter. Once more they embarked on strenuous bouts of exercise and training, which mainly consisted of target practice and route marches in the blazing heat. Unsurprisingly there were numerous cases of sunstroke and sunburn. But for the lucky ones who escaped illness there was plenty of time for rest and relaxation. They were near the Suez Delta and both the officers and the men would often swim in the Canal. Food was bountiful and cheap, which delighted the men after their gruelling diet on board the ships. For the officers there were excursions to Cairo and the pyramids, dinners at the celebrated Shepheard's Hotel in Cairo and visits to the casino.

Unfortunately for Rupert Brooke, he was one of the unlucky ones struck down by illness. His increasingly unpleasant malaise was blamed on a miserable combination of sunstroke and dysentery. He joined Patrick Shaw-Stewart, who was suffering from sunstroke, in the Casino Palace Hotel, where they shared a room in opposite beds. Shortly afterwards Brooke developed a swelling sore on the left side of his upper lip. The medical officer thought it was nothing serious. But while Shaw-Stewart gradually recovered, Brooke began to feel much worse. It was suggested he should be admitted into a military hospital, but Brooke insisted he stay with his comrades to fight with them in the forthcoming battle. In the first few days of April, the 29th Division—'the Incomparables'—arrived in Port Said, and the moment of battle could not be delayed much longer.

A CORNER OF A FOREIGN FIELD

Soon after the 29th Division arrived in Port Said, orders were given for the Royal Naval Division to re-embark and sail for Lemnos once more. The Naval Brigade staff left on board the HMS *Royal George* with the Howe Battalion. Johnny's Hood Battalion left Port Said on the *Grantully Castle* on 10 April. Rupert Brooke was on board, adamant that he would join his comrades in the battle, but confined for the time being to his bed on sick leave. Johnny, on the *Grantully Castle*, arrived at Lemnos on 14 April. Such was the size of the Expeditionary Force, that Mudros Bay could not accommodate any more Allied shipping and the *Grantully Castle* was redirected onwards to the island of Skyros, arriving in Trebuki Bay shortly afterwards. In a narrative of his experiences at Gallipoli, 'Opening Attack on Dardanelles', Johnny recorded his first thoughts about the herb-scented island, which had been Achilles' refuge from the Trojan wars in ancient times. 'It was most impressive,' he wrote. 'The high, desolate mountains of Skros [*sic*] on our right. The snow of Mt Olymus [*sic*] in front of us,— which glistened in vivid colours in the setting sun.'

The *Grantully Castle* had arrived just in time to witness the *Royal George* and two cruisers pick up the survivors of a ship that had been torpedoed that morning. Johnny watched as services were held on the quarterdecks of the ships and the dead were buried at sea, the corpses sliding from beneath

Union flags and into the mirror-like water. Once more the grim reality of war was brought home to those lucky enough to still be alive.

That night Johnny was on the 4.00 a.m. watch. It was a mild night and the moon cast dark shadows over the craggy hills rising high out of the sea to the sky above. It was in those early hours that he learnt he was to be the commanding officer of one of the first units to land on the Gallipoli Peninsula. The R.N.D. was to provide the Navy with 300 men and 8 officers for the landings. By early morning the complement were packed and ready to sail back to Lemnos in the *Royal George*. It was a bright and sunny morning but a dark cloud was cast over the day by a ceremony on the stern deck to bury those wounded from the torpedoed ship who had died overnight. Johnny recorded:

The ship stopped for the service, which was made very impressive by the roll of the muffled drum, accentuated by the beat of the Bass Drum, and the soft wail of the bagpipes. It brought death, for the first time, very near to our men, and made them realise what they were facing.

The *Royal George* arrived in Mudros Bay at Lemnos at about 4.30 p.m., just as the sun was setting. With the snow glistening on the mountaintops a pink glow was cast over the harbour crowded with Allied ships of every conceivable sort, from tugs and supply ships to cruisers and battleships. The *Queen Elizabeth* stood guard over them, wrote Johnny romantically, 'like a great watchful mother,' her huge 15-inch guns trained on the entrance of the harbour, and a torpedo boat slowly patrolled backwards and forwards. That evening of 18 April, the 300 complement of R.N.D. officers and men were addressed by a senior naval officer. He told them that he was sure they would live up to the best traditions of the Royal Navy. The men, wrote Johnny, were proud that both the navy and army wanted them. They were determined to do their best.

During the forthcoming days Johnny's time was taken up organising his men between transport ships and preparing for battle. He chose to make his headquarters in the transport ship *Aragon* and there was much to-ing and fro-ing between several ships in the harbour on organisational errands, fetching beer for his men and acquiring pay from the paymaster. Johnny was also given a guided tour of the sleek and modern *Queen Elizabeth*. He was impressed by the enormous gun turrets and the latest armoured range finder positioned high up on the mast.

As the Lizzie's engines were powered by oil rather than coal, and she made extensive use of electricity, everything appeared clean, neat and tidy—as well as quiet—compared to the older ships that Johnny was used to. 'One can't help being impressed by the great simplicity of the Lizzie's structure, the grace of her lines makes her size very illusive and she is a difficult target for this reason.' He was left with the impression of a happy ship. 'The officers' quarters were very cosy, and among their sports they played a good deal of hockey on board the broad quarter deck. All the officers were very cheerful and optimistic.' During the day men on the signal deck of the Lizzie were constantly running up and down flags sending messages to and from the dozens of other ships in the harbour. But after dusk the signalling method switched to Morse and, observed Johnny of the night of 20 April, 'The war ships rested like ghosts on the calm waters. Every light on them is extinguished, except those that danced about, now fast, now slow, transmitting their messages so pregnant with eventualities.'

During these innocuous interludes the serious business of battle was discussed. The plan, so vague and simple, that General Paris had outlined in wintry Blandford nearly three months previously had developed into a specific order of battle. The attack was to take place on the dawn of Sunday, 25 April, on the southern tip of the Gallipoli Peninsula. Parties were to land on five beaches known as S, V, W, X and Y beaches. Of these, the main landings were to be on the very westerly points of the peninsula: V, W and X. The landings on S (at the entrance to the narrows) and Y (on the opposite side of the peninsula on the Aegean Sea) were mainly to protect the flanks, disseminate the forces of the enemy and hold up his reinforcements. The French were to land a force of colonial troops at Kum Kale on the Asiatic side of the entrance to the Dardanelles. Another assault was planned some four miles north-east of Y beach, at Gaba Tepe, the place which became known as Anzac Cove because it was the landing site of the Australian and New Zealand Army Corps.

V beach, at Cape Helles, was, of all the beaches selected, the most suitable for defence and the most treacherous for the invaders. The beach itself was not more than 10 yards wide and edged by a small but perpendicular bank of sand not above 5 or 6 feet high; beyond was a broad amphitheatre rising over a gentle slope of some 200 yards to a height of 200 feet above sea level. The imposing fortress settlement around Sedd-el-Bahr Castle commanded the entire length of the beach. And the green and gentle slopes leading up to it were themselves covered with trenches and dugouts, invisible from the shore and beyond the reach of the preliminary bombardment. The dugouts were cut back in the slopes of the hill and the trenches were so deep as to be immune from anything save plunging fire.

To overcome these difficulties, the Allied commanders had devised a wily plan that they hoped would fool the Turkish defenders. A decrepit old collier would be beached on the shore in full view of the enemy. But while the ancient *River Clyde* might have looked like a harmless old civilian wreck she would in fact contain in her holds 2,400 troops. While a ferocious naval bombardment would keep the Turks pinned down in their defensive positions, the troops would pour out of two holes drilled in the bows of this modern-day Trojan Horse and storm up the hillside overwhelming the enemy by force of numbers and surprise. Simultaneously, other armed detachments were to be landed in an armada of small boats. Johnny was destined to act as an assistant landing officer on V Beach. The task for him and his 150 stokers was to man these boats that would take the attacking legions ashore. On the night of Thursday, 22 April, all the officers had been given their orders about their individual roles in the landings. They spent several hours studying maps and ensuring their men understood the situation. Afterwards

59

they joined one another to sing songs, make speeches and generally spread good cheer to each other.

During this preparatory period, Rupert Brooke's health had shown no signs of improving. Doctors diagnosed septicaemia, probably brought about by a mosquito bite that had caused the swelling on his lip. His transfer to a French hospital ship with no other patients on board and a complement of 12 highly trained field surgeons made no difference. On the afternoon of 23 April, Brooke died. England had lost not only the greatest of her young poets, but a voice that would have championed the cause of humane justice without discrimination in a world where, later, such voices would be few. His death came on St George's Day, and Shakespeare's birthday.

Brooke died at 4.46 p.m. on Friday, 23 April. The *Grantully Castle* received orders to sail for Gallipoli at six the following Saturday morning, so there was little time for elaborate funeral preparations. However, Brooke had expressed a wish to be buried on a Greek island and so at 7 p.m., three officers led by Freyberg set out for Skyros to select an appropriate resting place for the poet. They settled upon an olive grove where Brooke had rested some days beforehand. Johnny was among the fellow officers and men who helped dig Brooke's grave that evening.

At 9.15 p.m. the poet's coffin arrived, draped in a Union flag and accompanied by a phalanx of officers, to be greeted by a guard of honour on the quay. The procession, led by General Paris, progressed to the olive grove along a route lined with men holding lanterns, and Brooke's body was lowered into the grave decorated with sprigs of olive and flowering sage. A volley of three shots was fired into the air and the chaplain read the Church of England burial service. When it was over, officers heaped lumps of pink-and-white marble into a cairn over the grave. A simple white cross bore the inscription: 'Here lies the servant of God, Sub-Lieutenant in the English Navy, who died for the deliverance of Constantinople from the Turks.'

That night an officer telegraphed to Winston Churchill, 'He had a most romantic funeral.' Churchill wrote part of Brooke's obituary, which appeared in *The Times*:

> Rupert Brooke is dead. A telegram from the Admiral at Lemnos tells us that this life has closed at the moment when it seemed to have reached its springtime. A voice had become audible, a note had been struck, more true, more thrilling, more able to do justice to the nobility of our youth in arms engaged in this present war, than any other more able to express their thoughts of self-surrender, and with a power to carry comfort to those who watch them so intently from afar. The voice has been swiftly stilled. Only the echoes and the memory remain; but they will linger.

GALLIPOLI

On the late afternoon of the Friday, the *Aragon* weighed anchor and, following a transport ship full of Australians, began to slowly edge her way through the maze of warships in Mudros Bay. Great cheers went up from the crews as they passed by. Johnny captured the mood in his handwritten narrative 'Opening Attack on Dardanelles'. 'The ball had begun to roll at last . . . a gentle breeze blew causing small ripples on the water,—rather a cool afternoon.' He spotted one of his officers on the top deck of the *Andania* and they exchanged messages of 'good luck' via semaphore. Passing the French transport *Le Provence*, Johnny noted she 'looked very fine' with her graceful lines and red funnels. And as they approached the entrance to the harbour the crews of French and British ships cheered in unison. It was then that Johnny noticed another Australian transport racing past the *Aragon* dangerously close to them. The men were hanging from the rigging and over the side of the ship, swarming all over it, in fact, and loudly cheering their British counterparts. The British cheered back. But, noted Johnny, 'it was rather a close shave'. The two ships missed colliding with each other by barely 20 feet. That evening in the orderly room, the military officers went over the exact details of the plan for the landings.

On Saturday morning, the convoy arrived at the little island of Tenedos. Dozens of warships, torpedo boats and submarines bobbed in the sea off the coast. In the distance the gentle, undulating land looked well cultivated. To the east the mountainous scenery of Turkey's Asiatic coast stretched as far as the eye could see. To the north lay the opening of the Dardanelles, just nine miles away.

Rarely can such an inauspicious stretch of water have played such a critical role in the history of mankind. Since the dawn of time, control of the Dardanelles Straits has been the strategic objective of every great power with ambitions in the region. When the Ionian Greeks finally wrestled the Straits from Persia, the history of Mediterranean civilisation began. When Athens lost control of the Straits to Sparta, power passed to the Romans. For 1,000 years the Byzantine Empire ruled supreme, thanks to its dominance of these murky waters. Venice owed her greatness to the control of the Dardanelles. And with the defeat of Venice by the Turks, the renaissance of Mediterranean civilisation came to an end, and through her control of the Straits Turkey maintained a foothold in Europe for more than 500 years. Now it was the turn of the British and French to wrest control back into European hands.

The landings were due to begin the following day at 5 a.m. As night fell on the great armada, Johnny recorded in his narrative, 'The boats became gradually indistinct in the fading light until we seemed absolutely alone on the silent water.' That night at 10.30 p.m., the forward elements of the attack force embarked upon the short sea route to the peninsula. The boats—tugs, warships, sweepers—were hopelessly overcrowded and it was every man for himself as those on board attempted to find a place to rest for the night. Johnny bedded down under a lifeboat but later exchanged it for a warmer location on the iron gratings over the engine room. At 3 a.m., Johnny joined his fellow officers in the officers' dining saloon for tea and biscuits.

When dawn broke at 5 a.m., they could see the hills of Gallipoli some two miles away. Almost immediately the vast armada opened fire and a violent bombardment of the enemy's defences began. The troops were transferred to small boats and were towed ashore. To their surprise the enemy did not return fire except for shelling from the Asiatic shore. But they were being lured to their deaths. The Turks allowed the boats to go right inshore before they opened fire. At V beach below the village and fort of Sedd-el-Bahr, the Dublin Fusiliers were towed to shore in small boats, while the Munster Fusiliers, two companies of the Hampshire regiment and a party of the Anson battalion were hidden in the collier, the *River Clyde*. It was only when the small boats reached the shore and the *River Clyde* was beached that a tornado of fire swept over the scene, raking the little flotilla of vessels around the collier.

This is when the plan began to go disastrously wrong. The Turks were so well dug in that the pre-landing naval bombardment had little effect. Their return fire was far more effective. The few men who burst out of the *River Clyde* struggled to get ashore, as devastating rifle and machine-gun fire mercilessly mowed them down. Many of the Dubliners and seamen who manned the small boats were killed, and only a few managed to reach the low ridge of sand that ran across the beach and afforded some cover. Meanwhile the men aboard the *River Clyde* were stuck inside, unable to make a move. Some of them braved the firestorm to attempt to position lighters between the bows and the shore in order to form a bridge by means of which the troops on board could reach the beach.

Johnny found himself in the middle of this deadly maelstrom, ferrying troops back and forth between the beach and the ships moored offshore. When finally it was his turn to join the landings, it became obvious that the Turks had got the range of the small boat he was in because shells were crashing into the water only feet away and bullets whizzed past his ears. He was just about to jump out of the boat when a loud explosion 'like a firecracker' erupted in front of his chest and he felt a painful sensation in both his arms. He had been hit. Not knowing how bad his wounds were, he leapt over the side of the boat and swam the ten yards or so to the shore before scrambling along the beach to take cover behind the sandbank.

They huddled together, sheltering behind a sand cliff until night fell, and then constructed a barricade to give them as much shelter as possible using anything they could find, including the corpse of a dead officer. After nightfall, those men who were still on the *River Clyde* were able to get ashore, thankfully without loss. The attacking force took up a position on the right-hand side of the beach under an ancient castle, which had been shattered by the fighting. Under cover of darkness the wounded were able to crawl to their comrades and safety. The following afternoon they were evacuated to a hospital ship in an inglorious retreat. The war for Johnny, for the time being at least, was over.

THE WESTERN FRONT

The *River Clyde* tragedy was only the first of many in the course of the ill-fated Dardanelles disaster. Despite the courage of Johnny and thousands more like him, the campaign was so mismanaged by political, military and naval squabbling in Whitehall, as well as delays and faintheartedness on the part of commanders in the field, that in retrospect it seems clear it was doomed from the start. Winston Churchill took full responsibility and handed in his resignation on 11 November 1915. His name has been inextricably linked with the catastrophe ever since, and the memory of the huge loss of life produced a more timid frame of mind in him when it came to committing forces to risky adventures in later years. Because of his injuries, Johnny escaped the remainder of the fighting that went on for months and claimed 250,000 Allied casualties. His only significant wound permanently disfigured the fingers on one hand. By the time the remaining troops were evacuated in January 1916, Johnny had finally recovered and had been employed in the somewhat mundane task of training at Blandford.

In February 1916, Lady Cynthia Asquith, the Prime Minister's daughter-in-law, recorded meeting Johnny and his mother in London. Her description of Flora was not kind—she called her an 'astonishing voluble gushing American woman'—but she liked Johnny and said he had been 'recommended for the

VC'. In fact Johnny didn't get the VC. But he was awarded the Royal Navy's Distinguished Service Cross for his part in the landings. In the citation, Bernard Freyberg, his commanding officer, reported, 'When Johnny saw that all was not going according to plan, he led his platoon into the fighting with the utmost gallantry until he was badly wounded and he had to be sent home to recover.'

Training was too unchallenging an occupation for Johnny. With the help of his mother, who lobbied on his behalf, he was allowed to transfer to the Army and in April joined the recently raised 10th Battalion of the Queen's Royal West Surrey Regiment ('The Battersea Battalion'). Much to his satisfaction, he was back in the fray almost immediately. His regiment landed at Le Havre on 6 May and by the end of the month was in Flanders—just in time for one of the biggest bloodbaths in history. The first day of the Battle of the Somme, 1 July, claimed 60,000 British casualties. It was the worst day in the British Army's history and the slaughter was to continue for another four-and-a-half months.

Johnny's battalion learnt it was to become part of this titanic maelstrom of death and destruction when it was moved across the border to France in August and began training for a major attack as part of the wider offensive. They were about to take part in the Battle of Flers-Courcelette, the third and last of the great offensives of the Battle of the Somme. It would become better known, however (rightly or wrongly), as the debut of the tank: 49 of these newly developed monsters of warfare were deployed across the battleground. The Battersea Battalion was assigned two of them.

Their objective was Flers, a small village behind German lines. On the night of 14 September, the battalion moved through the shattered remains of nearby Delville Wood and, at 6.20 a.m. as the sun rose, began the attack. After 30 minutes of heavy fighting the first objective—the enemy's forward trenches—had been taken. By the early evening the village of Flers itself was in Allied hands. After the battle was won, one of the two tanks rolled down the main street 'followed by the whole British Army behind cheering' ran a newspaper report. It is not known why the second tank missed the celebrations. Perhaps it had broken down: many of the 49 did. But they were a great morale booster to the troops, who felt that they had a decisive advantage over the enemy.

The casualty rate in the Flers-Courcelette action for the Battersea Battalion was appalling: 335 men were reported dead, missing or wounded—half of the battalion's fighting strength. Johnny was among the wounded once more, and was forced to leave the front line for a period of recovery and recuperation in England. Once more the achievements of the offensive were questionable. The Army had made modest progress into enemy-occupied territory, but not so much that the decisive breakthrough British commanders had hoped for could be achieved. By the end of the Battle of the Somme the British had suffered more than 1,500,000 casualties, little had been gained and the area remained swamped in the stagnant quagmire of the Western Front.

Two months later, when Johnny had fully recovered, he was sent on a course to the Army's Machine Gun School at Grantham, Lincolnshire.

Thereafter he raised and trained the 188th Machine Gun Company, which was destined to be attached to an infantry brigade in France. They crossed the Channel on 26 April 1917. To Johnny's delight, his machine gun company was posted to the same brigade he had served with in Antwerp and Gallipoli. What remained of the Royal Naval Division had come back from Gallipoli and Salonica to France in 1916 to be reinforced from England and was now under army command as the re-named 63rd (Royal Naval) Division. (Though, to the irritation of some army commanders—and the amusement of others—its officers and men continued to adhere to the peculiar habits of the Royal Navy, which they respectfully but stubbornly refused to change.) They were now stationed on the Ypres salient. Within months they were in the thick of yet another gargantuan and largely futile struggle of the First World War.

The Passchendaele Offensive began in July 1917 with the Allied armies launching a blistering assault on German lines. The objective was the control of the village of Passchendaele, near Ypres. Johnny and his men of the 188th (which shortly became the 224th Machine Gun Company) were in and out of the trenches all through the summer and autumn of 1917. The climate was unusually cold and wet for that time of year. Since most of the battle took place over reclaimed marshland, which was unfathomably swampy in any case, the continual fighting and artillery bombardment resulted in a muddy quagmire in which men often drowned instead of being killed by the enemy. The filth and desolation of the trenches was rarely relieved. Worse still, the repeated attacks and counter attacks resulted in very little progress, while the death and casualty toll increased out of all proportion to the minuscule gains made. Johnny was gassed, but fortunately only mildly and he was not long away from the action. By the end of the action in November 1917, the Allies had gained no more than five miles of territory at the cost of hundreds of thousands of dead and wounded.

Within a few weeks of the end of the battle, Johnny was on leave in Boulogne. The war and its degradations might have been a million miles away and Johnny enjoyed a relaxing leave amid civilised surroundings and convivial company. One particular letter home from this period gives an early hint of his close connections with two important figures in the intelligence services. On 2 December 1917, he wrote to Flora, 'Rex Benson lunched w. me today at Mony's + Sir William Wiseman is crossing over w. him this afternoon to England. Rex's mother is ill. Rex is a Major on the Staff now.' Sir William Wiseman and Rex Benson were two of the most intriguing members of the British espionage community.

Wiseman had been sent by Britain's Secret Intelligence director, Mansfield Smith-Cumming, to establish the agency's office in the United States during the First World War. As the head of the British intelligence mission in Washington, D.C., Wiseman acted as a liaison between President Woodrow Wilson and the British government. Rex Benson, the son of a prosperous merchant banker, was the personification of the 'golden lad' at Eton. One of the most popular boys there, he was accomplished at polo and could play the piano non-stop for four hours.

Benson had been wounded and badly gassed in 1915, but served at Ypres in September 1916 and after that was transferred to the French counter-espionage service, the Bureau Interallié, as the representative of spymaster Stewart Menzies. Famously, Benson was instrumental in capturing the Dutch spy Mata Hari and served for most of his next four decades in intelligence, becoming, during the Second World War, Menzies' direct line to the 'exiled' Duke of Windsor. There is no evidence at all that Johnny was ever employed or paid as a spy. But given his proximity to such important members of the British intelligence community and connections in high circles with prominent personalities, and given his subsequent travels on the border lands of Soviet Russia, it would be incredible if they had not at least asked for his informal help from time to time.

On the eve of the New Year, Johnny received bad news about his friend 'Oc' Asquith. The former prime minister's son had been with his brigade in the trenches reconnoitring a position when he was badly wounded in the foot by sniper fire. 'I do hope his foot will be all right as men like him cannot be replaced easily,' Johnny wrote to Flora on 31 December 1917. Asquith was so severely wounded that his leg had to be amputated and he was saved from further active service for the rest of the war. By early 1918, Johnny had had a Mention in Despatches and was promoted to Major. He was appointed second-in-command of a battalion of 64 heavy Vickers machine guns.

In the spring of 1918, the Germans launched their last desperate attack. Johnny was gassed once more but not badly enough to warrant going to hospital. He continued in the fighting through the summer months and as the war approached its end was promoted to lieutenant colonel and given command of the 16th Royal Sussex, a yeomanry battalion. At 24 years of age he was one of the youngest battalion commanders in the British Army. The war was rapidly reaching its dénouement. He took command on 16 October and his battalion joined in the pursuit of the retreating Germans. It was Antwerp in reverse, Johnny wrote home. The war ended with the Armistice on 11 November 1918.

10

DEATH REVISITED

Johnny was to remain on the war-torn Continent for another four months after the Armistice, trying to keep his men occupied with sports and training classes and so forth while they waited to go home. Much of their time was also spent helping to clear up the devastated battlefields of Belgium. In March 1919, Flora and Lionel sailed across the Channel to be reunited with Johnny for the first time since he had last been in England. They spent four days with him, staying in a cottage near his headquarters at a hilltop chateau in Grammont (now Geraardsbergen) where he was stationed as Colonel of the 74th Division. They travelled around the devastated battlefields of Belgium and France with him, visiting some of the places where he had been stationed and witnessed action.

Flora wrote an account of their travels together, a 29-page typewritten document that is valuable, not so much for any insight into Johnny's life at the time, but because of the picture it provides of the sheer scale of the ruination laid waste across vast expanses of the Western Front. 'Account of trip to continent starting March 4, 1919' also reveals something of Flora's literary flair and spiritual awareness, as well as her indomitable spirit as she casually dodges sea mines in the Channel and picks her way through rotting corpses in the trenches.

The account begins with Flora and Lionel crossing from Harwich to Antwerp on a stinking

74

steamship crowded with refugees returning to what remained of their country. Unable to bear the two Belgian women—neither of whom washed at night—in her tiny hermetically sealed stateroom, Flora ventures above deck into the icy cold of the evening. She sees the boat passing perilously close to a mine bobbing in the water. It was shot at but not detonated. 'I wonder who struck it later!' she muses. In the once proud and prosperous city of Antwerp, where Johnny had begun his war, they encounter a swarm of desperate humanity and fighting on the streets. There are few taxis or horses; instead these are replaced with carts pulled by dogs three abreast, cows, goats and bullocks, and men who carried the Guests' baggage on their bare backs.

They met Johnny at the Hôtel Britannique looking very young in his colonel's uniform and 'tired, haggard and worn after the awful strain of 5 years [at war]'. 'An army of occupation,' Flora writes, 'is a restless thing to keep going—with the men's nerves all on edge . . . most officers consider since the Armistice, the most trying time of the war.' They spent most of the afternoon in Flora's room listening to Johnny's accounts of the last battles. It was raining and cold outside. On the following Sunday, they set off for Ypres with a rented car and driver 'to go over the road Lionel and Johnny knew only too well during the war'. (Lionel had also been fighting.)

They passed through villages, some of which appeared unharmed by the war, others of which had been bombed by the British and Germans. Lunch was 'pale soup, roast horse flesh, boiled potatoes and greens' with good coffee. They

75

encountered Menin, which was the first town virtually flattened by the hostilities. 'A few melancholy looking people dressed in deep mourning, looking among the ruins of their homes in vain. The town is practically uninhabited, but a few brave people had arranged walls and roofs of straw and paper, and crept into one end of a derelict building.'

They drove on in the drizzling afternoon rain. The stillness of the surrounding countryside, reported Flora, was awful:

> the country all pitted with shell holes and the debris of battle everywhere; shells exploded; discarded rolls of barbed wire; machine guns old and new, French, German and English; broken down tanks and aeroplanes. There was not a note of life anywhere,—only death and destruction—a strange bird occasionally swooped down and quickly disappeared,—a weird grey and white bird of prey that hovered close to the ground.

In Ypres itself the sun finally shone down but they discovered 'wet ruins glistening like useless jewels. We could see through them the blue sky.' They climbed over the ruins and motored around the silent streets. They drove out to the St Julien Battlefield where Johnny's Machine Gun battalion had fought in 1917 in the great Passchendaele offensive. The dugouts were still intact, coats hung on hooks and bottles stood on tables. They struggled through the mud to Johnny's brigade headquarters, too full of water to step into; but they managed to salvage some relics: French and

German helmets and English shell casings.

There were a good many live shells and hand grenades lying about and we had to pick our way carefully not to slip into the great craters of blood coloured water . . . Discarded kits lay everywhere on the ground; the worms had begun to get into them. There were many dead bodies lightly covered with a bit of carpet or thin carpet of earth;—some skulls and endless graves of French, English and German buried side by side.

Flora seemed to be uplifted to discover a note of humanity: one French soldier was buried with a tumbler upside down on his grave and a note inside it, probably found in his pocket, with a request to have it buried with him. The grave had been fought over for four years, but the poignant memorial had remained undisturbed. Next to the Frenchman's grave was that of a German.

They found the grave of Captain Guy Drummond, the only son of a friend of Flora in Canada, killed in action on 24 April 1915.

Here I knelt down in the mud between my precious husband and son, and said a prayer of thanks to my Father in Heaven for having spared Lionel and Johnny through this awful war; they stood bare-headed beside me and made their prayer—we three alone together the only living things for miles and miles around—in the sunset light—and I realised for the first time in my life that life is a moment in eternity, and the great deeds, the great suffering, the wonderful cheerfulness and courage of the men that slept around us, had a message to the world that would in time be heard—probably more through Death than had they lived. Foe and Friend,—side by side in the great peace.

They visited Arcq, where Johnny's 16th Sussex Yeomanry fought for four days just before the Armistice, and walked from his trenches across no man's land, which now bloomed with pink-and-white marguerites, to the German trenches only 200 yards distant. The road toward Brussels was littered with shells and all kinds of explosives thrown away by the Germans in their haste to escape the British advance. The railway tracks were blown into 'grotesque festoons'; the ground as far as they could see was riddled with shell holes. They finally reached Grammont and Johnny's 74th Division headquarters in a huge chateau high on a hill over the village. Flora and Lionel were billeted in a house on the village square owned by two Belgian women who had lost everything in the war.

The town appeared completely unscathed. The Royal Engineers gave a concert in the theatre. The next day Flora and Lionel lunched in the mess in the chateau and were amused to see that all the officers under Johnny's command were at least ten years older than him. 'He looked so very young and so dignified at the head of his table.'

As they continued on their journey they heard many stories of German brutality and pillaging and were received with several encores of 'viva l'anglais! [sic]' They visited Mons, where the legendary Angels appeared during the British withdrawal toward Maubeuge. (The legend of the 'Angel of Mons' was a popular myth repeated for propaganda purposes about a group of angels who were said to appear over the trenches protecting British troops during the Battle of Mons.) Finally, on Monday, 17 March Flora kissed her precious son goodbye. Two of his soldiers loaded her and Lionel's luggage onto their rented car as a crowd gathered around to wish them farewell, and Johnny gave them a salute as they disappeared from sight. They returned to England from Ostend on 18 March.

Flora ended her account with a curious ode to England describing her feelings as they boarded the little boat home:

Oh our wonderful British Navy who only had individually and collectively [a] quarter the praise they deserved in their courage, their inventions, their absolute silence sacrificing the praise due to them to their country's need. The great Army, the impossible—always made possible by the Englishman in all his classes.

He is sportsman on land and sea—a generous victor—an admiring foe, for all the qualities there are to be admired in the opponent of a great game—he only asks 'keep the rules—keep the rules' we have sometimes broken the rules ourselves in greed, in ambition but the world is still unsettled and Britons sense of justice and order will always win out even among ourselves give us a little time.

Both paragraphs have been scrubbed out. Perhaps even Flora realised her rosy-eyed vision of her adopted country was hopelessly sentimental. Shortly after Flora and Lionel arrived home, Johnny was presented with the Distinguished Service Order. He was demobilised that spring. It would be more than a year before he relinquished his commission in the Army, on 18 December 1920. In the meantime, he became immersed in an intriguing diversion that would take him to the ends of the earth.

TO THE ENDS OF THE EARTH

On 1 January 1919, three months before Flora and Lionel's visit to the Continent, Johnny had received an appealing offer from his uncle, Poultney Bigelow. Poultney was Flora's older brother, a fascinating man, almost as accomplished in his own right as their illustrious father, the modern-day Renaissance man John Bigelow. During the years when Bigelow senior was American envoy and minister to the court of Napoleon III, Poultney attended Potsdam preparatory school near Berlin. There, he became friends with Prince Wilhelm, the future King of Prussia and last Emperor of Germany. They played 'cowboys and Indians' together and their friendship grew and strengthened over the years. After they left school, Wilhelm and Poultney began a correspondence that continued throughout their lives, though it became frosty just before the Second World War.

The land of Goethe, Schiller, Bach and Beethoven exercised a compelling hold over Poultney: he was a great admirer of most things German. (An early enthusiast for Adolf Hitler, Poultney's support waned considerably when the brutality of the dictator's regime was exposed.) Poultney was also a great explorer, once sailing to the Orient and becoming shipwrecked off the coast of Japan. An international newspaper correspondent who covered the Spanish–American Civil War for *The Times* of London, Poultney was, like his father, a prolific man of letters who would go on to write 11 substantial tomes during his lifetime, many about German culture and politics.

Now Poultney invited his favourite nephew to become a member of an exclusive international dining fellowship, which celebrated the urge for travel and adventure. 'The Ends of the Earth Club' had been founded in the early days of the century by a group of artists, explorers and entrepreneurs who had travelled widely. It was broadly intended to be a forum in which they could pool the lessons they had derived from their experiences, amid convivial company and civilised surroundings. Among the founding members of the club was Rudyard Kipling, whose celebrated poem 'The Ballad of East and West' no doubt inspired the name . . .

> Oh, East is East, and West is West, and
>   never the twain shall meet,
> Till Earth and Sky stand presently at God's
>   great Judgment Seat;
> But there is neither East nor West, Border,
>   nor Breed, nor Birth,
> When two strong men stand face to face,
>   tho' they come from the ends of the earth!

Every year, members of The Ends of the Earth Club would descend upon New York City, and later London, for their annual jamboree: a white-tie dinner over which they would exchange their experiences of exploring the world, much of which was then still undiscovered. For many years this elite gathering was held at the Hotel Savoy in Manhattan, though subsequently Claridge's in

London became a favoured venue during Ascot Week. The club had neither a constitution nor rules; however, the *New York Times* summarised its somewhat vague principles thus: 'A member must be a good fellow, who has no axe to grind, and who speaks our language.' But from the very beginning, the *New York Times'* correspondent reported waspishly, the members broke their own strictures: at the first official dinner in March 1904, 'The menus were printed on cardboard compasses, and, untrue to the principle of the organisation, the dishes were all in French.'

A central assumption of The Ends of the Earth Club was, undoubtedly, the innate superiority of the Anglo-Saxon world, hardly unusually, since that was the generally held belief of much of humankind at the time. At the March 1904 dinner, General James L. Wilson, addressing his dining companions, stated:

> There are . . . about four hundred millions of white people on the earth and about twelve hundred millions of coloured people. What will become of the white people when these coloured inhabitants of the earth really start up in business you can imagine for yourselves.

Mark Twain, who was adopted as the honorary head, had a slightly jaundiced view of The Ends of the Earth Club. After General Wilson made similar comments at the September 1906 get together, Twain observed privately, 'and when the Anglo-Saxon wants a thing, he just takes it'. Twain depicted Americans and Englishmen as thieves, highwaymen and pirates, and proud of it. He couldn't help but note the slightly ambiguous nature of the association. At the 1906 dinner, he commented, 'I don't quite get the hang of this club.' He was greeted with laughter and hailed with 'For He's a Jolly Good Fellow'.

The Great War had almost destroyed the cradle of the Western civilisation that The Ends of the Earth Club held dear. And it had put the transatlantic alliance between Britain and France on the one hand, and the United States on the other, under great strain. In many American circles, Britain was regarded with intense suspicion: the ever-perfidious Albion, who, with France, had retained her colonial pretensions, and who had lured her 'cousins' in the United States into a costly and ruinous conflict. For many Americans, their overwhelming desire was for a return to 'normalcy', which in their terms meant extricating themselves from engagement with the rest of the world and particularly from their troublesome European 'cousins'.

It is no secret that before, after and during the war, Washington and Whitehall maintained exhaustive plans to wage war on each other's countries. This air of mutual suspicion had by no means been allayed by the temporary exigencies of the wartime alliance. After the Armistice, the Hearst newspaper empire railed against the British, claiming that they were operating 5,000 agents in America attempting to influence elections. There was indeed a 'special relationship' between Britain and the United States (though not as empathetic as the one between republican America and republican France), but it was fraught with the frisson of perpetual suspicion, mutual self-interest and ill-disguised ill will.

However, there was a small but influential group of Americans and a larger group of Britons who believed passionately that a strong and sustainable Anglo-American compact was fundamental to their future survival in the newly evolving world, the world in which they were already a minority. Pivotal to their convictions was the continuance of Anglo-American laissez-faire economics, practised within a framework of democracy, liberal or otherwise. Utmost in their fears was the menace of Bolshevism. Among the eclectic collection of American businessmen, stockbrokers, philanthropists, writers and academics who shared these views were Winthrop Aldrich, Vincent Astor, Nelson Doubleday and Johnny Dodge's great friend Kermit Roosevelt.

These profoundly influential people acted in informal unison to propagate their Anglo-American view of the future, often congregating in private clubs. One informal gathering, known enigmatically as 'The Room', worked with Sir William Wiseman, chief of the British secret service in America during World War I. Wiseman remained in America after the war to become a partner in the Kuhn, Loeb & Company investment bank. He belonged to both The Room and a similar, connected grouping called—even more enigmatically—'The Walrus Club'. So did 'Wild' Bill Donovan, who would go on to become the founding father of the Office of Strategic Services, forerunner of the CIA. In his biography of the British spymaster Sir Stewart Menzies, Anthony Cave Brown described these people and their clubs as: 'Essentially, a private intelligence service that worked in collaboration with the British secret service.'

Both The Room and The Walrus Club maintained close links with The Ends of the Earth Club and another establishment with the unfathomable name of 'The 1b Club'. Prominent among their members were Wiseman, Menzies and Johnny's chum from days of fighting in France, Rex Benson. Thus, when Johnny accepted his Uncle Poultney's invitation to join The Ends of the Earth Club, he found himself in familiar company. Shortly after joining the club, Johnny embarked upon a voyage that would take him around much of the world. He would visit the New World and the antipodes, but it was to the outlands of Soviet Russia, where the latest episode of the 'great game' was unfolding in the form of the Russian Civil War, that Johnny would devote his most assiduous attention.

While the war on the Continent had ceased with the Armistice of November 1918, turmoil continued to wrack the former Russian Empire and political unrest was spreading throughout Europe like a contagion. The Russian Civil War had been raging since 1917 and would continue until 1923. Though it was ostensibly being fought between the 'Red' forces of the October Revolution and the reactionary 'White' forces of the former czarist regime, these predominant elements were themselves divided between a multitude of factions, and a half-dozen outside states—many with conflicting agendas—were actively taking part in the hostilities.

Soviet Russia had been reduced to a state of poverty even more abject than it had endured under the czars. Pandemonium reigned everywhere in an enormous country whose borders touched upon those of so many others. Britain, fearful that the revolutionary contagion would spread into India and its other colonial possessions in the East, was giving active support to the Whites. China and Japan, concerned about their own territorial integrity on the far-flung fringes of Siberian Russia, were also lending tacit assistance to the supporters of the former czarist regime. The United States shared these wider strategic worries and, under the veil of protecting international trade routes, President Woodrow Wilson had dispatched engineers and a force of 10,000 troops to protect the Trans-Siberian Railway stretching between Moscow and Vladivostok. It was into this unholy maelstrom of international intrigue and internal chaos that Johnny threw himself in the immediate aftermath of his four exhausting years in the Great War.

There are three main items of documentation that can be relied upon to account for the more than two years that Johnny devoted to his voyage of discovery, most of which was spent in the warring outposts of post-Revolutionary Russia. The first, written by himself, is a published account in a now defunct magazine entitled *The World's Work*, and relates to his commercial activities in Persia and the Caucasus, ostensibly attempting to establish an import-export business. The other is an unpublished and untitled document in his archive in Toronto that gives an expanded version of his activities in this region, including many absorbing episodes he obviously thought it wise to omit from the publicly published article. These episodes display an intense interest in the activities of the

Soviet forces in this widespread region. The third is an infuriatingly incomplete and muddled folio of 30 or so out-of-sequence pages covering his travels through China, Mongolia, Japan and Russia, including a 1,700-mile trek on horseback. This was written, it appears, some five years after the fact and parts of it were intended as the basis for a book.

These accounts broadly conform to one another, but curiosity is piqued by the slightly changing nuances. For instance, in *The World's Work* magazine article, published in 1922, Johnny writes:

> Faced after the War, like so many others, with lack of definite occupation, it occurred to me to set out upon an investigation of my own into the problems of trade congestion resulting from a four-years upset of the ordinary channels of commerce. It was necessary to visit various countries not only in order to discover the best possible trade openings, but also to learn what each country needed most. This was perhaps not an original idea on my part, but at least I had enough faith to invest in it my own moderate supply of money.

But Johnny was not an independently wealthy person. His London home had been presented to him by his stepfather, and before the war he had not advanced beyond being a junior stockbroker albeit a successful one. He certainly didn't have the sort of money required to finance a more-than-two-year-long gallivant around the world. Lionel did, and according to Phyllis B. Dodge's notes for her potential biography of Johnny, it was Johnny's stepfather who financed the mission. Though Phyllis cites no sources, she writes that in return Johnny was to report on business investment opportunities for Lionel and his business colleagues in America and Britain, and on potential settlement schemes in Canada and Australia for British ex-servicemen.

This, again, provides a different motivation to that which he enunciates in the third source—the muddled and incomplete notes mentioned above. In those he states that once the war was over he looked on with alarm as trouble brewed everywhere—'strikes, riots, bankruptcies, dissentions'—while 'the greatest statesmen of Europe did not know what to do'. Everyone was frightened, 'and many were thinking that the whole fabric of civilisation was tumbling down'. He writes:

In those troubled days, all of a sudden Europe began to hear of a new remedy for all evils. The remedy was an extraordinary one, private initiative was to be prohibited and everything was to be entrusted to the State. The whole of industry, trade, railways, and banks had to be nationalised.

This was such a drastic measure that people were not prepared, anyhow in England, to accept it as a solution unless they were satisfied that it could work in practice. In those days we read out of the newspapers that the experiment had been tried in Russia . . . I was free, I was seeking together with many men of my age the truth, and I decided to go to Russia and to see how nationalisation worked.

Thus we have a completely different motivation for the trip. Comrades who subsequently found themselves incarcerated with Johnny in various Second World War prison camps insist he said he went to Russia as a confirmed socialist and only became disillusioned when he saw how badly socialism worked.

So we are left with a melee of subtly different motivations. Travelling international businessmen are often enlisted to assist the intelligence-gathering forces of one country or another, without being formally paid as agents. It would not be surprising if this were Johnny's real role: a gentleman spy operating behind the perfectly legitimate facade of business.

Whatever the truth, and whatever the differing nuances of Johnny's various explanations, there is no doubt that his travels began in a completely uncontroversial way. As the spring turned to summer in 1919, he set sail from England for Canada with Flora and Lionel, and stayed in Montreal, no doubt visiting relations and friends, and addressing himself to family business. In the autumn, Johnny left Flora and Lionel behind and went out to British Columbia, presumably as part of his role in assessing the potential for ex-servicemen's resettlement schemes. He didn't spend much time on this assignment, and soon left North America. His peregrinations took him across the Pacific to Australia and New Zealand, where he sent regular reports back to Lionel. He remained in the southern hemisphere until June 1920. It was around about this time, he later stated in yet another account, that he decided to travel to Russia.

A GREAT GAME

Over the forthcoming months, Johnny's travels would take him into the darkest corners of the Russian colossus where the shadows cast by the abuses of the czars had not been lifted by Soviet misrule. Johnny would meet some of the more exotic—and bloodthirsty—elements of this enormous and mysterious land at a crucial moment in its history and the history of the wider world. Tellingly, though Johnny would acknowledge the abuses of the 'noble' classes who formerly ruled it, he seemed perfectly oblivious to the atrocities that their supporters were committing under his nose while he was there. And he rarely held up their behaviour to the critical scrutiny that he invariably applied to 'the Reds', often, instead, parading his own prejudices for the upper classes, approvingly describing their smart uniforms, clean-cut features and 'civilised' behaviour. As much as Johnny attempted to be the unbiased observer, he really could not shrug off the assumptions of his class and background.

Only a fragmentary record of Johnny's wanderings around China, Mongolia and Russia survive, but we know from them that his journey took in Beijing—or Peking as it was then—possibly Hong Kong and certainly Japan. He eventually arrived overland through Mongolia at his ultimate destination, the Communist-held Russian town of Verchne Udinsk (now Ulan Ude) near Lake Baykal

(Baikal). Given that this expedition involved, according to his own account, a 1,700-mile horseback ride 'beyond the railway into Siberia'—more or less the distance between Hong Kong and Verchne Udinsk—it is likely that his route started in the British colony, took him thence to Peking, from where he might have made a side-excursion to Japan before continuing into the vast and untamed expanses of Mongolia. Scant details of this remarkable odyssey survive, except a few scraps of manuscript that refer to Chinese rest stations made of mud, and meals of 'inevitable mutton, unleavened bread and tea'. We also know, from what remains of the manuscript, that Johnny travelled with an interpreter ('almost certainly a Red sympathiser').

Verchne Udinsk was the capital of the Far Eastern Republic, a puppet state that the Soviets had created as a buffer to placate the Japanese, who still occupied Vladivostok and were apprehensive about Communist incursions into their territory. Situated in the middle of the Siberian steppes, the settlement is some 60 miles south-east of the vast Lake Baykal and, at nearly 2,000 feet above sea level, stands at the foot of two huge mountain ranges. Verchne Udinsk was, and is, an important stop on the trans-Siberian railway between Irkutsk and the great railway junction of Chita which, when Johnny was travelling, was occupied by pro-czarist White forces. Before arriving in Russia, Johnny and his interpreter had heard all manner of rumour about the plans of the feared White warlords, the Cossack general Grigori Semenov (or Seminoff) and his sidekick Baron Roman von Ungern-Sternberg, a descendant of

German crusaders. It was said that these two reactionary officers, staunch defendants of the czarist empire, were planning a decisive offensive against the Reds. It was certainly true that they deployed ruthless and bloodthirsty tactics against their opponents.

After an arduous trek across Mongolia, Johnny and his interpreter crossed into Russia at the frontier town of Troitzkosavok. The morning after their arrival, they went to see the president of the local Communist Party. In his manuscript Johnny recorded: 'The objects of my journey were Russia and the unbiased study of Socialist rule, and now I found myself, with a certain feeling of excitement, on the threshold of the Soviet domain.' (Interestingly, in this record, made some five years after the event, he made no claim to being a 'confirmed socialist'.) He continued:

> Moscow was still far; even Verchne Udinsk was some days' journey away, but from now onwards, with a mind unclouded by prejudice and free from bias, I could commence the collection of impressions of Red Administration which would give me an opinion, accurate as to fact, and honest as to expression.

His first interview with a Bolshevik official left a lasting impression on Johnny. The individual was a collarless and unshaven 'but not unattractive little man', who received them at once and addressed Johnny in perfect English. It turned out that he had spent 15 years in America. Unfortunately, Johnny's notes about this meeting come to an abrupt halt before we learn much more about it but, interestingly, the very last line before the narrative is severed reads, 'I as a journa— . . .', which hints that Johnny was likely to be adopting a familiar ruse in the espionage trade. He never before or after made any effort to portray himself as a journalist, or showed any inclination to that calling. His family have always presumed he was acting as a spy.

Johnny eventually made it to Verchne Udinsk. He was to spend three weeks there during which any objectivity he might once have entertained for the socialist cause rapidly evaporated. On one occasion he was walking along a road with his interpreter when he saw a man with a rifle, but not in uniform, savagely beating a 'wretched looking fellow'. The victim of this assault made no effort to protest or fight back, which puzzled Johnny. He later discovered that the poor man had been a priest. He concluded that 'centuries of slavery had crushed in them [the ordinary Russians] the spirit of protest and power of resistance'. And now, under the Soviets, 'there was no legal institution the man could complain to because the "People's Courts" were little more than kangaroo courts presided over by drunken soldiers which dispensed not justice but retribution against the once rich—and priests'.

As he wandered through the streets of Verchne Udinsk he saw only wretched and tired people, all miserable and hungry despite Lenin's promises to bring them salvation. Shops were closed and food was outrageously expensive. There was no work to be found because factories had shut down. The right to freedom of speech, for which the

95

proletariat had perished fighting the czarist regime, had been abolished by the Soviets. In his narrative, Johnny acknowledges that there were serious abuses of power during the czarist years, but doesn't see Communism as a remedy to these reactionary depredations. He wrote: 'I sometimes wish that our advocates of Bolshevism would emmigrate [sic] to Russia for a year and take part in the farce there which is called political life.' They would, he was sure, be soon begging to come home.

Johnny summarised his stay in Verchne Udinsk as 'three weeks of cold and hunger and dirt'. But, he later wrote, 'worse to endure than all the physical discomfort was the atmosphere of suspicion and distrust'. While he was there he became enmeshed in the 'web of fear and hate' spun by Moscow. On several occasions he returned to the bedroom in his hotel (which was bereft of a bed) to find it had been ransacked and his diaries had been read. 'People with whom I had made friends suddenly disappeared.' He observed:

> no dictatorship is possible in a country, unless the whole population is kept in a state of abject fear and of an obsession, which the Russians would express in their own language by saying that, 'All the walls seem to have ears.' Such a state of fear prevents people from coming together; their discussing anything, even from thinking, and effectively prevents the existence and the rise of public opinion.

He was presumably relieved to leave this bastion of Bolshevism. He did so on a 'well appointed' train with good food and 'cheerful company'. It took him some 400 miles to Chita, one of the few strongholds of the White Army. There he was met by a Japanese officer who spoke English and escorted Johnny to the headquarters of the *Ataman* (Chief) of the Cossacks, Grigori Semenov. Semenov was waiting for him in another train standing in a siding. Semenov and his staff impressed Johnny with their willingness to help him with the questions he had about their army, its aims and activities. Johnny betrayed his respect for order and civility when he contrasted their well-run and tidy offices with the chaos of the semi-civilian administration of the Communists at Verchne Udinsk. He wrote:

> Staff officers in the glittering, if worn, czarist uniforms, passed and re-passed, exchanged chits, summoned orderlies and dispatched them into space amid that peculiar atmosphere of noiseless confusion which pervades the homes of the high command in any country.

Johnny insisted throughout his travels that he took no sides, and that he had sympathy, to a lesser or greater extent, for both the Reds and the Whites. He also acknowledged the serious abuses of czarist Russia that had brought the country to a state of revolution, chaos and despair. It is clear, however, that he felt more comfortable in the presence of the smart and decisive General Semenov and his entourage than with the shambolic Communist authorities of Verchne Udinsk.

Johnny might not have been fully aware of Semenov's reputation for ruthless savagery or, for that matter, of Baron Ungern-Sternberg's bloodthirsty temperament. It was said that war, bloodshed and massacre were the natural elements for both these warlords. Both were devoted to imperial autocracy and fanatically opposed to any kind of democracy. Semenov's rule in the region had been known as the *Atamansjtsjina*: the *Ataman*'s reign of terror. His roving trains carrying men armed to the teeth terrorised the locals. Other trains would transport Bolshevik prisoners of war to their doom. They were either executed along the way at conveniently discreet locations, or they were simply allowed to starve or freeze to death (a tactic that was adopted in Russia by the victoriously advancing Nazi armies of the Second World War). It was said that when the trains stopped at stations the stench of corpses from the wagons was unbearable. Ungern-Sternberg's troops were wild and sadistic warriors who gloried in terrorising whoever they came across. It was his heartfelt hope to see every Bolshevik and Jew between Mongolia and Moscow hanging from gallows.

Given Johnny's gentle temperament and his unswerving optimism about human nature, it is unlikely he was acquainted with these unsavoury truths. Perhaps there is a more simple explanation. The world was a savage place in Johnny's day. He had witnessed some of the most dreadful depredations of human behaviour during the Great War, which was fought among those countries regarded as the most civilised in the world. Is it any surprise that similar depravities committed among those who were widely regarded as less than civilised fell short of exciting his interest or concern?

Johnny eventually bade Semenov farewell and continued his journey, apparently hoping to go to Moscow on board the trans-Siberian railway. This crucially important railway was operated with the help of an American delegation of railway engineers, and parts of the line were protected by a force of some 10,000 US troops sent by President Wilson. But it was under the control of the Communist Russian authorities, who were obviously suspicious of Johnny because they refused him permission to go to Moscow ('although my ends were not political, M. Lenin's government did not trust me, and I was refused the necessary passports'). Thus, rebuffed but not dispirited, he determined to enter Russia by a western route and set off through the more friendly lands of India, Mesopotamia and Persia to the Black Sea.

Johnny first went south to Siam (now Thailand) and Bangkok where he met Arthur Stannard Vernay, a British-born, New York-based antiques dealer, who had embarked upon an adventurous exploration of the Far East, to collect specimens for the American Museum of Natural History. Together, it appears, they travelled and mapped a new route to Mandalay, one which Vernay published a year or so later, before they parted company. Sadly, yet again, no recollections of Johnny's chart-making journey survive.

Subsequently Johnny went to India where he felt more at home. He paid a visit to Field Marshal Sir William Hardwood at Rawalpindi, the Commander-in-Chief of the subcontinent. Johnny noted:

when I saw him taking part in the men's

99

sports—pig-sticking as well if not better than most—and the obvious way in which he was beloved by all the troops under his command, I breathed a sigh of relief and thanked God that England still had real leaders of men.

In Bombay, he stayed with Sir George Lloyd: 'what his energy, foresight, courage and determination has done for improving the people of Bombay and the surrounding country will be remembered with gratitude . . .' And he met the Duke of Connaught. ('Everywhere I read of instances of his thoughtfulness for others. So long as we have men like the Duke of Connaught and the Prince of Wales in England, we need never fear that Bolshevism will get hold here.')

After some time in these comforting surroundings, Johnny set off for Mesopotamia and the Caucasus, where he would once more become embroiled in the struggle between the Whites and Reds of post-Revolutionary Russia. By the time he arrived, Baron Ungern-Sternberg had invaded Mongolia with a cavalry division of Cossacks, Mongolians and Tibetans. They had been sent to him by the Dalai Lama in the hope that the force would free Mongolia and Tibet from China. They stormed the capital of Ulan-Bator (then Urga), sacked the city and massacred the Chinese garrison with medieval-esque ritual. Ultimately his forces were crushed and Ungern-Sternberg was executed by a Bolshevik firing squad. Grigori Semenov's fate was longer in coming. He escaped across the Pacific and attempted to find sanctuary in the United States. But the American press branded him a war criminal and he was forced to return to the

Japanese puppet state of Manchuria. From there throughout the 1930s and 1940s he agitated against Communist Russia. But he was finally arrested by the Bolsheviks and in 1946 died an agonising death at the end of a Soviet noose.

13

OF BANDITS AND BRIGANDS

Johnny's next destination was Mesopotamia, as it was referred to, practically, in Johnny's day: the area between the Tigris and the Euphrates, taking in modern-day Iraq and parts of Iran, Syria and Turkey. It was a fertile terrain of vast and mostly un-tapped natural resources—oil, lead, copper, silver and other minerals—tantalisingly close to Western Europe. Johnny's mission was to explore the prospects for trade and investment in this bountiful land of enormous commercial potential.

Johnny arrived in Mesopotamia in May 1921, tempted by the commercial prospects of this lush, though politically unstable, region at the confluence of Asia and Europe. It was natural that he should make his first port of call Baghdad, the principal city of the newly formed state of Iraq, and until recently part of the Ottoman Empire. Iraq had, since the end of the Great War, come under League of Nations mandate and British control. Then, as now, it was an unstable territory of many warring factions, mainly the Kurdish and Shahsavan tribes to the north, which were steadfastly resisting the ambitions of both their old and new colonial masters.

The Kurds and the Shahsavans occupied the large tracts of lawless lands on the borders of the three so-called Transcaucasian republics in the northern uplands that separated Persia from Russia. The small Transcaucasian states of

Armenia, Azerbaijan and Georgia were equally unstable entities, traditionally fought over by their neighbours, the imperial powers of Persia, Russia and Turkey, who coveted them for their immense economic potential. The great Western powers waited eagerly in the wings. To the east, by contrast, Iran, or Persia as it was alternatively called, was an oasis of comparative stability. Persia had proved remarkably resilient to the ever-expanding ambitions of Europe's great powers. Despite the endless and mendacious machinations mainly between the imperial powers of Britain and Russia in the Great Game, Persia had survived with her sovereignty intact. Indeed, in 1906 she had established her first parliament within the framework of a constitutional monarchy.

Johnny visited the capital of Iran, Tehran, immediately after he arrived in Baghdad. When he crossed the border between the two territories he discovered that despite her newfound stability even Iran was not without her difficulties. Her government and civil service were in such a fragile state that the country had descended into a state of internal administrative disorganisation. The Iranians for their part, and not without some justification, cast a suspicious eye on the old colonial power on their doorstep, running Iraq under post-war mandate. British agents in the region were widely supposed to be fomenting dissent among the many unruly tribes in Persia's far-flung regions that were attempting to throw off the shackle of Tehran's wavering authority. Johnny's presence in the country would undoubtedly have attracted the attentions of the powers that be.

He did not stay in Tehran for long. Before the temperate warmth of springtime had been replaced by the oppressive heat of a Persian summer, Johnny set off for Tabriz. The small, civilised northern city was close, or at least closer, to the frontier with Armenia and Azerbaijan, and beyond these tiny satellite states lay the great trading confluences of the enormous Black Sea and Georgia. Tabriz was an ideal base for Johnny to launch his investigation into the commercial and trade opportunities in the region. It was also a staging post to the wild uplands that divided Persia from Soviet Russia. Populated by bandits and brigands—and fiercely anti-Bolshevik tribesmen—these mountainous regions were a tempting destination for anybody curious about the advance of Communist power in the borderlands of Asiatic Europe.

Johnny travelled comfortably by railway at first before being obliged to hire a four-wheeled carriage drawn by a pair of indifferently tendered horses, and to arrange for relays of horses every twenty-five miles. His journal notes, 'In this archaic, almost spring-less vehicle I was jolted and pitched about for eight days over a track plentifully sprinkled with ruts, crevasses and mounds of hard mud.' Everywhere he passed through in Persia's East Azerbaijan Province (bordering Azerbaijan proper), Johnny found the shepherds and the tillers of the soil fearful of raids by Shahsavan nomads. The Shahsavans' Turkoman ancestors received their name, Guardians of the Shah, because Shahs (Persian kings) had relied upon their ferocious fighting abilities and unrestrained savagery to defend the northern and western frontiers from invaders. The Shahsavans were ferociously anti-

104

Bolshevik but they also refused to acknowledge the authority of Tehran. They complained that the officials appointed by the Persian government were corrupt and their taxes were never expended on local roads and institutions. They were striving for independence, Johnny observed, but because of their complete illiteracy and unrestrained savagery, they were unable to translate this otherwise commendable aspiration into even the semblance of ordered administration.

Johnny found that the Shahsavans in the mountains east of Tabriz lived in tents made of felt and shaped like a sphere cut in two. They were first-class shots and first-class horsemen. But rather than deploying their undoubted fighting prowess to pursue their more justifiable political aims, they used it as often to terrorise the weaker communities in their localities. Whenever they needed sheep or cattle or foodstuffs, the Shahsavans descended from the mountains to pillage their more peaceful neighbours. The regular mail coaches in the region were not safe from arbitrary plunder. To add insult to injury, on the many occasions when the Shahsavans held them up, the coach drivers were not just deprived of their mail and horses, they were stripped of their clothing too and left, humiliatingly, stark naked.

One afternoon, Johnny almost witnessed one of these terroristic incidents. His driver and he were about a mile outside a village when rifle shots rang out. They pulled up suddenly and noticed that the men of the village were running in all directions to occupy defensive positions that had been readied for the event of an attack. Others were escorting their women and children to safety, or driving the sheep and cows into the village. 'The scene indeed was suggestive of what must have occurred many times among the pioneer settlements in America when Indian raids were threatened.' In the event, nothing happened and Johnny was cheated of an encounter with the legendary Shahsavan tribesmen.

Eventually he and his driver arrived at Tabriz. Despite his declared aim of investigating trade opportunities, Johnny's lodgings were to be the comfortable and accommodating surroundings of the British Consulate rather than one of the many hotels that were available to other commercial travellers. His host was the affable and efficient British Consul, Ernest Bristow, who made Johnny very much at home. Within days of arriving in Tabriz, again despite his prospective interest in the commercial potential of the area, Johnny found himself plunged into the quagmire of post-war Eurasian politics.

He met the destitute Nestorian Christians—the Assyrians—who had migrated during the war to the region of Urmiah to the west of Tabriz after the Turks drove them out of their homelands. They were trying to regain possession of their lands and homes. But Johnny learnt from the Assyrians that the tyrannical and ruthless Kurdish warlord Simko Shikak now held complete sway over the territory they once inhabited and was constantly expanding his powerbase—much to the consternation of Tehran as well as the Assyrians. Like the Shahsavans, Simko and his Kurds had all the qualities that make first-class guerrilla fighters, such as endurance and courage in extreme measure. But like the Shahsavans they were in the habit of expending these admirable warlike talents

106

with wanton lack of mercy on innocent bystanders.

It was said that Simko enjoyed rolling those who offended him down hills and shooting at them with his rifle as they descended the slopes. If the human moving target reached the bottom unharmed, he was benevolently allowed to go free. Simko displayed many of the traits of a certain type of totalitarian leader that has become wearily familiar. He and his Kurdish followers had inherited—or had sequestrated—enormous tracts of rich and fertile agricultural land from the Assyrians, but lacking any sense of the importance of systematic husbandry they had allowed it to fall into privation. The result was that poverty and famine followed Simko in his tracks.

In Tabriz Johnny also found a Mr Vatzrian, who called himself the President of the Armenian White Republic. Vatzrian told him that a little band of Whites under the leadership of a charismatic general called Nejdi was holed out in the Zangezur Mountains north of Tabriz. The Zangezurs stretch eastwards from the Armenian towns of Natchivan (now Naxçıvan) and Erivan (Yerevan), and north and eastwards of the river Araxes (now Aras). The region was mostly in the hands of Reds, but General Nejdi, an Armenian born in Bulgaria, was using the natural fortress that the mountains created there to form a pocket of resistance to their ever-encroaching power. Vatzrian asked Johnny if he could do anything to provide arms, munitions, food and uniforms to his followers and Johnny volunteered to telegraph England. He was disappointed, however, to discover that people at home knew nothing of that part of the world and cared even less.

Perhaps it was through a sense of guilt at letting Vatzrian down that Johnny resolved to go to the Zangezur Mountains himself and make an independent assessment of the situation. In gratitude for his offer, Vatzrian presented Johnny with a beautiful black stallion with 'long flowing mane and tail' and also provided him with a guide. For the next few weeks Johnny spent his time wandering through mountains and valleys, huge plains and high plateaux populated by tribal chieftains and villains. None of this time was spent investigating trade possibilities between the Caucasus and Persia, and all of it seemed to be spent in the company of various White factions, weighing up the relative strengths of their forces verses the Reds. He learnt much, and quickly. Johnny and his guide almost immediately encountered scores of Armenian refugees fleeing Zangezur for the safety of Tabriz: men, women and children, some on foot, others on horseback. They heard from these people that General Nejdi and his little army of Whites were on the verge of capitulating.

Undeterred, Johnny and his guide proceeded apace and found the dusty little village of Midi on the Araxes River, which offered a little mud house to sleep in. When they awoke in the morning they found General Nejdi himself had arrived in Midi and was in the town square haranguing his gathered men. Nejdi, observed Johnny, wore riding breeches with jackboots up to his knees, and a black shirt; from the belt around his waist hung a sword and a pistol. His men were all similarly dressed; dirty, unshaven and covered in dust, they looked as if they had not rested for many days. The sight conjured up for Johnny images of 'the crusaders of old who fought in Palestine and Turkey'.

Johnny couldn't understand a word Nejdi said, but through his mannerisms he gave the impression of being a fine leader of men. Johnny's guide explained that Nejdi had abandoned Zangezur because of a lack of supplies. It was his intention to withdraw into Persian territory and, when rested and re-supplied, to return and drive the Reds out of Armenia. Johnny never saw Nejdi again.

Since the Whites no longer controlled Zangezur, Johnny decided it would be fruitless to continue there. After swimming across the Araxes River to explore the north bank and discovering a railway under construction, he set off for Ardebile (Ardabil), which was close to the Caspian and controlled by Shahsavan nomad tribesmen. During the following days and weeks he encountered a veritable fiesta of humankind, such as only an extraordinarily colourful and complex region can provide. His travels encompassed a cross-section of the region stretching from north of Ahar, the capital of East Azarbaijan province, to as far as Ardebile in the east, and beyond Sarab in the south.

One memorable evening he was given dinner on the roof of a mud house, after which an ancient travelling storyteller entertained him with recitations of Persian poetry.

He stayed with warrior tribesmen, with 'one or two' ex-czarist officers among their number, who occupied a grand home arranged around a delightful courtyard of trickling fountains and beautiful flowerbeds. It was furnished with French-style gilt, hard-backed chairs as well as huge silk cushions on the floor and Persian carpets hanging from the walls. His newfound companions wore fur hats and jackboots, and two or three bandoliers of small munitions draped around their waists and shoulders. 'The crowd looked very picturesque and rather like a scene in a comic opera, where the bold bandit hangs out in some remote mountain retreat.' It was here that Johnny had his first experience of smoking a Persian water pipe, which he thought was a 'very luxurious way of smoking'.

Soon he was to meet the elusive Shahsavans of whom he'd heard so much. They were encamped among their flocks of cattle and sheep on a vast plain high in the mountains. One of the local khans immediately invited Johnny to lunch in his tent, a round affair, shaped like half an orange and covered inside with rugs and carpets. About 16 or so Shahsavans sat in a circle with Johnny and they shared a delicious lunch of mutton and rice, which they ate with their fingers. The khan was 'perfectly charming and,' wrote Johnny, 'I felt very much at home in the surroundings.'

Johnny's journal gives a taste of his romantic outlook on life:

For a rest-cure, to live with this gentleman, two to three thousand feet above sea level, to go to bed at sunset and to rise at dawn, to ride about on horseback seeking fresh grazing ground for one's sheep is hard to equal. An occasional skirmish with some other khan, who with his followers tries to rob you of some of your belongings, or else drives you off your grazing ground because he has taken a liking to it, relieves the monotony of the situation and gives a zest for life.

110

On his travels, Johnny wore a black Persian lamb hat to be as inconspicuous as possible, and bodyguards provided by his various hosts accompanied him through some stages of his journey. Eventually, the relentless exposure to the elements took its toll even on his robust constitution. Soon, 'most of the skin was off my face, due to the sun, my eyes were half-closed, very sore, red and bloodshot'.

A Shahsavan khan Johnny encountered had enjoyed some success against the Bolsheviks in the district of Lenkoran. Short, stocky and full of life, this new acquaintance entertained Johnny with the usual fare of mutton, pilaf and cheese before showing him some of the Russian machine guns and artillery he had captured in Lenkoran—along with several Bolshevik prisoners. The prisoners assured Johnny that their captors had treated them well. After sleeping the night once more in a tent full of Shahsavans, he bade a reluctant farewell to his 'kind' host, a 'child of nature'.

Once more Johnny's notes reveal his inner romanticism:

It is curious how one meets a man like this, illiterate, uneducated, simple, without any of the superficial conventions to which one has been used, in the remote places of the world, and one feels that truly there is a brotherhood of man, irrespective of religion, nationality, or anything else. He was looked upon by many as a rebel against the constitutional authority of the Persian government in Tabriz and Tehran, and yet it was this rebel who was keeping the

111

Bolsheviks from seizing Ardebile, whereas the pusillanimous Persian Governor there was, if anything, seeking the assistance of the Bolsheviks to overcome the Shahsavan.

At one stage, Johnny became short of funds and was compelled to telegraph his bank in Tabriz to ask for 15 pounds in Persian silver tomans. When they were handed over, the coins filled two small canvas bags that Johnny attached to either side of his saddle. It was time to return to Tabriz. With two bodyguards provided by the Governor of Ardebile to accompany him, Johnny set off. But after two days he made a fateful decision. 'So peaceful . . . did the countryside seem, that on the evening of the second day I sent them back with thanks and a small present.' It was a big mistake.

About an hour later, his black stallion suddenly turned its head, obviously interested in something behind. Johnny followed its gaze and saw a man riding up behind, levelling a rifle at him. He was dressed in the usual manner with a sheepskin hat and draped with bandoliers. Johnny was ordered off his mount and another bandit emerged from some rocks nearby. The interlopers beckoned Johnny to follow them down into a steep ravine of giant boulders, strewn with rocks. He contemplated trying to overwhelm them but could not be sure if they had any accomplices lurking behind the boulders nearby. While one of them kept an eye on Johnny, the other rifled through his canvas bags and was, unsurprisingly, delighted when he found the 15 pounds of silver tomans. They were intrigued by his Gillette razor and Johnny was amused to see them debate among themselves what on earth it could be.

Both men, however, turned out to have more than a modicum of decency about them. Using sign language and facial expressions to communicate with the brigands, Johnny explained that the stallion did not belong to him. Not only did they allow him to keep the horse, they also spared him the ritual Shahsavan humiliation of stripping him of his clothes. All three men were amused by the situation and they sat down on a log and sang Persian songs together.

With the coming of dusk Johnny became numb with cold.

> They then, in the most courteous manner, put me on my way, returning me two shillings and sixpence for a night's lodging, as they feared I would not reach my destination . . . I could attribute this forbearance from the usual methods of the Shahsavan robbers only to the high prestige in which Englishmen are still held in this part of Persia.

Wishing him 'Godspeed', they disappeared into the night. Afterwards, while the stallion was cantering along it stumbled and threw Johnny from the saddle.

When he finally reached Sarab, Johnny's host the Governor suggested that he avail himself of a bath in the little lily pond at the front of his house. 'This caused great amusement to all of his retainers who watched me from all sides. It was customary for everyone to wash their hands and face before and after meals in this pond, but I think it was the first time they had ever seen a guest bathe in it.' On reaching Tabriz, 'I was as brown as a berry and hard as nails, as I had been in the saddle day in and day out practically ever since I left.' He threw himself happily on the mercy of Ernest Bristow, the British Consul, whose hospitality he had enjoyed before.

He was delighted with his expedition. He wrote:

> The country I had traversed gave me the impression of having great agricultural possibilities in the valleys and having excellent grazing grounds in the hills, and I am convinced that some day, when there is a railway line from Tabriz to Ardebile, and thence on to Astara, Lenkora and Baku, the area around Ardebile would prove to be rich, not only in oil, but in lead, copper, silver and other minerals.

This passage leaves little doubt that the primary purpose of Johnny's excursion had been trade. But he must surely also have presented Bristow with a summary of the situation regarding Red Russia.

TRADING WITH THE ENEMY

By now Johnny was convinced that his mission had been a success. Mesopotamia and the south Caucasus *did* hold out the promise of economic prosperity. Johnny was confident enough of the commercial prospects of the wider region to open an agency in Tabriz for his nascent company: J. B. Dodge & Co., South Russian and North Persian Merchants. The key to making the enterprise a success was to reopen the old trade route between Europe and Asia through the Caucasus and the Black Sea—a route that had been closed during the post-war political upheavals. Johnny was delighted to discover, therefore, that the Tehran government was sending a delegation to the Transcaucasus with this specific object in mind. When the special plenipotentiary leading this delegation invited Johnny to accompany him on the trip, he jumped at the offer to travel in the private railway car of His Excellency Moutaz-el-Dowleh.

Their ultimate destination was Tiflis (T'Bilisi), the capital of Georgia, which stood centrally between the Caspian Sea and the Black Sea. Tiflis was linked by a modern railway line to the Black Sea port of Batoum (Bat'umi) and thus was a natural centre for international trade. Tiflis was a prosperous and civilised city with an excellent electric tramway system that compared favourably with those of Western Europe. The roads in Georgia were generally maintained in excellent condition and the pavements of Tiflis were neat and clean. With an exchange of more than 300,000 roubles to the pound sterling, an American or Englishman had no difficulty in purchasing any of the amenities he needed. The average weekly wage of a clerk was about six pence a day. As a result most trade was done by barter.

Tiflis had been the first province under Soviet domination to resume foreign trade on an appreciable scale, made possible by a decree permitting private trading and private ownership of property. Houses, factories and oilfields were being restored to their former owners. Georgia was also the first part of the former Russian Empire in which foreign consuls were welcomed and recognised, with consular offices representing all the major European powers (Switzerland representing Great Britain). Thus foreign firms hoping to set up businesses were given a reassuring sense of security. Johnny had also heard from many people that life and liberty were then reasonably secure in Georgia and it was very rare that a foreigner was imprisoned.

Tiflis and Batoum were rapidly becoming distributing centres for foreign imports destined for Turkestan, north Persia and the Russian regions of the Volga basin. And since ships of the Lloyd-Triestine line had begun plying once more between Constantinople and Batoum, commerce was beginning to pick up. Johnny was convinced that he could build a viable business importing much-needed items, such as food, clothing and machinery from the West, and sending out equally needed raw materials from the East in return.

It must have been with high hopes that one

afternoon in June 1921, Johnny boarded the private car of el-Dowleh on the trade delegation's train. The little steam engine left Tabriz station thronging with well-wishers and set off on its 300-mile journey to the frontier station at Julfa (now Dzhul'fa) on the Araxes river. The train was a wood-burning one and so proceeded at a stately pace interrupted by frequent stops to resupply timber for burning. As it puffed its way towards Erivan (now Yerevan), the capital of Armenia, Johnny couldn't help but contrast the splendid scenery with the sparsely tilled countryside he had become accustomed to in north-west Persia. The mountain grandeur, the gorgeous, fantastic forests, the rising torrents all reminded Johnny of the backgrounds to Russian ballets. After Julfa the party changed to an oil-burning steam train and it was not long before they arrived at Erivan, in its splendid location on two mountain-river banks, with its views of Mount Ararat looming majestically in the distance, still covered in snow.

But if the natural surroundings were impressive, the condition of those who lived in them was both pitiful and deplorable. The world now knows of the appalling misery and destitution that had been inflicted upon the inhabitants of Armenia since 1917. It was only when Johnny arrived at Alexandropol (Gyumri), some distance north of the capital, that he first learnt of the dreadful Turkish outrage that had occurred in this former Russian garrison town. After the Turks, during their temporary occupation of the town in the autumn of 1920—the previous year—had looted it of as much furniture and valuables as they could carry away, they signalled their evacuation by herding 1,500

117

men, women and children into a ravine and shooting them down. The winter snows covered the corpses, and so thorough was the massacre that nothing was known of it until the following spring. Some American friends of Johnny, out riding one day, just months before Johnny's visit, discovered the bodies, which were beginning to be exposed by the melting of the snow. This, and other systematic massacres, had occurred at a time when the Turks were protesting that in future it would be their policy to show every consideration to their Christian neighbours.

Johnny was pleased to note that his own native country was among the first to come to the Armenians' aid. The American Near East Relief charity in Alexandropol baked five tons of bread each day for local distribution. The bread helped to support 60,000 orphans, besides keeping alive thousands of homeless adults who roamed about the city in search of scraps of food and lodging amid the ruins of houses senselessly destroyed by the Turks.

After his brief stay in Alexandropol, Johnny pressed on to Tiflis. He set off by a night train that climbed up the steep and somewhat bleak hills that divide Armenia from Georgia. Once over the summit, though, the train descended through beautiful hill country of running streams and fruit orchards. It was hard to believe that this enchanting scenery had witnessed some of the bloodiest encounters between Armenian and Georgian patriots between 1920 and 1921, on the eve of Johnny's arrival in the region. Shortly before the train pulled into Tiflis station, it passed an ominous site. Johnny saw several artillery batteries manned and guarded by Red Army troops, their guns

118

trained on the city below. He later learnt that the Russians were so unpopular they feared a popular uprising. The guns were trained upon the main squares and thoroughfares where the rioters would most likely gather. It was the first sign that perhaps all was not as well in Tiflis as Johnny had imagined.

Otherwise, Johnny found the Georgian capital city just as he had hoped. It was like a modern European metropolis: mostly clean, neat and tidy; efficiently run and with many of the cultural amenities of modern civilisation. He found lodgings with a French family who had a house with a charming little garden. He spent the nights sleeping on the veranda covered with ivy and vines. His host, the landlord, a young man of 34 or so, worked for the railway company. The Frenchman had an amiable disposition and had been very rich before the Revolution. He spoke openly and volubly about how corrupt the Soviet authorities were, much to his guest's amusement but to such an extent that Johnny warned him to be careful. The Frenchman said he had no fear—he was far too valuable to the Soviets in his role for the railway line. To Johnny's distress, he was subsequently taken away and shot by the authorities.

During his stay in Tiflis, Johnny had several meetings with a Fyodor Rabinovich, the commissar for foreign trade. It appears that these talks must have offered some promise of success if not an outright commercial pact, because the Soviet authorities were in desperate need of flour and Johnny was in a position to provide it. He promptly resolved on returning to Tabriz to telegraph his business contacts in the United States and ask them to send some consignments to Batoum.

Johnny's return journey proved to be exciting. When people travelled by rail in that region, it invariably meant passengers were consigned en masse in freight cars, often with the freight—various food stuffs, animals and so forth. Sometimes fifty or so people would be squashed into one car, many of them refugees who hadn't washed for days, if not weeks and months. On the leg of his journey between Julfa and Tabriz, Johnny found himself confined in such conditions. The smell was indescribable, and he chose to abandon the freight car and sleep in the open air on an open flat car. Lying on a Persian rug he fell asleep in the 'delightfully cool' night air. Unfortunately for him, at about 2 a.m., the direction of the wind changed and cinders from the engine came raining down on him. Johnny awoke to find his clothing and the rug alight and, after desperately stamping the flames out, reluctantly returned to the stinking freight car. These unsuitable travel arrangements, however, were to be the least of Johnny's problems.

On finally returning to Tabriz and the comfort of Mr Bristow's hospitality at the British Consulate, Johnny found it was not so easy to arrange a business transaction between the free West and the Communist East. His friends in New York refused to extend credit to the Russian authorities and insisted any shipments would only leave port when they had been fully paid for in advance. This the Russian authorities were unable or unwilling to do, and Johnny reluctantly concluded that the only way to arrange the appropriate credits was for him to do it from London. Johnny asked the Russian trade representative in Tabriz to supply him with the necessary visa to allow him to return to Georgia and travel from Batoum to Constantinople and thence to London. This, too, proved problematical, but after much dragging of feet the necessary paperwork arrived and Johnny set off on his travels once more.

Again, Johnny accompanied his old friend His Excellency Moutaz-el-Dowleh, who was leading, it appears, another trade delegation north of the border. Johnny was glad to join el-Dowleh in his private car, not least because of the comparative comfort it provided, but also because he and many of his staff spoke French. It was fortunate that Johnny found himself in such distinguished company. Shortly after crossing the border Johnny became an object of the unwelcome attentions of the Cheka, the Soviet state security organisation. They were in Natchivan, a dreary outpost of the so-called 'Tartar Republic' and to Johnny's eyes, 'one of the most God-forsaken places I have ever set foot in'. During an inspection of everyone's passports, Johnny was singled out and told that he would not be allowed to continue to Tiflis. He would have to take his luggage off the train and accompany the Cheka official into town.

It was only because of the intervention of his friend el-Dowleh that this did not happen. His Excellency insisted that he would not allow his train to leave Natchivan without Johnny. The Cheka official reluctantly backed down after extracting a promise from el-Dowleh that he would not let Johnny escape en route. When the train pulled into Tiflis, Johnny fully expected to be arrested at the station but nobody took the least notice of him. So he headed into town to make some last-minute arrangements with business contacts in the Georgian city. It was only a day or so later, on 9

December, when Johnny was boarding a ferry steamer at Batoum, that he felt a hand firmly grab him on the shoulder. He turned around to see a Red soldier.

PRISONER OF THE CHEKA

Despite his remonstrations, Johnny was put into a carriage with his luggage and, guarded by two Russian soldiers, taken to the headquarters of the secret police at Batoum. There, he and his baggage were searched and he was shown into a modestly sized cell with some 45 other prisoners in it. It was so crowded there was hardly any space to lie down to sleep at night and Johnny was to discover that the electric light was kept on 24 hours a day. The following morning Johnny found that the rations the prisoners lived on consisted of a cup of 'coloured water' masquerading as tea but with neither milk nor sugar at the beginning and end of the day, with one pound of black bread and some boiled haricot beans for lunch. Regulations allowed prisoners to receive food parcels from their families but, of course, Johnny had none. He was touched therefore when some of the men shared theirs with him.

One of the prisoners was in a terribly nervous state thanks to his treatment at the hands of the Cheka. He was only young, perhaps 20 years old, and had been an officer in a cavalry regiment of the czarist regime though he was really just a boy. The Cheka had accused him of 'counter-revolutionary' activities and threw him in an underground hole of a cell, which contained cold dank water that came up to his knees. There was no platform or bed with which he could keep himself above the water, and he was forced to endure several days and nights in these barbaric conditions terrified, presumably, of falling asleep and drowning. The wretched boy had practically been driven mad by the experience.

Johnny discovered that there were all sorts of men among his fellow prisoners: czarist officers, merchant traders, engineers, professors, peasants who could hardly read or write, robbers, highwaymen and counterfeiters. Some had been behind bars for only a few days and were airily confident of their imminent release; others had been compelled to endure these conditions for as long as nine months. Their complexions were a ghostly yellow, having not had the benefit of sunlight except for a few brief minutes' exercise every day in a tiny courtyard.

This was to be the first time in his life that Johnny experienced the strength of his fellow man's fortitude when subject to the most beastly of circumstances. Some of his fellow prisoners coped by sleeping all day long. Others fashioned chess and draught figures out of pieces of bread and cheerfully played games. They played charades. And every evening there was chorus singing and dancing. 'Cheerfulness rather than despondency was the dominant note of their captivity— cheerfulness which was none the less admirable because it was born out of fatalism.'

He later wrote: 'I shall never regret, however, the weeks of detention that followed, uncomfortable though they were at the time, for they gave me opportunity at close quarters to appreciate the extraordinary quality of Russian endurance.' Despite this sunny note, it was likely that Johnny was relieved when on his third day of captivity he was told he would shortly be taken to Tiflis to face a Cheka tribunal that would decide his fate.

The journey from Batoum to Tiflis proved to be one of the most miserable of his life. It was in the third class carriage of a very slow train, which had no windows in the frames to fend off the bitter December cold, and hard seats that were impossible to sleep on. The prison officials had at least given Johnny some of his money back, some ten shillings, and he was able to buy bread and fruit, which he shared with his three Red Army guards. The discomfort did not stop Johnny appreciating the beautiful vistas of pine forests and snow-topped mountain ranges, even if, as he did so, he was wondering whether his own experience in a Russian prison would be as harrowing as some others of which he had read. The journey took 48 hours. When they finally arrived at Tiflis, Johnny was informed he would have to spend another night in a huge waiting room teeming with so many peasants he could move only with a vast amount of difficulty. Somehow or other he managed to persuade his escort to allow him to sleep at the offices of the American Near East Relief charity.

There, his guards were no doubt delighted to be offered steaming hot chocolate, boiled eggs and bread by the officials and, given the munificence of their treatment, were happy to allow Johnny to sleep alone on a bed in a little cubicle. Replenished by his own rations of the above, Johnny was able to settle down to the task of writing two letters. The first was to Sir Horace Rumbold, the British High Commissioner in Constantinople, then under Allied occupation, explaining what had happened to him. (Sir Horace was later to become the

Ambassador to Berlin and an outspoken anti-Nazi.) The second letter was to his mother Flora telling her, regretfully, that he would not be home for Christmas as he had planned. A great weight was taken off his mind when these two missives were deposited in the American Near East Relief mailbag.

Johnny at least now knew that within days the Foreign Office would be aware of his plight and where he was being held. He promptly fell asleep. Next morning, 'after one of the most pleasant nights I ever remember spending', Johnny was able to persuade his guards to allow him to visit a barber's shop close by. They watched him closely as he was shaved. Afterwards he felt like a new man, and he was ready to start off for the Cheka headquarters, refreshed in body and soul.

The Cheka building was a former school that stood high on a hill on the other side of the Kura River. Johnny was marched there by his three guards and once inside was taken down a corridor lined on both sides with cells and the occasional soldier with rifles and bayonets. When he was shown into his own accommodation he was dismayed.

> The first impression I got was distinctly unfavourable, for I found it a much smaller room with a lower ceiling than the one I had been in at Batoum, with about 50 men in it. There was no ventilation except from a little window at the far side of the room, which was below the ground, and the room was so crowded that the atmosphere was positively stifling until one got used to it. I noticed that

126

the faces of the men, as they scanned the new-comer, looked distinctly annoyed . . .

It was not until he had made friends with a Polish engineer who spoke French and a Russian who spoke a little English that Johnny learnt the reason for their scowls. The room was so crowded there was barely enough space to lie down at night. Naturally, the prisoners didn't like the idea of new people coming in until some had been released.

Thankfully this happened quite regularly but that wasn't necessarily a happy thing for the prisoners involved. It was the practice of the prison authorities once or twice a week to take out inmates who were to be shot. 'The Death Commissar, who was a little Jew called Schulmann, would come into the room with a sheet of paper in his hands and call out the condemned man's name and age and then the man would go out, occasionally not until a struggle had taken place.' Outside they were stripped of their clothes except for their shirt, and handcuffed. Johnny was told that once a lorry load had been assembled, they were taken to an execution place some miles out of town. The wretched souls were led to a pit and before they could take in what was happening they received a bullet in the neck.

Yet again, though, Johnny discovered that despite the pitiful conditions of their existence, and the possibility of being shot, the prisoners did not allow themselves to become desolate. Every evening, as in Batoum, there was singing and dancing; they played board games and parlour games. The prisoners were similar in variety to those Johnny had shared the cell with in Batoum:

127

there were three generals of the old czarist regime, various professionals accused of 'counter-revolutionary' activities, bona fide criminals, counterfeiters, bandits and highwaymen. Next door to their cell was a group of women, perhaps as many as 12 of them, including, Johnny was told, princesses but also humble peasants. They were made to scrub the floors of the Cheka rooms. The sanitary arrangements for the prisoners were, however, 'revolting'.

One day the casual carelessness of the Soviet criminal system was brought home to Johnny and his fellow inmates. Among their number was a nice young boy of sixteen who had already served six months for the trivial offence of stealing two shillings' worth of vegetables. Despite the harshness of his sentence he was forever high-spirited and smiling. He had never learnt to write but one of the czarist generals wrote a letter on his behalf to the authorities suggesting the boy had already undergone enough punishment to expiate the offence. Much to their surprise, he was promptly released. It turned out the authorities had no record of him at all. Two days later he turned up as one of their prison guards. They had fed him, given him a good bath and presented him with a uniform about three sizes too large for him.

Thankfully for Johnny, he too was due a similar fate. On his sixth day of confinement, the prison commissar turned up and told him to 'clear off'. There would be no charges against him. No reason whatsoever was given for his imprisonment. But Johnny wasn't going to hang around for one. Rolling his flea-ridden bedding beneath his arm, he bade his erstwhile companions 'adieu' and was soon out of the prison walking down the hill with three days' growth of beard on his face. One of the first things he did was visit the local Turkish baths for a thorough wash and scrub up.

After his body and soul had been restored to health, Johnny called upon Fyodor Rabinovich, the commissar for foreign trade with whom he'd had earlier dealings.

Mr. Rabinovich showed little concern at my having spent two weeks in prison, and rather treated it as a common, everyday, occurrence for businessmen with whom he had to deal, and when referring to it shrugged his shoulders, smiled and said, 'It is all in a good cause, you have suffered for the Revolution.'

Rabinovich assured him that his arrest had been a mistake and expressed the hope that Johnny would not be put off by the 'untoward experience'. He was good enough to put these sentiments in writing to Johnny who replied that he was quite prepared to treat the incident as 'an unfortunate misunderstanding'.

Johnny stayed in the Caucasus long enough to receive more written assurances from other Russian officials that they were not hostile to foreign trading. Once these assurances were put in writing, Johnny set up two agencies, one in Tiflis and one in Batoum, for the company he was planning to call 'J.B. Dodge & Co.'. In January 1922, he set off to complete the journey he had begun many months previously to London via Constantinople.

In London, Johnny discovered what had happened after Sir Horace Rumbold received his letter in Constantinople. The contents had been divulged to Winston Churchill, the Colonial Secretary, who was attending the Genoa Conference. Churchill in turn told Lloyd George who promptly asked Lord Curzon to telegraph the appropriate Soviet authorities. Johnny was convinced that if it had not been for this sequence of events, he would have been left to rot in his Tiflis cell for many months.

In England, Johnny spent two busy months arranging credit for J. B. Dodge & Co. and buying consignments of flour, clothes and other goods to be shipped. He later admitted that he made mistakes over his first export shipments, holding out for higher payment, but was pleased that he had at least proved that business could be done in that part of the world. By the beginning of March he was on his way back to the Caucasus, ready to set up and start running the newly formed company. He also became involved in an attempt to get concessions for the Baku oilfields of Azerbaijan on behalf of Baku Consolidated Oil Fields Ltd, a British firm with 'over six million' invested in the Baku oil industry. In the days of the czars, British interests had invested heavily in what was the second largest oilfield in the world. It had been operating under British technical direction until the Russians took over after the Revolution.

Johnny believed that it was only a matter of time before the Soviet government would return appropriated property to private ownership. He had been approached by several people in Tiflis asking if he could obtain British capital to finance the oil industry in the region. He thought an arrangement could be made to acquire part of the

Baku oil fields in Azerbaijan for British investors. The local authorities, however, did not like the renewed interest that the British—in the form of Johnny—were expressing in their part of the world. His ambitions would lead to his second encounter with the Cheka.

APPOINTMENT WITH DEATH

One evening in Tiflis in the first week of July, Johnny was enjoying supper in a public garden. A young friend came up to him and whispered in his ear that he had heard Johnny was going to be arrested 'on account of the oil business' and he had better watch out. Johnny told him not to worry, as he was certain nothing of the sort would happen. Two evenings later, he attended a performance by a visiting Moscow ballet company at the opera. This show was of particular interest to him because the leading lady was said to be a Cheka informant who had been responsible for the deaths of many White Russians.

Later, when he arrived at his apartment in the very early hours of the next morning, he discovered two Cheka officials there lounging on the settee of his sitting room. They searched the place from top to bottom and sealed all his luggage and boxes before marching Johnny off to prison once more. This time though, and worryingly, it was to the military Cheka prison quite nearby, rather than the civil facility on the hill that he had unfortunately become so familiar with. And this time he was thrown into the solitary confinement of a cell some nine feet long by four wide, with no natural light except that which percolated through a tiny grate in the cell door.

Johnny seems to have been genuinely puzzled about his arrest. 'I thought of all the things the

Soviet authorities might have arrested me for, but for the life of me, could not fix on one,' he confided to the journal he wrote after returning to England in 1924. He was further concerned the following morning when he saw the manager of his Tiflis office being led down the corridor outside. He never saw the man again, but later gathered he had been sent to a prison camp in the White Russian sea port of Archangel: 'from what I gather most people who go there either die from the cold, scurvy or starvation'.

Johnny spent the next day lying on the wooden plank in his cell, allowed out only to go to the latrines, which were 'perfectly filthy'. At 2 o'clock the following morning, an armed guard arrived to take him across a courtyard and up some narrow steps. They arrived at a large room containing a large desk behind which sat a man about 35 years old. He was wearing a black shirt buttoned up to his neck, black riding breeches with top boots, and in his waistband was stuck a revolver. The door was shut behind Johnny and, as the soldier stood sentry inside, the man behind the desk introduced himself as Solomon Mogilevsky. He told Johnny that he was vice president of the All Russian Cheka, and had been sent from Moscow to combat counter-revolution and espionage.

Solomon Grigorevich Mogilevsky, born of Jewish parents and a confidant of Vladimir Lenin, was responsible for intelligence in Iran and Turkey, so it was no wonder that Johnny Dodge's activities had come to his attention. It was likely that Mogilevsky knew quite a deal about Johnny. 'He asked me to sit down and offered me a cigarette,' Johnny recalled. 'We spoke in French and as I had had no conversation with anyone in twenty-four hours I found it rather pleasant to have a little human intercourse.'

The interrogation that followed was a baffling one. During it Mogilevsky opened a dossier which showed Johnny that there was very little his interrogator did not know about him or his family. For about an hour and a half, Mogilevsky asked Johnny about his travels in Australia and the Far East, Mesopotamia and the Caucasus. He asked about his relationship with Winston Churchill and Lord Curzon; when Johnny replied there was none, he didn't believe him. He demanded to know if Johnny was connected with the Standard Oil Company of America (a well-known front for American espionage) and, again, Mogilevsky didn't believe him when he replied, 'No.'

At one stage, with a smile Mogilevsky said, 'One fisherman knows another fisherman a long way off.' Johnny replied, laughingly, that Mogilevsky was quite wrong if by that he meant that because he, Mogilevsky, was an agent of the Soviet government, Johnny was an agent for the British government. Implying that Johnny's answers were untrue and evasive, Mogilevsky said, 'Come now, Mr Dodge, let us talk frankly together, there is nothing to hide.' Johnny said he was talking frankly, and he had nothing to hide. Finally Mogilevsky said he had asked all the questions he wanted to, and that he was sure Johnny had been arrested in error, and would be free to go quite soon.

But Johnny was not free to go soon. Instead he was dragged out of his cell at a similarly ungodly hour the next morning and subjected to another interrogation. This time the subject concentrated on was his trip to Baku. Mogilevsky opened a long discussion about the intricacies of foreign and private enterprise business involvement in Soviet territories. There was a difference, Mogilevsky insisted, between a Russian individual attempting to procure British capital to finance a concession which might or might not be granted, and a Russian endeavouring to sell oil property which was once owned by him but, under the Soviet government, was now nationalised.

His point was that to lead Russians, who had been disposed of their property, to entertain any hope that foreigners might be induced to give them money for the rights they used to have on the chance that the Soviet government would alter their policy or be overthrown with the result that the rights of the former owner would become valuable, was a criminal offence in as much as it was actually counter-revolutionary and so most dangerous.

Johnny objected that this was a 'ridiculous' interpretation.

Johnny had another encounter with Mogilevsky, this time at the more seemly hour of 8 o'clock, on the following evening. On this occasion Johnny was asked to fill in a questionnaire, which consisted of all the same subjects he had already been interrogated about. It took him about an hour and a half to write down the responses. After he had done so Mogilevsky dismissed him. At around noon the following day, Johnny was taken to the prison commandant's office and told he was free to return to his apartment but that he must not try to leave

Tiflis. When he returned to his office, he discovered that an office courier and a Russian–Armenian interpreter had been arrested, effectively grinding the business to a halt.

With his nascent business at a standstill, Johnny could find little to do except spend his days playing tennis with the few Americans who lived in Tiflis. After the days had stretched into weeks, a Russian acquaintance explained that by not protesting about the arrests of his three employees, Johnny's behaviour might be construed as an admission of guilt. Johnny duly lodged complaints, which only provoked the Cheka into ordering him to report to them twice a week. This led to another meeting with Mogilevsky who, some days later, produced a written charge sheet.

The document stated that Johnny had been found guilty of (1) being a British secret agent (an offence punishable by death), (2) having four tête-à-têtes towards buying oilfields that had been nationalised and (3) having given bribes to Soviet officials in order to obtain secret information. Added to the end of the sheet was a statement that his punishment was expulsion and he must leave Soviet territory within 48 hours. Johnny was ordered to sign the charge sheet to certify that he had read it. Reluctantly he signed but wrote that the charges were 'damned lies' and added that he would 'make it very hot for the Russian trade representative and his staff' in London when he got home to Britain.

Two days later a Cheka agent came to Johnny's apartment saying he had orders to escort him from Tiflis to Batoum and see him off on a boat to Constantinople. After sharing his breakfast with the man, Johnny packed a single bag and was taken away to the railway station in a touring car carrying the Soviet flag on its radiator. At Batoum, there was no boat in the port and no prospect of one for several days, so Johnny was lodged in the local jail. He was not allowed to visit his local branch office in the town but they did let his Armenian manager come to see him in jail. Johnny never saw him again.

He shared his confinement with some three dozen other would-be merchants, mostly Greeks and Italians who had been arrested for breaking laws related to dealings in foreign exchange. As one of them had a mandolin they amused themselves with impromptu concerts, singing and dancing. Finally an Italian ship arrived and Johnny was driven under armed guard in a carriage from the jail to the quayside and put on board with his luggage. He later wrote: 'and that was the last I saw of the Caucasus'. He arrived back in London on 8 October 1922.

Had Johnny been lucky to get away with his life: a spy who had somehow managed to dodge the wrath of the Soviet counter-espionage agents by some peculiar quirk of fortune? Or had he been, as he always insisted, a bona fide entrepreneur attempting to set up a business in a part of the world that was sorely in need of the commerce that would bring it affluence? The answer is probably a bit of both. In the end it was one of Johnny's best friends who let the cat out of the bag, after Johnny had died. At his memorial service in November 1960, Johnny's old commanding officer Bernard Freyberg spoke glowingly about his friend's colourful life and many achievements. He stated,

'Ultimately he was taken prisoner fighting against the Communists on the Russian Front.' Thus in Freyberg's mind there was never any doubt what Johnny's mission was in the East after World War I. He was not exploring trade possibilities, but 'fighting' the Communists 'on the Russian front'—if not overtly then certainly covertly. Among Johnny's family, nobody doubts that he was a spy.

FROM FAR EAST TO EAST END

Despite all his experiences in the Caucasus, Johnny attempted to continue to trade with Russia. He formed a company with impeccable City connections. Among its directors was Rex Benson, the Old Etonian and former operative of the French counter-espionage service, the Bureau Interallié, who was closely linked to the spy master Stewart Menzies. Johnny's new company bought a consignment of goods and was preparing them for shipment when the Soviet authorities banned such imports, scuppering the deal. After acquiring a special licence from the Russian trade mission in London, the consignment finally left Britain in August 1923. Benson was allowed to go to Batoum, where he purchased a quantity of lambskins for export to England. These were being prepared for shipment when the Soviets raised the duty on such commodities, thus turning a profitable trade into an unprofitable one. Once the lambskins had been exported the Russians reduced the export tax to its previous level. Then, in June 1924, an order was issued calling for all foreign firms to liquidate and clear out of the country.

From these experiences, Johnny came to the conclusion that the Soviets were simply bluffing the West into thinking that they sincerely wanted to conduct international trade. In reality, Johnny decided, they were intent on sending their own trade representatives into the countries of the outside world with instructions to foment unrest among the working classes and, eventually, produce a worldwide Communist revolution. And they were deliberately keeping foreign traders out of the Soviet Union because they didn't want exactly the same ploy played upon them—albeit through the natural means of free forces rather than the underhand methods of sedition and subversion. Of course, it might equally have been possible that the Soviets objected to a British spy ring masquerading as a commercial endeavour. It is tempting to suspect, nevertheless, that it was this aspect of Communist behaviour that turned Johnny so insistently against the Soviet Union and not, as so often is assumed, the two weeks or so he spent in the abominable conditions of the Cheka's cells. In fact, as we have seen, Johnny adapted to these atrocious circumstances with his usual equable spirit. He was not a man to hold a grudge against an enemy over a few minor discomforts.

Johnny appears to have abandoned his efforts to forge trading links with Russia. His life through the rest of the 1920s was largely taken up with stockbroking and politics with a large dose of social work in between, the latter inspired by his mother's example and that of Lionel who, besides his interest in astrology, was a noted philanthropist of his day and age. And if Johnny had once genuinely flirted with socialism (and there is no real evidence he did) his experiences in the East had put paid to that. He had returned to England a fervent anti-Communist. It was probably his passionate belief that Communism threatened Western civilisation that propelled Johnny forcefully into the political arena. It was the staunchly conservative Unionist Party to which he turned in the mid 1920s, when he attempted to carve a place for himself in the political landscape of England. In 1923, he was adopted by the Unionist Party to be its prospective parliamentary candidate for Mile End. This was possibly the poorest part of the East End of London, which in turn was one of the most destitute parts of the United Kingdom. Unemployment and bad housing in the area were perhaps worse than anywhere else in Britain. The very phrase 'East End' had become a leitmotif for the evils of poverty and social deprivation.

The local Member of Parliament in Mile End had been a Conservative until he was unseated by a charismatic Labour candidate, John Scurr. An Australian, born in Brisbane, Scurr's family had moved to England when John was a baby, and he had spent most of his life in the East End, an unswerving supporter of Labour and champion of left-wing causes. These fearsome credentials would have deterred a lesser soul, but not Johnny. With his eternal optimism and faith in the innate fairness of his fellow man, Johnny embarked upon the conquest of his prospective new fiefdom with typical unflagging energy, verve and panache.

He rented a house at 62 Beaumont Square and soon became a familiar figure in the constituency and at public meetings where he assailed all who would listen with his faith in conservatism, democracy and the Empire, oblivious to the accusation that some of those beliefs he held dear to his heart would appear to some to be at odds, on occasion, with one another. He enlisted the aid of Flora and Lionel for his campaign. Over the forthcoming weeks and months they arranged between the three of them, and their prosperous and well-connected friends, diversions and distractions that would bring some colour into the bleakness and dreariness of everyday life in Mile End.

They laid on fetes and fairs, concerts, dances, sports events and even outings in charabancs to the country estates of their titled friends. Johnny arranged visits to Mile End by members of the Royal Family, Prime Minister Stanley Baldwin and Mrs Baldwin. These were just a few of the long list of famous people drawn from Johnny's family's wide circle of friends who found themselves tramping into territory it is unlikely they would ever before have given a second thought. A typical event was the Conservative Women's Association's Fayre and Fete at Beaumont Hall on 25 July, at which Johnny escorted Mrs Baldwin and which was attended by Lady Denbigh, Lady Beaverbrook, Lady Gould Adams and the Duchess of Sutherland, no less.

On 25 August, Johnny took a party of boy scouts to the Sutherlands' palatial Sutton Place home where they camped for a week and the duchess gave them golf lessons. In September, he took more boy scouts camping, this time to the Sussex coast where his stepfather Lionel Guest had bought land and was in the process of building a number of properties. Blessed with good health and physical prowess all his life, despite the ravages of the war, Johnny never failed to emphasise the importance of fitness and regular outdoor exercise. Gamely, he did not hesitate to test his prowess against some of the more proficient Mile End boxers by going several rounds with them, an egalitarian gesture that was much appreciated.

Johnny matched these displays of social graciousness with a vigorous campaign in which he did not mince his words. He stated his principles forthrightly and confidently with passionate inflexibility. He proclaimed that during the war he had leaned towards socialism and the Labour party (of which there is no evidence whatsoever), but that his adventures in the Transcaucasus had convinced him that Communism was not just a discredited notion but an outright evil force. He maintained that Communist agents were everywhere infiltrating the Labour party. 'The menace of Communism' was a theme at the core of virtually every speech he gave. Johnny told one reporter that after his experiences in the Caucasus he was determined to stamp out socialism in Europe.

At the same time Johnny unstintingly supported the British Empire, claiming it was not a case of the privileged few exploiting the weak, but a case of all classes working together (which was to stretch the *actualité* to say the least). It was socialists, he stated, who perpetrated class division and war. He insisted there should be no class consciousness. Instead there should be unity of all sections of society against Communism, which was directed towards the break-up of the British constitution—one of the greatest achievements of the modern age. On a practical rather than ideological level, Johnny believed that unemployment benefit should go up while taxes should be reduced, prompting, he hoped, a welcome drop in the cost of living, and the costs of production. He wanted to see some of the 'dole' money used to help the unemployed move to the Dominions overseas.

143

The people of Mile End came to love the tall, handsome Anglo-American army officer with his disarming manners and lack of pretension, and they adored his energetic mother with her southern drawl. They called Flora 'the Duchess of Mile End', and Johnny was their 'Squire'. They were two people who seemed to epitomise to many the true values of noblesse oblige that were supposed to be a characteristic of their class. But in the general election of 1924 the incumbent Labour MP, John Scurr, successfully withstood the challenge from his popular opponent and won the election. Johnny's reaction is not recorded but it is more than likely he accepted his defeat in good heart and wished his opponent well.

Happier developments were afoot that would bring greater comfort to Johnny over the years. In the early 1920s, his stepfather, Lionel, had begun buying up large amounts of land around an idyllic rural settlement on the south coast of England called Ferring. A hamlet of some 300 souls near Worthing in Sussex, Ferring was little more than a patchwork of sandy lanes surrounding thatched farm workers' cottages. It overlooked a wide pebbly beach that sloped gently into the English Channel. The most prominent building in the village was the Norman church of St Andrew's. Lionel began building a number of houses and cottages on his newly bought land, mostly in the white-walled timber-framed style that is common in America. The biggest house, in Sea Lane, was to become Flora and Lionel's country home, a large and rambling villa set in 60 acres. When it was finally completed Flora called it 'Wookyi-Tipi' after her Sioux Falls residence. Lionel had a small building that housed a telescope constructed in the grounds, to cater for his own particular tastes. A small staff of loyal retainers administered to Flora and Lionel's needs and the estate was populated by a menagerie of dogs, chickens, cows, bulls and goats. Flora was particularly fond of her four Pekinese dogs, upon which she doted as if they were her own children. Wookyi-Tipi soon became the local manor, with Flora its much-loved queen.

A local girl, Beris Collins, and her brother would often be sent to Wookyi-Tipi with baskets of fresh fruit, dead chickens and rabbits. They were told to present themselves at the big white gates of the estate where they would be admitted via a small opening. An underling would take the basket and instruct the children to wait for the Honourable Mrs Guest. A formidable figure, invariably wearing a big floppy hat and long flowing gowns, would eventually arrive. Thanking the children, Flora would make two of her Pekinese dogs, Mr Woo and Mr Chang, perform a dance. Beris and her brother would then be presented with two sweets each and allowed out of the smaller gate.

Lionel began renting out some of the homes he had built as holiday cottages. Whether this was the catalyst or not, the little village of Ferring was soon to be transformed from a rural backwater into a honey pot for the rich and famous. Shiny limousines were to become as familiar along the quiet hedge-lined lanes as farm carts pulled by antiquated nags. Among the first of the newcomers was the Prince of Wales, who brought his mistress Mrs Dudley Ward and occupied a pretty house called 'St Malo'. The Prince became a familiar figure strolling along the beach, sometimes alone, sometimes with Mrs Ward.

Later his equerry Piers Legh also rented one of the Guests' houses, which they had called 'Lullaby'. Johnny would spend many happy years in Ferring and it would become one place on earth that he could truly call his home.

In the meantime, Johnny had not given up his political ambitions. After his failure to win Mile End he was presented with a consolation prize, of sorts, when he was elected to the London County Council in 1925. His stepfather followed suit in 1928, also winning a seat on the council. Johnny served a five-year term. But when it came to the next general election in 1929, Johnny's second attempt to win the Mile End seat was once more a failure and the people of the East End again returned John Scurr to the House of Commons. Throughout his life Johnny was loved and admired, but he rarely persuaded anyone outside the tight circle of his wealthy and privileged friends to endorse his conservative view of the world.

Johnny was to have more success in business. It was Lionel who introduced Johnny to Nathan & Rosselli, a small but successful stockbroking firm in the City. Lionel had been one of their most notable customers and was instrumental in obtaining Johnny a job with the company. His stepson started as a humble clerk but within a year or so was a partner. By all accounts he was a great success: no doubt his natural charm attracted a great deal of business. He was to remain a stockbroker until his dying day, but there is a lingering suspicion among those who knew him well that he would have preferred to have been known as a politician, and that he could never quite understand why popular opinion was so out of kilter with his own.

146

Major Johnny Dodge. (courtesy of Jane Aitken)

Johnny as an infant in the arms of his mother,
Flora, with Lucy. (courtesy of Jane Aitken)

Johnny in Royal Naval Division uniform at
Blandford Camp, late 1914 or early 1915.
(courtesy of Colonel Lord Freyberg)

Johnny and Minerva, possibly at Fred Dalziel's
Palm Beach estate. (courtesy of Jane Aitken)

Minerva on her and Johnny's wedding day.
(courtesy of Jane Aitken)

Uncle Poultney in characteristic macho pose.
(courtesy of Jane Aitken)

Johnny's mother, Flora. (courtesy of Jane Aitken)

Johnny's stepfather Lionel Guest. (courtesy of Alice Berkeley)

Johnny (far right) in pyjamas, recovering in Dulag Luft's medical facility, 1940. (courtesy of Alice Berkeley)

Wings Day on a walk in the woods near Dulag Luft. (courtesy of Alice Berkeley)

John Casson.
(courtesy of Alice
Berkeley)

Jimmy Buckley, the
original 'Big X'.
(courtesy of Alice
Berkeley)

MINERVA

After losing the parliamentary election of May 1929, Johnny turned his attention back to business, which he had necessarily neglected during the years of attempting to carve a career in politics. Nathan & Rosselli sent him to his native New York to drum up new clients. Stockbroking was, as Johnny later commented, more about who you knew than what you knew. His work in America involved an endless series of lunches and dinners with potential clients, glittering parties thrown by plutocrats to which socialites fluttered as moths do to a candle and weekends spent at the country estates of the great and the good—and the not so great and not so good. It was during these hectic and exciting post-war years that Johnny met the woman he was to spend the rest of his life with.

Minerva Arrington was a bright and bubbly debutante from a wealthy Charlotte, North Carolina family. A great-granddaughter of a former governor of the southern state, Minerva was an archetypal 'southern belle'. She had been briefly married to her childhood sweetheart, Charles Austin Sherman, who boasted an ancestor who had been a founding father of the American constitution. The marriage produced one child, a boy, Peter, but it had ended in divorce. When Minerva embarked upon the life of a single mother—albeit a somewhat glamorous one—in Manhattan, a long line of suitors were eager to take her out. There were other enticing possibilities that presented themselves to Minerva at this moment in her life. Peter Sherman, her son, in his unpublished autobiography, 'Memoirs of Another Time', writes that for a while Minerva considered a career on the stage. She made several appearances in productions in North Carolina and on Broadway. At one point she formed a friendship with the composer George Gershwin, and was on first name terms with Jimmy Durante, Al Jolson and the Broadway musical star Marilyn Miller. According to Peter, Gershwin's 1925 song Dinah was written for and about Minerva.

Among her closest friends was Fred Dalziel, a larger than life explorer and big game hunter, very much in the mode of Kermit Roosevelt and a host of other wealthy Hemingway-esque adventurers that proliferated during that time. It was at Dalziel's home that Johnny first met Minerva. There is some dispute as to whether it was at his oceanfront estate in Palm Beach or at his Manhattan apartment on East Seventieth Street. Peter states that Minerva found herself in difficulties swimming off the coast of Palm Beach when Johnny swam out to save her like a dashing hero in the romantic make-believe of a Barbara Cartland novel. Others insist the first meeting was in New York. But there is no doubt it was love at first sight on both sides. Less than three weeks after Minerva and Johnny met, they announced their intention to marry.

How Flora received the news is not recorded. But soon the whole of Manhattan and Mayfair were talking about the impending nuptials of the handsome Great War hero and his 27-year-old southern belle. The *New York Times* gushed:

> New York society is today busily discussing the announcement that . . . two of its most popular figures will be married here tomorrow . . . Although the couple have been together at ultrafashionable society gatherings, the announcement has come as a surprise and a revelation to their friends.

The night before the wedding, Johnny held a bachelor dinner party at the Knickerbocker Club. The following day's ceremony was held at Fred Dalziel's New York residence. Minerva wore a gown of printed chiffon and a striking velvet turban, and carried a large bouquet of orchids and roses. Dalziel gave the bride away and Poultney Bigelow was his nephew's best man. The assistant rector of St Bartholomew's Church read the rites. A wedding breakfast followed. Among the many cables the joyful couple received was one stating, 'All Mile End Conservatives wish you happiness and best of luck.'

Minerva and Johnny spent a brief honeymoon in Canada. By September, their sojourn was over and they were heading back to England with seven-year-old Peter. The party travelled on the French liner the *Île de France*, a voyage that proved to be a whirl of cocktail parties, dinners and dances. Peter Sherman was hurt by the apparent coldness towards him of the new man in his mother's life, but it is clear from his memoirs that even during these uncertain early days of his new life, Peter was in awe of Johnny. One evening in the middle of the Atlantic, Peter hid behind the pillars at the top of the stairs leading down to the liner's elegant dining room. Below him the women in evening gowns and glittering jewellery danced with their handsome partners in black tie and tails.

I was watching the glamorous scene from the top of the stairs, the dessert was being served, and the dance band struck up. I saw Mother and Johnny rise from their table and joining the many other dancers already on the floor. They were a dazzling pair, Johnny with such a dominant presence, such a wonderful strong face, carrying himself like an emperor, and my gorgeous mother happier than she had ever been, in the arms of this gallant husband whom she was to adore for the rest of their lives. Everyone seemed to be looking at them, and many stopped dancing to admire them and to give them more room. I was so proud of them.

They were to arrive in England to find that they had been given a generous wedding present from Flora and Lionel: a house, no less, in one of the most fashionable parts of London. The handsome terrace at 6 Connaught Street in Bayswater came with a small staff of Irish retainers, including a cook and personal maid for Minerva. It was around the corner from 26 Connaught Square, where Flora and Lionel had held court in London since moving from Seymour Street. The newlyweds would invariably spend the weekends at Wookyi-Tipi in the delightful seaside retreat of Ferring under Flora's watchful eye. It was evident that Flora was not going to let her beloved son too far out of her

150

sight.

The young Peter was the first to feel the force of Flora's overbearing personality. Her presence in the drawing room of Wookyi-Tipi, he later wrote, scared him even before she spoke. She referred to him as a 'wretched boy' and mocked his American clothing (though Peter could see no difference between his clothes and those of the English boys he knew). In time Peter came to believe he understood the deep-seated cause of Flora's simmering anger. He thought she had set her mind on marrying a duke or earl but had ended up with the miserable consolation prize of an 'Honourable'. 'Poor Flora Guest,' he writes in his memoir:

> I really think that, if she had been a 'Duchess' or even a 'Lady', she would have been in seventh heaven, her whole attitude improved, instead of being married to an 'Honourable Mister' and serving out her youth into middle-age bulk, her looks fading and her companion of a husband to be coddled and cared for until the end of time. Only her beloved child, Johnny Dodge, saved her sanity, and now he had gone and married an American woman, of all people—she having carefully forgotten that she had been an American before her marriage to Lionel and still had her American passport.

Peter formed an affection for 'Uncle Lionel', suspecting, perhaps, that Flora's husband suffered as much from his wife's overbearing manner as he did. They spent hours together in Lionel's observatory in the seclusion of the extensive lawns

151

at Wookyi-Tipi. 'But as soon as Flora realised that he and I enjoyed each other, she stopped my visits to the telescope,' Peter writes. He continues, 'He was a nice gentleman, but completely under the thumb of Flora, who treated him as if she were his nanny and he her child.'

After their first weekends at Wookyi-Tipi, Peter didn't raise Flora's rudeness with his mother because he sensed she was also the victim of her new mother-in-law's sharp tongue.

I could feel that Mother was somewhat on edge and apprehensive, and, when we got a moment together on the last day of an interminably long weekend, I asked her how she had enjoyed the weekend. 'Enjoy?' she cried. 'Enjoy! This whole visit has been a nightmare. Between Flora's efforts to undermine our marriage and with all her criticisms of my clothes, my hair, my Southern drawl, and my bridge playing, not to mention those damned dogs from hell, I'm about ready for the crazy house!'

Flora's attitude to Minerva, it appears, never softened and mother and daughter-in-law had a fractious and confrontational relationship to the end of their lives.

Fortunately Flora's attitude did not dampen Minerva's sunny disposition. Shortly after moving into 6 Connaught Street, Minerva had the house redecorated from top to bottom. The *Daily Express* described how it was being decorated in a 'most unusual and charming way' under the direction of Minerva and Mrs Gordon Ives, Lord Wimborne's niece. The new colour scheme was a cacophony of bright colours, soft primrose yellow, duck-egg blue, soft salmon pink and Venetian red. One room opening onto a courtyard was painted with a cheerful scene of a cottage surrounded by hollyhocks against the backdrop of the sea. 'All this sounds a trifle gaudy, but it is not. The effect is most charming and cheerful, like Mrs Dodge herself,' trilled the *Express*. Over the years the house at Connaught Street was to witness a parade of glitterati traipsing through its gaily decorated reception rooms, among them the Duke of Windsor and Wallis Simpson, Princess Marina of Kent and Noel Coward.

At a later date, Flora and Lionel would present Minerva and Johnny with another house, a modest 'cottage' in Ferring, albeit a cottage with eight bedrooms, set in eight acres with oak trees arching over the circular driveway. The pretty thatched, white timber-framed house looked directly over the wide pebble beach and was a ten-minute walk from Wookyi-Tipi. Minerva and Johnny called it 'Florida' in honour, according to Peter Sherman, of the American state where they met and which for them held such happy memories. (Compelling evidence, perhaps, that it *was* Florida and not New York where Minerva and Johnny first met.)

By then Ferring was attracting more of the glitterati from London besides the Prince of Wales and his mistress. The actor Raymond Massey bought a house near to Flora's estate on Sea Lane, and the popular comic Arthur Askey lived there too. Among those who frequented the pretty seaside hamlet were Laurence Olivier and Vivien Leigh, golden couple of the stage and screen; the

153

Hollywood heartthrobs Robert Donat and Ronald Coleman, two of the biggest movie stars of the age; and the Shakespearean actor Ralph Richardson. Lord Beaverbrook and Anthony Eden were said to be regular visitors, as were Lord Evan Tredegar and Kermit Roosevelt, Johnny's best friend. Many of them stayed with Minerva and Johnny at Florida; others stayed at a local hotel that became something of a chic place to be seen. Peter wrote that the American aviator Charles Lindbergh and his wife Ann were frequently guests at Florida after they moved to England, grieving for the death of their first-born child. 'They told Mother that their weekend with us had given them their first real desire to get on with their lives since the tragedy.' To complete this picture of the international socialite, Johnny also became the proud owner of two yachts, which he moored at the Royal Yacht Squadron in Cowes. *The Windstream* was an auxiliary Bermudan cutter of 14 tons, and *Rose of Sharon*, also 14 tons, was a schooner-rigged motor yacht. Johnny used them for private pleasure but also to entertain Nathan & Rosselli clients with trips up and down the coast, occasionally across the Channel and sometimes to the Riviera.

Minerva and Johnny's first child, David, was born in 1930. His arrival was greeted by an adulatory notice in *The Times*:

Few children have such well-known godfathers as David, the son of Colonel John B. Dodge and Mrs Dodge, who was christened yesterday at St John's Church, Southwick Crescent, London. His godfathers are the Honourable Piers Legh, Equerry to the Prince of Wales;

154

and the Honourable Lionel Guest. Colonel Dodge is the son of the Honourable Mrs Lionel Guest. Lord Desborough, Lady Lily Fitzgerald, the Dowager Marchioness of Blandford, the Honourable Mrs Piers Legh, and the Honourable Mrs Lionel Guest were present at the ceremony.

Their second son, Tony, came three years later. He was christened Lionel Arrington Bigelow but at the outset Minerva and Johnny had vowed to always call him Tony. General Lord Bernard Freyberg and Victor Cazelot were his godfathers. Tony was christened in a church in the East End of London, a gesture which suggests that Johnny's commitment to that impoverished part of the world was more than that of mere political opportunism.

The 1930s provided Johnny with many diversions besides politics and business, not least a holiday on Sir Samuel Courtauld's yacht in the Mediterranean. The other guests included Winston Churchill and his wife Clementine. Johnny impressed them all by swimming the Hellespont one fine day. It was in between the births of David and Tony that the arrival of a colourful woman in Britain was to prove a portent for the uncertain times to come. Wallis Warfield Simpson bore certain superficial similarities to Minerva and Flora, inasmuch as they were all American beauties (and divorcees) who chose a husband from the other side of the Atlantic, and preferably a titled one. According to Peter, his mother and Wallis became close friends, almost bosom buddies, after a chance encounter outside the Hungria restaurant during a rainstorm when they shared a cab together. Wallis, and subsequently her Royal consort, became frequent visitors at Connaught Street. But the impact that Wallis Simpson was to have on the British establishment far outweighed anything thus far achieved by the many hundreds of other wealthy socialites engaged in this rather unseemly transatlantic marital trade.

The story of Wallis Simpson, her cuckolded husband Ernest and Edward, the Prince of Wales, the future King of England, has been related ad nauseam. Peter's account is that the crisis that their love affair provoked and which culminated in the King's abdication of 1936, was followed closely by Minerva and Johnny, who were hosts to the couple at Connaught Street on several occasions. There is no independent verification of this amid the mountain of literature devoted to Wallis and Edward, but there is no particular reason to suspect Peter might be wrong. They moved in the same circles as so many celebrated personalities that it is hardly likely every social encounter would be recorded.

In the summer of 1936, as these momentous events unfolded, Johnny and Minerva with Peter in tow embarked upon a trip to Europe in the old tradition of the 'grand tour'. They flew to Paris and stayed at the Crillon Hotel, where Flora's Ferring chauffeur had delivered their car a few days before. The first night began in the company of Viscount Evan Tredegar (owner of the eponymous park in Monmouthshire), who occupied a suite at the Crillon. Tredegar had hired Edith Piaf and Maurice Chevalier to perform for the benefit of his guests and the entertainment was followed by dinner at Maxims. It was an evening that, quite naturally, made a deep impact upon young Peter's mind.

Throughout this grand tour Johnny was in the habit of absenting himself, sometimes for hours at a time, according to his stepson. Peter is convinced that during these 'lost' moments, Johnny, at the behest of the intelligence services in Whitehall, was meeting various senior ranking foreigners. The discussions were mainly aimed at providing him with objective assessments of the state of their preparedness in the event of the expected war breaking out. Peter claims Johnny had been in touch with some unnamed and mysterious people who had 'drawn up a list of certain VIPs in the top echelon of the government and military of the countries we were visiting who were deemed favourable to the British'.

Sadly, there is no proof of this but then nor would there be and, again, there is nothing intrinsically improbable about such discreet liaisons being arranged among people of high rank during those worrying times. In those rapidly darkening days, men—and women—of Johnny's social class and political standing were engaged in exactly the sorts of exchanges Peter alludes to, whether officially inspired or simply through private connections. There was an enormous communal effort among the political cognoscenti to avert the forthcoming crisis or at the very least to understand the minds and motivations of the enemy rising ominously out of the dark heart of Europe.

The travels of Minerva, Johnny and Peter subsequently took them to Vienna. Peter found the old Hapsburg capital beautiful but he was struck by the apathetic expressions on people's faces, and the evident poverty that was not easily masked by the fading glamour of the city's *fin de siècle* glory years.

In Munich, by contrast, they found the people celebrating life with fine food, good beer and inimitable Bavarian humour. Peter could not help but be impressed by a potent manifestation of Nazi power.

> . . . the uniforms! You would have thought you were already in a war, as one in every five or ten people displayed a uniform from one or another of the military services, not to forget the policing services. And then there were the Nazi posters displayed in wearying profusion on almost every wall and building, exhorting the multitudes to ever higher goals for the Führer and the Fatherland.

Johnny explained to his stepson that the only countries on the Continent which were doing well were Germany and Italy, the former in particular because its factories were churning out the planes, tanks and ships that were turning the Third Reich into the mightiest military power in Europe. Johnny warned Peter that there were only two possible consequences of such extraordinary industrial output: abject bankruptcy or outright war.

Peter's young eyes could see the benefits of Hitler's three years in power.

> To Hitler's credit, though labour unions had been banned, almost all workers were receiving an adequate pay check, plus free medical and hospital care, plus subsidized vacations at seaside resorts that they would never have dreamed of visiting before Hitler. Furthermore, there was no unemployment.

Peter even had a flattering word or two to say about Hitler's strict anti-pollution laws, which, it is universally acknowledged, were half a century ahead of their time.

They drove to the Berchtesgaden, location of Hitler's famed alpine retreat. Peter was thrilled to get a glimpse of the Berghof perched high on the mountainside. That night they dined at a restaurant crammed with families wearing traditional clothes and lederhosen and eating enormous plates of sausages, fried potatoes, beets and sauerkraut. Above the almost deafening sound of happy banter, a band played in the background. It proved to be a convivial evening for all. Johnny found a Great War veteran who had to have been on the opposite side of the Western Front to him in 1917. He introduced him to Minerva and Peter and presented him with one of his favourite Romeo Y Julieta Cuban cigars. At the end of their meal, Johnny left a generous tip for both the waiter and the band leader. They left to tumultuous applause and banging of beer glasses on tables.

From Germany their journey took them to Budapest and thence Venice where they booked into the Danielli Hotel. Johnny's sister, Lucy, was already lodged there with her husband Walter Rosen and their two children, Ann and Walter Junior. The Rosens enjoyed spending their summer vacations in Europe, visiting the great chateaux that had fallen into destitution and decay, and salvaging vast quantities of furniture, chandeliers and works of art from certain doom. Lucy and Walter sometimes bought whole rooms, which were broken down and packaged to be shipped back to the US and reassembled as part of the mansion they were building in upstate New York.

Peter was struck by his first meeting with his stepfather's sister:

Aunt Lucy was a knock-out of a lady, about five feet eight inches tall, with a pompadour hair style that increased her height by another foot or so, it seemed, and with a beautiful, elegant face on a long neck, plus a slim figure. She also had a presence that, like her brother Johnny, could get the attention of a room full of chattering people without her saying a word. She was graciousness personified, and yet, like her husband Walter, a down-to-earth person, generous with herself and her influence in the world of young, underfunded artists pursuing careers in voice or instrumental music, never denying a more than generous scholarship if the professors in their field verified that the talent was indeed there . . . Aunt Lucy found joy in almost everything she was interested in, and, like Mother, she loved to laugh. These two sisters-in-law got along wonderfully well, mainly, I think, because they were both very giving of themselves, and poured their energy into any project, big or small, that they felt worthwhile and worth doing.

Peter recalls that on the third day of their visit, Johnny received a call from Count Ciano, Mussolini's son-in-law and his secretary of state. Ciano invited Johnny to lunch and sent a launch to pick him up from the Danielli Hotel. While Johnny was having lunch with Ciano, Peter and Walter Junior spent the day at the Lido gazing at the suntanned beauties sprawled on the sand half naked. According to Peter, when Johnny returned from his luncheon with Ciano, he told how the Italian count had stated Mussolini's great regard for Britain. He had assured him Italy would act in its own best interests, not Hitler's interests.

Minerva, Johnny and Peter left two days later for the final stop of their grand tour: Switzerland. In Switzerland, at the quiet mountain resort of Château-d'Oex, Minerva, Johnny and Peter relaxed, exploring the countryside and enjoying long picnic lunches. The layover had a double purpose. Johnny wanted to take Peter out of Eton and enrol him for a year in an exclusive school nearby to learn French. They visited the school together, and Peter agreed. The following day they left for England. Peter never saw Walter Junior again. Walter was killed in an air accident while training at flight school in World War II.

19

A FINAL NOTE

There are some veiled hints that during this period
Johnny and Minerva's marriage came close to
breaking up. On New Year's Day of 1937, just after
the abdication crisis, Johnny wrote disapprovingly to
Minerva of her 'flashy' clothes and penchant for
foreign, cafe society friends such as, no doubt, Wallis
Simpson. He said he much preferred English ladies
and gentlemen, old friends of his family. It appears
too that Johnny had found another woman upon
whom to pour his affections—presumably an English
lady of long-standing family connection if he were
being true to his expressed sentiments. His mystery
lover is referred to in Phyllis Dodge's notes, but
her identity is not revealed. Surprisingly in the
circumstances, he was dissuaded from divorcing
Minerva by his wife's greatest antagonist, his mother
Flora. The exact details of this marital disharmony
have been successfully buried. And whatever
domestic woes Minerva and Johnny might have been
enduring were rapidly cast into the shadows by
events of a far greater magnitude in the outside
world.

Germany invaded Poland on 1 September, its
blitzkrieg tactics swiftly turning the neighbouring
nation to rubble, the scale of its sledge-hammer
attack reducing her proud people into a state of
abject terror. The governments of Britain and
France, which had proved so pusillanimous in the
face of Hitler's demands on the Ruhr and

Czechoslovakia, finally made a stand against the German dictator. But they were too late. On 3 September, Britons gathered around their wireless sets in silent apprehension to listen to their prime minister tell them the grim news that they all half expected. Shortly after the broadcast began at 11.15 a.m., Chamberlain's weary and tremulous voice, full of remorse and sorrow, crackled over the airwaves . . .

> This morning the British Ambassador in Berlin handed the German Government a final note stating that, unless we heard from them by 11 o'clock that they were prepared at once to withdraw their troops from Poland, a state of war would exist between us. I have to tell you now that no such undertaking has been received, and that consequently this country is at war with Germany.

For the younger members of the Dodge family, the onset of the second great conflagration in Europe meant several years of separation from the parents they adored. David, who was nine when war broke out, would spend the rest of the conflict mostly with his grandmother Flora, sometimes at her estate in Ferring, and at other times in the suite at the Dorchester Hotel, which she had hired in London for the duration. (The Dorchester was a popular haunt for the rich and wealthy during the war, as it was one of the few steel-constructed buildings in the capital, thus offering an almost indestructible refuge from the Luftwaffe's bombs.) Tony, who was six, would be dispatched to a house in Wales where he would see his mother only intermittently over the next five years. Both boys would no longer be able to look forward to the blissfully happy weekends and summers they had spent at Ferring with their mother and father. Johnny was soon to sign up, and would disappear from their lives for nearly five years. Minerva spent the war working for various servicemen's charities. Florida was cleaned and mothballed as if for the winter, but in fact for good.

Peter Sherman was nearly 18 when war broke out. Bidding Florida farewell was particularly hard for him. 'It was no longer the centre of entertainment and laughter, with guests from all over the world coming and going, enjoying the company, the various activities available, and above all the presence of their hosts, Johnny and Minerva.'

With the help of Winston Churchill, Johnny and his friend Kermit Roosevelt joined the Middlesex Regiment. Johnny was reduced from the rank of lieutenant colonel to that of major. He joked that he didn't mind being demoted but feared that if he went on at this rate he would be a private by the end of the war. Johnny returned to the machine gunners and began the tedious task of training. When it became apparent that the 'phoney war' was going to continue for some months to come, Johnny decided to have one more go at realising his ambition to achieve high political office. The incumbent member of parliament for Gillingham in Kent had announced that he would not stand at the next general election, which would not now be held until the war was over. Thus encouraged, Johnny determined to become the prospective Conservative candidate for the seat. After visiting the constituency he was swiftly selected by his local party. Soon after, he returned to his military unit, confident, as many were, that the war would be over by Christmas and he would be contending the Gillingham seat in the near future. It was not to be, however.

Disconcertingly, the phoney war stretched long into the new year, lulling many people into a false sense of security. Perhaps there would be no war in the West after all, now that Hitler was happily sated on his acquisitions around the borders of his thousand-year Reich. But as the summer of 1940 approached, these optimistic hopes were thoroughly dashed. In April, Germany attacked Denmark and Norway. Britain's response to the latter proved ill conceived and ill led. Once more, the inadequate British reaction was neutralised by Germany's nimble action and overwhelming force.

During these disastrous days, Johnny's machine gunners were dispatched with the 51st Highland Division to France with the British Expeditionary Force (B.E.F.). The possibility that Germany might launch a blitz on its old enemy on the other side of the Maginot Line no longer seemed quite as far-fetched as it had done so many months ago. On the Continent the Highlanders were detached from the main body of the B.E.F. at the Belgian border and sent to do a tour of duty with the French Army along the heavily fortified 'impregnable' line of defences. It was one of the most formidable military obstacles ever constructed, but it would not be formidable enough. On 10 May, the Wehrmacht swept through Belgium, Holland and Luxembourg, sidestepping the Maginot Line and bulldozing its way into France through the Low Countries at

165

lightning speed. For France the phoney war was over and the debacle that would bring the sacred home of *liberté*, *égalité* and *fraternité* to her knees had begun.

As scores of German divisions stampeded across France driving the B.E.F. inexorably toward the sea, Johnny's 51st Division put up a fighting retreat. Within ten days of the invasion, the division learnt that the Germans had broken through the French lines separating them from the rest of the B.E.F. They were on their own. After a period of indecision it was decided to move the men back some 300 miles into a position overlooking the River Bresle near Abbeville. Some of the 51st Highlanders were lucky enough to be transported to their destination in the relative comfort of trains. The remainder, Johnny among them, had to slog their way through roads crowded with panicking civilians, a spectacle all too familiar to him from his experience during the Great War of the defence of Antwerp.

While the bulk of the B.E.F. beat its retreat to Dunkirk and hoped-for salvation at the hands of the Royal Navy, the Highlanders were to fight on with the French Army as part of the French IX Corps. Their task was to hold a line along the Somme from Erondelle to the south-east of Abbeville to the coast at St Valéry-sur-Somme. But their numbers were thinly stretched over the 23 miles of the line. When the German attack on the Abbeville bridgehead began on 4 June, the British and French defenders put up a heroic fight. But the flood of German armour and troops was too much for them to stem. They were forced to retreat slowly. After the Germans cut off their supply route to Rouen, they

166

were compelled to fall back to a line on La Béthune, with nearby Dieppe a possible port of evacuation. But the German advance was swift and sure and the Highlanders' situation was becoming increasingly desperate. Commanders turned their attention to Le Havre much further west; when even that possibility was ruled out they settled on the midway point of St Valéry-en-Caux instead, from where they hoped to be evacuated. It was 13 June.

In fact there was no possibility of evacuation and no chance of reinforcements. The division had run out of artillery shells and all other ammunition was almost exhausted. The men were broken by fatigue. It was more than a week after the 'Miracle of Dunkirk'. Some 340,000 Allied troops had been rescued by the famous armada of little boats that had crossed the Channel in the much celebrated Operation Dynamo. When Johnny and the bedraggled ranks of the 51st Highlanders arrived in the little port of St Valéry they could see no sign of any evacuation vessels save for a single lone steamer, presumably friendly, about three miles out in the Channel.

Johnny was ordered to swim to the vessel in the hope that he might alert the ship's skipper to the fact that the 51st Highland Division was in St Valéry and possibly effect a rescue. He was accompanied in his endeavour by a private who swam valiantly with him to the distant steamer. But the ship began moving away and Johnny realised his mission was futile. Carried westward by the wind and tide, the private and he were about a half a mile from the shore when they came under fire from small shells. The private told Johnny that he was becoming tired and so Johnny handed him an oar which he had found in

167

the sea. That was the last he ever saw of his erstwhile companion. By then, back on shore, the 51st Highland Division had been left with no choice but to surrender to the Germans in the form of a then little-known German general officer called Erwin Rommel. Though the war in the west had hardly begun, it was nearly over for Johnny.

Out at sea Johnny was unaware of this turn of events. He tried to swim back to the place at St Valéry where he had left his clothes, but the tide was running out and it forced him to spend an uncomfortable four or five hours in the water. Eventually he reached the beach some four miles west of his departure point, at the foot of some high cliffs. He was naked. Someone threw him an overcoat and trousers from the top of the cliff, and he gratefully donned them. Realising that St Valéry had probably fallen to the enemy, he resolved to walk towards Le Havre along the shoreline. On the way, as he stumbled across shingle and rocks, he came under occasional sniper fire. But it was his lack of shoes, rather than a sniper, that brought his heroic struggle to an end. His feet became badly bruised and cut, and eventually he could continue no more. Johnny took refuge in a cave in the cliffs where he stayed until dusk fell.

Outside, the Germans continued to fire shots from the cliffs in his direction. Fortunately the shells splashed harmlessly into the gently lapping water. Somewhat more alarmingly, the Germans dropped hand grenades in front of the entrance to the cave. But fortunately the blast from these infernal devices did not penetrate the cold interior where Johnny sheltered. When darkness fell, he emerged to continue his painful slog to Le Havre, slipping and sliding over the wet rocks on his way. At about 3 a.m. the following day, 14 June, Johnny ran into a party of officers and men from the 51st Division making their way to the beach in the hope of getting away. Lights of a ship were visible and they signalled it with a torch but they were disappointed that no boat came to their rescue. The men retreated to a cave and fell asleep exhausted.

They were awoken in the morning by the sound of a revolver firing. When they looked out of their hiding place they saw a car containing Germans standing about 75 yards from the mouth of the cave. They could see another 100 or so Germans armed with machine guns a little further along the coast. After being fired on by machine guns and having grenades thrown in their direction, the men decided the wisest course of action was to surrender. Johnny emerged from the cave waving a white handkerchief, the firing ceased and they were all taken prisoner. It was the beginning of almost five years in German captivity for Johnny.

The men were marched north by the Germans and a few days later they joined the main column of Allied prisoners being evacuated eastwards. There were about 1,000 of them in all, and with them Johnny endured a fortnight's trek across France and Belgium. Fortunately he had managed to borrow a pair of someone else's boots. But marching over many miles in the wrong-sized footwear proved to be unbearable and Johnny's already injured feet became even more blistered and infected. Eventually the weary column reached the banks of the River Scheldt in Holland. It was a river he had first encountered some 26 years earlier when, as a young man in the Royal Naval Division, he had taken part in the evacuation of Antwerp. Once more Johnny approached the famous Dutch river as part of the defeated side but, as ever, he refused to be a defeated soul.

When the column of prisoners arrived at the Scheldt they were herded aboard the ship that was to take them back to Germany. Johnny had different ideas, however, and the following morning he jumped overboard. It was his first attempted escape of the Second World War. Sadly, it was a short-lived one. Soon afterwards he was picked up by a small Dutch passenger boat and handed over to the nearest German military authority. By chance it happened to be the Luftwaffe and as a result Johnny was taken to German air force headquarters in Amsterdam. It was a stroke of luck that was probably to make Johnny's war behind the wire considerably more comfortable than it would have been if he had remained a prisoner of the Wehrmacht.

After a cursory interrogation (which appears not to have questioned the suitability of a British army officer being held by the Luftwaffe) Johnny was driven through the night into the heart of Germany. His destination proved to be on the outskirts of the small town of Oberursel near Frankfurt-am-Main at the foot of the Taunus Mountains. At the end of the journey, Johnny found himself in an unassuming setting: a collection of anonymous brick buildings supplemented by more modern timber huts, surrounded by hastily erected barbed wire and guarded over by a handful of watchtowers. In the distance was what appeared to be a pretty village. Johnny had arrived at Dulag Luft, the first prisoner-of-war camp he would inhabit over the forthcoming years in captivity.

PRISONER OF WAR

Before the war, Dulag Luft's ramshackle collection of buildings had been an experimental agricultural centre, of the sort the new National Socialist authorities were keen on. The pretty village in the distance had been just that: a model settlement for the new agrarian labourers in the new ideal order that the Nazis were planning to impose upon the world. Once hostilities had commenced, however, the agricultural centre had been hastily turned into a makeshift prison camp for air force prisoners. After December 1939, Dulag Luft was the first point of call for most Allied airmen captured in German-occupied Europe. From there they would be dispatched to the permanent air force camps under construction in other far-flung corners of the Reich. The name Dulag Luft was a contraction of the phrase 'Durchgangslager der Luftwaffe', meaning 'transit camp of the air force'. But Dulag Luft was to become much more than a mere transit camp. The facility was also turning into an interrogation centre, the purpose of which was to extract every ounce of valuable information from the downed Allied air crew it found in its grasp.

It remains a mystery why the Luftwaffe authorities in Amsterdam sent Johnny to this air force facility and not to an army camp where he rightfully belonged. By the time he arrived, the original farm buildings were supplemented by a compound of three purpose-built timber barrack blocks (designated East, West and Middle blocks) providing dormitories and cooking and cleaning facilities, all surrounded by a perimeter fence overlooked by watchtowers. Despite these intrusive security precautions, however, Dulag Luft was to be by far the most comfortable and civilised prison camp that Johnny was ever sent to during his long unwelcome stay as a guest of Adolf Hitler.

The Luftwaffe commandant presiding over Dulag Luft was an urbane and congenial former World War I flier who would figure largely in Johnny's life over the next few months. Major Theodor Rumpel was a tall, thin officer of aristocratic mien who had the habit of tucking his right hand into his jacket in the style of a latter-day Napoleon. But Theo Rumpel was far from being a figure of caricature. A former cavalry officer of great distinction, Rumpel had ended up, during the First World War, in Hermann Göring's air force squadron. Flying an Albatross, the dashing young German pilot was unfortunate enough to be on the receiving end of a burst of fire from a British machine gun over Rheims. The result was a shattered right shoulder, which Rumpel endured for the rest of his life. He never, however, let his occasionally painful disfigurement sour his feelings towards the enemy who had inflicted the injury upon him.

In the interwar years, Rumpel had been a commercial trader in the Dutch East Indies where he acquired an appreciation and respect for the colonial power's commercial modus operandi in the Far East. He also found himself a beautiful wife from an aristocratic Dutch dynasty. Two years after Hitler came to power, and as the Germans began secretly rebuilding their armed forces, Rumpel was invited to rejoin the revitalised Luftwaffe. Subsequently, in 1938, he was recruited into the British Section of Abteilung V, the Luftwaffe intelligence service commanded by Lieutenant General Josef Schmid, a favourite of Hitler and Göring. Rumpel only accepted the job with the proviso, it is recorded, that he did not have to become a member of the National Socialist Party. Like many people in Germany, he resented the inequities of the Versailles Treaty and wanted to see his country take her rightful place as a modern and respected industrial nation alongside the other great powers of Europe and the world beyond. But while he may have sympathised with many of Hitler's achievements and ambitions, he harboured a distinct distaste for some of the more crude aspects of Nazism and its Führer.

Rumpel was regarded as the best intelligence officer the Luftwaffe had. This, combined with his courtly charm and almost perfect English, made him a natural choice for the job of running Dulag Luft, where most of the early Allied inmates were of a similar background. Rumpel was reluctant to accept the job of being, in his own words, a 'common jailer'. But he obeyed orders and sought to institute at the camp a regimen in keeping with the *esprit de corps* that he considered bound all air force officers, regardless of what nationality they might be or which side they were on. The tone and tenor of the German command at Dulag Luft towards the Allied inmates was one of politeness and courtesy. There was plenty of heel clicking and head bowing, but no Nazi salutes. Rumpel himself was friendly and solicitous of his prisoners' needs, often apologising to them for the role that he found himself in, and invariably engaging them in apparently inconsequential conversation.

Rumpel was well liked by most of the Allied officers who passed through his hands. They included at that early stage of the war several personalities who would become central to Johnny's life in captivity, and pivotal to the many escape plans that were hatched over the years. Among them was Wing Commander Harry Melville Arbuthnot Day, a Royal Marine in the First World War who had become an RAF pilot in the Second. 'Wings', as he was known to all the Allied officers, was an elderly 41 years old when the war broke out. He became the Senior British Officer (SBO) at Dulag Luft, and would maintain that position for much of the war. Other early Dulag Luft prisoners who would become friends and fellow escapologists included Roger Bushell, a South African-born lawyer who had become a Hurricane pilot; Jimmy Buckley, a Fleet Air Arm pilot; John Casson, the son of the distinguished Shakespearean actress Sybil Thorndike; and Peter Butterworth, a Royal Navy flight lieutenant who went on to become a famous character actor perhaps best known for his appearances in British television's *Carry On* series of comic capers.

These first British officer prisoners in captivity during the war (and those from other Allied nations) came from the same elevated social class as their German captors, and they treated one another accordingly. It was not unusual for Rumpel to invite the Allied airmen to his office in the evenings for convivial drinks parties. Occasionally he had them for more lavish buffets or meals to his private quarters, a well-appointed bungalow a few hundred yards or so away, beyond the barbed wire and watchtowers of Dulag Luft on a gentle slope of a hill in the Taunus Forest. Rumpel was a good host: the repartee was amusing and the conversation illuminating, as would be expected. Dinners of smoked eels, thick soup, sauerkraut, ham and boiled potatoes would be accompanied by dessert of Apfelstrudel and fine wine and whisky (much of it plundered from the French people and the retreating Allied forces).

Rumpel often sent the prisoners casual gifts of fresh fruit, alcoholic beverages or cigars, invariably accompanied by brief notes containing inconsequential pleasantries. His prisoners, in turn, were fulsome in their gratitude. 'On behalf of all the P of W's in this camp I wish to thank you for your very generous gift to us,' wrote a grateful Wings Day on 22 November 1940, after receiving some unidentified offering. He added, 'I hope very much that your wife is continuing to make a good recovery from her illness.' In another letter Peter Butterworth thanked Rumpel for a birthday present the commandant had sent him. 'It converted my birthday from what promised to be only an anniversary into a celebration . . . I am very sorry you were unable to come and join us.'

When Rumpel contributed some prizes to be awarded in one of the prisoners' six-a-side football competitions, Jimmy Buckley wrote to thank him 'for the cigarettes you sent over yesterday and for your many handsome gifts of whisky and wine which you so frequently give us'. After Roger Bushell celebrated his birthday in fine style, he wrote: 'This note is to thank you very much for your birthday presents which made possible, for me at any rate + I hope for you, a most enjoyable party. Believe me we appreciate these acts of kindness very much indeed and will not forget them.'

When Johnny arrived in Dulag Luft he found himself on the receiving end of a typical Rumpel charm offensive. The commandant gave his distinguished new prisoner some Player's cigarettes and beer as a welcoming gesture. On 29 June 1940, only a matter of days after he had been admitted to the camp, Johnny wrote home a glowing report of the camp commandant. Rumpel was 'most intelligent + kind . . . If he is rep. [representative] of the German people, we should be able to work together . . . some day.' Rumpel saw to it that the new arrival had a deck chair to rest his body and his badly scratched and bruised feet. Together Johnny and Rumpel sat in the sun and chatted amiably like old friends.

On account of his wounded feet, Johnny was put into a private room in the Dulag Luft hospital and later a nearby convalescent centre. He was treated there by a young medical orderly called Heinz Dörrfus, with whom he formed a bond of mutual affection that would outlast the war. The military situation at the time was somewhat depressing, at least for the Allies, with Germany triumphant in every endeavour she undertook and Britain seemingly on the verge of a crushing invasion defeat. It was hardly surprising that some of the less gracious German functionaries among the Dulag Luft staff would brashly predict, *England in sechs Wochen* ('England in six weeks') or alternatively, the self-explanatory *'England kaputt'*. But despite the dire straits his adoptive home appears to have

177

been in at this time, Johnny seems to have maintained his equable spirits. He sent Rumpel several letters thanking the German commandant for the hospital treatment he had arranged.

When Rumpel first learnt of Johnny's high connections in England and America is not known. It is possible that Johnny might have told the Luftwaffe interrogators in Amsterdam, which would explain why he was sent to Dulag Luft in the first place. Maybe Rumpel's contacts in Abteilung V had informed him. Rumpel was the recipient of a letter from a Frankfurt bank that arrived at Dulag Luft shortly after Johnny. It advised the commandant that the director of a bank in New York, John Bigelow Dodge, was a prisoner in Germany and should be supplied with anything he wanted. When Johnny was told by Rumpel of this intervention on his behalf, he replied, 'Tell them I've got everything I want.' Rumpel enjoyed having Johnny in his camp. One day the commandant picked up a list of his prisoners and wrote against Johnny's name, 'abkommandiert zur RAF' ('transferred to the RAF'). Rumpel told Wings, 'You and Johnny both belong to the same London club . . . so I have arranged for him to stay with the RAF prisoners.' Thus Johnny became an air force prisoner and would escape, for the most part, the deprivations and indignities entailed by imprisonment at the hands of the less respectful Wehrmacht.

Famously, on 19 July 1940, the Führer spoke from the Reichstag in his impassioned entreaty to Britain to grasp one final chance of making peace with the Reich before Armageddon would be released upon her. By now, Churchill was in

Downing Street. Rumpel went to great pains to ensure that the wireless broadcast could be heard by his prisoners in Dulag Luft. He made sure the loudspeakers were wired up throughout the camp so that it could be heard in even the most remote corner. Rumpel himself enjoined his captives to listen to the historic broadcast. It is difficult to comprehend from the perspective of seven decades after the event, but at that time, many Germans believed that their cause was just, and some believed that Hitler's final plea to Britain would be the moment that her stubborn bulldog of a leader would finally see sense.

Indeed, many of the Allied prisoners in the Führer's audience at Dulag Luft might very well have agreed with some of the sentiments the German leader expressed. It was not only Germans who thought the Versailles Treaty was an abomination that merely stoked up trouble for the future. This had been a widespread feeling throughout Europe before the ink had dried on the controversial pact. But, as the Führer's words came over the airwaves at Dulag Luft, they did not go down well with the audience. Major Rumpel was put in the uncomfortable position of having to listen to some highly colourful Anglo-Saxon expressions of disapproval in vocal reply to his great leader's impassioned entreaties. It was swiftly evident to him that the war was not going to be over by Christmas. The commandant, nevertheless, distributed a translation of the main points of the speech directly afterwards. Johnny, who was still recovering in the medical quarters, was one of those to receive a copy of Hitler's speech (along with a selection of fresh fruit). He sent a note thanking Rumpel for the 'beautiful fruit' and describing

179

Hitler's speech as, somewhat ambiguously, 'very fine'. He ended the letter: 'I hope you and your family are well and that we shall meet again before long.'

Johnny—in common with many others from all shades of the political spectrum—was by no means unimpressed by what he had seen in the Germany that Hitler had transformed since his visit there in 1936. 'Hitler certainly has given his people work, food and their self respect back,' he wrote in letters from Dulag Luft to Minerva and Flora. 'There are many leaves we can take out of the book of Nazi-Socialism with profit to ourselves. Anti-Bolshevik that I am, I long for the day when there will be a just and honourable peace between Britain and Germany.' He concluded, however, 'While England is at war, I wish I were able to fight for her.'

Despite the apparent comfort of his new surroundings, Johnny quickly embarked on an energetic campaign to canvass for his release from German captivity. It is testimony to his importance, perceived or otherwise, that his efforts, and those on his behalf, occupied the attention of some of the busiest diplomats and civil servants in Europe and America during that hectic time in world affairs. Not only did underlings in Whitehall and Washington find themselves embroiled in the bid to get him released: the offices of both Winston Churchill and Franklin Roosevelt were to be drawn into his plight.

Johnny would neither be the first nor the last prisoner of war (POW) to conceive of the possibility of being exchanged on medical grounds for an enemy prisoner. 'I want vy much to get back to England + hope some scheme of exchanging prisoners can be arranged,' he wrote in October

1940 to his cousin Olive Pell in neutral Portugal. Olive was the daughter of his uncle Poultney Bigelow. Her husband Herbert ('Bertie') was the US minister in Lisbon at the outbreak of war. 'Thank God he is alive, and has only a "slight ailment",' Olive wrote to Flora on hearing the news of Johnny's captivity. 'Let us thank God for his sunny and genial disposition and handsome appearance, both of which will go a long way toward ameliorating the relations between him and those in charge. Nobody could be unkind or even rude to Johnny . . .' Olive and Bertie brought the matter up in Lisbon in January 1941 at dinner with the former US presidential candidate Wendell Willkie when he was on the way to London on his well-publicised drum-thumping mission from Roosevelt to Churchill.

Johnny wrote to Minerva and asked her to appeal on his behalf to Herschel Johnson, the *attaché d'affaires* at the US embassy in London. Relatives and friends serving in various diplomatic posts and the Red Cross in Hungary, Germany and Switzerland were all enrolled to lend whatever assistance they could muster. Unfortunately for Johnny, he was told repeatedly that his efforts were most likely to be of no avail. One typical response was quite blunt. There was 'not a chance as he is neither old enough nor wounded enough . . . only the severest cases get xchan'd,' wrote one US intermediary.

Undeterred, Johnny persisted. Poultney Bigelow wrote to Flora that he had personally approached Franklin Roosevelt. The President's Hyde Park estate in upstate New York neighboured Poultney's own rural retreat. It appears that the possibility was mooted of exchanging his nephew with Prince Frederick of Prussia, a grandson of Poultney's old friend of Potsdam days, the former Kaiser and King of Prussia. Prince Frederick had been shooting on a grouse moor in Scotland with a duke when he was arrested and sent to Canada. Frederick was at that time interred in Ottawa as an 'enemy alien'. This plan to exchange him with Johnny sadly came to nothing.

Winston Churchill also became embroiled in Johnny's plight. Flora wired his 'cousin' at Downing Street only to receive a somewhat disheartening reply. 'Mr Churchill is sorry he will be unable to see you personally as he will not be in London,' wrote his personal private secretary Kathleen Hill. Subsequently, Mrs Hill was able to write that, 'The Prime Minister has now completed the inquiry which he made about Colonel Dodge, and he asks me to say that the War Office have sent his name to the Foreign Office with a request that they will employ the diplomatic channel (which is the United States Embassy) with the object of securing his examination by the Mixed Medical Commission now functioning in Germany.' She warned that even if the commission recommended Johnny be repatriated there was likely to be a substantial delay. She ended the letter, 'Mr. and Mrs. Churchill wish me to express their sympathy with you in the very anxious time you are passing through . . .'

It was all to no avail. Despite the painful injuries to his feet, Johnny was fitter and healthier than many men half his years, and the blisters and bruises swiftly healed to prove the point. His wounds had been treated quickly and effectively by his German doctors. Johnny was fully recovered within three months of entering the convalescent unit at Dulag Luft. The vice consul of the US Embassy in Berlin visited Johnny there and found him in good shape and 'hale + hearty'. Intriguingly though, a US inter-embassy memo between London and Berlin acknowledged that the 'desire of the British government to nominate him for examination . . . was being brought to the attention of the appropriate German authorities for future reference'. It is possible that these fevered efforts on Johnny's behalf at the beginning of his captivity led the Germans to believe later that their prisoner was indeed a valuable bargaining chip worth hanging on to.

These letters began at the height of the Battle of Britain, when the RAF's Fighter Command was desperately holding off the Luftwaffe's attacks. In these darkest hours for Britain, Flora was dividing her time between Wookyi-Tipi on England's south coast, where a German invasion was expected any day, and the Dorchester. (Johnny's older son David stayed with Flora until he was sent away to boarding school in the north of England.) Minerva and the younger boy Tony were in London until the Blitz began and their house in Bayswater was badly bomb damaged. They took refuge on a farm in Wales. Eventually, Minerva returned to London and worked for the rest of the war at the English Speaking Union, arranging hospitality for American military officers in London. ('She certainly kept them entertained,' one of her relatives commented waspishly in an interview for this book.)

On 19 August 1940, the Gillingham Conservative and Unionist Association sent Minerva a letter to say that they had passed a resolution regretting that Johnny was in the hands of the enemy, and resolving to do anything within their power to maintain full support for his candidacy.

OH, WHAT A LOVELY WAR!

At Dulag Luft Major Rumpel established what became known as 'the British Permanent Staff'. The officers he selected for this privileged group all shared similar qualities. They were mostly older individuals who could provide guidance to the more immature and hotheaded Allied airmen who would be brought to the transit camp on their way to other Luftwaffe camps. They were mostly 'well-bred' men from distinguished families who satisfied Rumpel's own personal prejudices as to how gentlemen should behave towards one another. A few were put on the Permanent Staff because they were of bona fide intelligence interest to the Germans. Johnny fulfilled, possibly, all three of these criteria.

The leader of the Permanent Staff was Wing Commander Day, the Senior British Officer and the man who would increasingly become Johnny's best friend behind the wire. Harry Melville Arbuthnot Day was born and brought up in Borneo, but educated in England. A Royal Marine in the First World War, he was decorated for gallantry after twice braving fire and flames to save two members of the crew in a torpedoed ship sinking fast. After the war he acquired a taste for flying and, joining the newly formed RAF, Wings became a stunt flier. He led the aerobatic flight at the Hendon Air Display in 1932. One of the more colourful members of his team was a tearaway pilot called Douglas Bader.

From the moment Wings was shot down over Germany in October 1939 (he was flying an ancient Blenheim on a reconnaissance sortie), he was treated with great decency and kindness. He determined that he would fight his war from behind the wire with the same courtesy that had been extended to him by the enemy. He always insisted on a sharp turnout for roll-call (Appell) and he snapped to salute a senior Luftwaffe officer just as sharply as he would have done an RAF one. After a brief spell in various makeshift prison facilities including Spangenberg castle, the ancient schloss near Kassel, Wings had been sent to Dulag Luft.

One of the first requests that Wings made of Rumpel when he arrived was to be given a kitten. He hoped the presence of a living creature would dull the pain of the many hours spent alone in captivity. Rumpel said he would look into the matter and some days later turned up with a cat. Wings remarked that the kitten seemed on the large size but Rumpel insisted it was only a few weeks old. 'In that case I will call it "Ersatz",' said Wings, comparing his substitute kitten to the substitute ersatz coffee, cheese and meat that were the staple of the prisoners' diet when not being entertained by the commandant's largesse. Some weeks later a photograph of Wings and Ersatz appeared in the German Luftwaffe periodical *Der Adler*, in which the British officer was labelled 'ein grosser Katzenfreund' ('a big friend to cats'). The photograph was to rile many other POWs in other camps whose circumstances were not quite as comfortable as those of their lucky counterparts at Dulag Luft.

Indeed, the relatively benign conditions that the

Permanent Staff at Dulag Luft enjoyed provoked widespread accusations of betrayal and collaboration. Wings discovered this to his great discomfort one day when Rumpel showed him an intercepted communication. The letter had been written from Stalag Luft I, a new camp in the windswept and inhospitable surroundings of Barth on the Baltic. In no uncertain terms the writer accused Wings, Johnny and his fellow officers of pilfering Red Cross parcels intended for others and enjoying the high life courtesy of the Third Reich. Ugly rumours persisted beyond the end of the war, so much so that in the RAF's own 'official' history of escape activity during the conflict, the officer commissioned to write it felt obliged to address the issue.

The author, Aidan Crawley, a future Tory MP, was a famed escaper himself during his captivity in the war. In *Escape from Germany, 1939–45: Methods of Escape Used by RAF Airmen During the Second World War* he wrote: 'In later years a myth grew up that in these early days relations between the Germans and their air force prisoners had been almost medieval in chivalry and that prison life had been more like life in a country house.' But, the author claimed, 'The facts were otherwise . . . Far from being lenient German discipline in the first few months was strict . . . The officers . . . for many weeks were locked in cells and prevented from having any communal life.'

Few Permanent Staff prisoners of Dulag Luft between 1940 and 1941 would recognise the austere picture painted by Crawley. Rumpel and Wings often went for walks together in the surrounding forest, the German commandant unarmed and

187

unguarded. On Wings Day's first birthday in captivity, 3 August 1940, Theo Rumpel invited the British officer to lunch at the Forellen Gut, a pleasant restaurant attached to a trout farm in the woods near Dulag Luft. They chatted over drinks as if they were old friends. In fact, they were beginning to become old friends. The two men remained in touch long after the war ended. According to Wings's daughter June:

> They were very fond of one another. Daddy used to go on the most marvellous fishing expeditions with Rumpel. He always promised Rumpel that he would not attempt to escape while on parole. But on other occasions, Wings reminded him, it was the sworn duty of all officers to escape. Rumpel told my father that he must of course do his duty. And he promised to send him a fine bottle of champagne after he had been recaptured.

Rumpel was to share an equally equitable friendship with Johnny. After the war Johnny became Rumpel's stockbroker.

As a Kriegie (derived from the German word '*Kriegsgefangener*' for 'prisoner of war'), Johnny became used to the meagre and almost inedible German rations. Usually they consisted of ersatz coffee made from acorns with dry black bread of questionable provenance for breakfast, sauerkraut soup and a portion of mouldy potatoes for lunch, followed by some sausage or a peculiar cheese made from fish by-products. It was the Germans' standard diet for a non-working civilian, but at 800 calories per day it offered far less than the optimum 1,200 calories recommended for a normal healthy, though sedentary, adult.

However, supplies of Red Cross parcels were plentiful and the Luftwaffe made sure their prisoners were well fed. In fact there were so many Red Cross parcels that the Germans served up banquets of four or five courses every two weeks just to keep the surplus down (lending credibility to the accusation that parcels were being 'pilfered'). In addition there was plenty of wine and spirits, and culinary delicacies looted from occupied France. Theo Rumpel was unstinting in his generosity in dispensing these supplies among the prisoners for birthdays, other anniversaries or farewell celebrations.

Instead of ten to twelve officers per room, which became the norm in later camps, the rooms at Dulag Luft housed as few as two or four men.

Walks out on parole were frequent for visits to church or recreational outings, even holidays with German officers and their families. It would have seemed remarkable to prisoners at a later stage of the war, but for the first two winters some officers enjoyed skiing holidays with their German counterparts. In the summer, it was not unusual for the commandant to give permission for berry-picking excursions into the woods. Sometimes walk parties would be allowed to stop—with their single German officer accompanying them, and a Luftwaffe guard—at one of three big terraced beer gardens in the surrounding Taunus forest. If the prisoners wanted beer or wine their escort would pay for it, the sum to be subsequently deducted from their pay allowances.

Sonderführer Heinrich Eberhardt, the chief

189

interrogator at Dulag Luft, a brisk, highly educated man in his mid twenties, was a frequent and popular escort on these occasions. Eberhardt was a typical product of the Hitler Youth but he had had the Nazi edges rubbed off his character by having studied at an English university, and many visits to Britain. In the circumstances it is hardly surprising that Johnny wrote home, 'we are treated as officers, gentlemen and equals'.

The prisoners were allowed to write three letters and four postcards home per month, and some excerpts from his letters home give an impression of what Johnny's life was like in the camp. On 21 October, he wrote: 'We have lovely long walks through the woods here once a week, a concert every 3 wks. gotten up by the prisoners, & had sports 2 days ago wh. was great fun.' On 26 October, he mentioned some of his fellow prisoners (including John Casson, the son of the distinguished Shakespearean actors Sybil Thorndike and Lewis Casson) and said they were all 'delightful'. 'At this camp we are treated as offrs, gents, + =s, wh. is much appreciated by us all.' He said he washed all his own clothes, which, if such domesticity was alien to him, he did not complain about.

Three days later, he was writing about some of the outdoor sports they had been enjoying such as the high jump, long jump, putting the weight and tossing the tabor [sic]. He mentioned that Buckley and Casson had recently produced 'a very good theatrical show' and that there was a model farm at the camp where bees and angora rabbits were raised. He wrote that he got thirty-six marks every ten days from the German government. And at the

190

end of November after a walk in the woods he and some other officers 'stopped at a delightful little inn en rte for some wine + beer'.

They played football on Christmas Day and the commandant presented them with crates of good wine for their celebratory dinner. More excerpts provide an insight into his life behind the wire and, once more, belie the 'official' version of camp life depicted in Aidan Crawley's RAF history. At one point the commandant presented them with a radio on which they could listen to the BBC (an illegal act punishable by prison for anyone in the German population). 'I have been digging in the garden lately + helping to plant peas, [?], beans, radishes etc . . .' Johnny wrote that, 'Day is charming + vy clever. We are lucky to be in this camp and have such an exceptionally kind person as cdt.'

Two episodes of that winter illustrate the extraordinary indulgence with which the officers of the Permanent Staff were treated. On the first, Rumpel invited Wings to his office for drinks. The commandant's office was an L-shaped room. The shorter arm was occupied by Rumpel's desk and telephones. The longer part was a homely room with low tables, deep leather armchairs and a buffet table bearing bottles of schnapps, port, Scotch, and Rhine and fine French wines. During the course of the evening, presumably after several drinks had been consumed, Wings jokingly demanded to be allowed to sit at the commandant's desk. He wanted to telephone Hermann Göring in Berlin and demand that the British prisoners be sent home immediately. Rumpel vacated his chair after first instructing Dulag Luft's switchboard operator to go along with the joke and pretend that he was the head of the German air force. Thus, for several moments, Wings enjoyed a long and boisterous wrangle with the imaginary air Reichsmarshal at the other end of the line.

The other evening of note was at a party thrown by Rumpel at his bungalow in the woods for half a dozen or so members of the RAF Permanent Staff, among them Johnny, Buckley and Casson. As usual, the long dining area table was laden with food and drinks. Rumpel regaled his happy audience with stories about Göring and other luminaries of the Reich, with whom he was on first-name terms. At one stage he called his wife in Berlin, and handed the receiver to Wings. Both had lived in the Far East, and they spent several minutes recounting nostalgic reminiscences about their time there. Jimmy Buckley told some of his hilarious stories and Casson, a member of the Magic Circle, mesmerised the assembly with card tricks.

Johnny, ever the benign controversialist, tried to get the men to discuss more serious affairs. When somebody voiced views diametrically opposed to his own, he was perplexed, 'spreading his arms and hands to say "My dear friends", with an expression of compassion, hurt or astonishment on his face depending on the ignorance, rudeness or imbecility shown by the person addressed'. Casson's parents were pacifists and his brother was a conscientious objector. Casson had been beginning to hold similar views and had been on the point of resigning his navy commission when the war started. He and Johnny often had lively exchanges. 'My dear chap, I agree with you entirely,' Johnny would say. 'But you don't agree with me,' protested an exasperated Casson.

192

As the Rhine wine flowed, the men found themselves descending into a drowsy haze. Rumpel slumped drowsily under the dining table. Before he fell into a deep and happy slumber, he advised his English guests that he would be unable to take them back to the camp. They would have to find their own way. And so they did: squelching through the deep snow of the forest that separated the commandant's bungalow from the prison enclosure of Dulag Luft. As they progressed, it occurred to one of their number that this might be a suitable opportunity to escape. But the consensus was that to do so would represent an unforgivable breach of social etiquette. Shortly afterwards they arrived at the camp gates, where they had to argue with a sleepy sentry to allow them back in.

WITH MAJOR RUMPEL'S COMPLIMENTS...

That Christmas was a sombre affair for Johnny. Rumpel did his best to cheer his charges up, providing them with ample supplies of food and wine for a festive feast. A picture of the somewhat subdued affair shows Johnny at the top table surrounded by smartly turned out officers in a room festooned with bunting and balloons. A dartboard hangs from the wall behind him. It could have been an RAF mess in Sussex or Kent. The photograph eventually appeared in the local newspaper in his prospective constituency of Gillingham some months later. The same newspaper reported that Johnny whiled away his time in captivity by rereading the works of Rupert Brooke.

But the easygoing air of chivalrous civility that prevailed at Dulag Luft disguised a deadly serious war that both sides were waging secretly and assiduously. Rumpel had wired the prisoners' barracks with secret microphones. His men were routinely reading the prisoners' letters to and from family and friends. Through these means Rumpel was building up a formidable data bank of information on his charges, including their personal circumstances back home, their worries, their love affairs and so forth, which it might be possible to use against them in the future. The English officers knew about Rumpel's microphones but pretended they had not detected the bugs and said nothing indiscreet within range of them. At the same time the prisoners were communicating valuable intelligence in their letters to wives and family, but written in a pre-determined code. And, while they were enjoying the Germans' hospitality, they were planning to break out of the camp. Their weekly parole walks provided them with useful information regarding the lie of the land, transportation links and so forth, and with escape resources.

By midsummer 1940, Wings Day was able to assemble in his mind a fairly accurate map of the paths and roads leading from the camp. After one visit to a restaurant, Wings returned with a wireless stuffed down his tunic. He cut out the photograph that had appeared in the Luftwaffe periodical *Der Adler*, showing him stroking his cat Ersatz, to use in a bogus pass. Even as he dined with Rumpel at the Forellen Gut on the occasion of his birthday, Wings was overseeing the construction of a tunnel out of Dulag Luft.

Rumpel had sometimes discussed the possibility of escape with Wings and later he did so with Johnny, the two most senior Allied officers in his camp. The commandant accepted that there were compelling motivations to try to get away. 'For young men forced to sit back and do nothing but eat German bread and Red Cross food while their friends are dying, escape is perhaps alright.' For the older officers, however, he counselled against hazardous escapades. They had children, he pointed out. 'Why get shot for fun? Because that is all it is, this escaping: you'll never get anywhere in this country. Leave it to the young boys.'

The prospect of escape had always been talked of. But any plans the RAF prisoners entertained had been nebulous, based upon the widespread

195

belief that the war would soon be over in a negotiated peace, and they would all be home for Christmas. When it became apparent they would not be home for Christmas, one of the first things Wings did was appoint an 'escape committee' with the responsibility of overseeing escapes. Wings taught the men that even though they were behind barbed wire in enemy territory, the war was not over for them. They could collect valuable information about German operational methods and send it home in coded messages. Above all they could help to build up an integrated, effective escape organisation. Though relatively few men had the temperament or talent for escaping, all could help the actual escapers in a variety of ways. The rationale for organised escapes was not only the obvious one of getting back to England, but also of creating as much trouble and panic as possible within Germany.

Wings appointed a young lieutenant commander of the Fleet Air Arm as the committee's first chairman. Lieutenant Commander Jimmy Buckley was a Dartmouth-trained Fleet Air Arm pilot. He had been shot down over the coast of France in May 1940 while strafing German lines at Dunkirk. A small man with dark hair and eyes that always seemed to twinkle with laughter, Buckley was a born comedian: he occupied much of his time in captivity writing and acting comic sketches for the theatrical shows that would become such a part of Kriegie life.

Buckley appointed an equally strong character as head of intelligence on the escape committee. Squadron Leader Roger Bushell was a Hurricane pilot of 92 Squadron who had also been shot down over France during the evacuation of Dunkirk. Twenty-nine years old when he fell into enemy hands, Bushell was the wealthy son of a South African mining engineer. He had moved to Europe to graduate from British and French universities. He studied engineering at Cambridge University, but ended up practising as a barrister. Bushell was a man of formidable build and an equally formidable personality. Thickset and of aggressive appearance, he was a fearless skier of Olympic standard, and sported a permanently drooping left eye, thanks to a skiing accident before the war. He had joined the RAF long before the war began and before joining 92 Squadron had belonged to 601 Squadron of the Royal Auxiliary Air Force. This 'County of London Squadron' was dubbed 'the Millionaires Squadron', thanks to the wealthy former public schoolboys who mostly made up its number, and it had a reputation for louche ribaldry. In the air Bushell displayed all the characteristics that he possessed in his career on the ground, not least his outrageous daring and complete fearlessness.

Buckley and Bushell had hatched their first escape plan by the summer of 1940, before Johnny arrived in Dulag Luft. Their idea was to build a short tunnel from the East Block (the nearest hut to the fence), under the perimeter wire, and emerging in the side of a small ditch some two to three feet deep that ran parallel to it. The tunnel would begin in East Block's washhouse. The total distance to cover was just 60–70 feet. As soon as the plan had been hatched, Wings climbed into the roof of the barrack block and disconnected Rumpel's microphone wires. (It was only later that he

197

discovered the Germans had long given up on listening to the devices.) All the 'permanents' were on the tunnelling roster, and when the men began digging both Wings and Johnny joined in. Quickly, however, it was decided that both should stay above the surface. Because Wings was such a prominent figure, his absence would be noted; Johnny was so big he was liable to get himself stuck in the tunnel.

Work began with an open trench under the washroom that sloped gradually until it became a tunnel just before leaving the barrack block. The heavy clay, rocks and gravel from the tunnel were dispersed under the three huts without, apparently, arousing suspicion. But progress was not encouraging. The diggers encountered an enormous boulder, which took an eternity to remove. Unfortunately the water table proved to be higher than they had calculated, and they soon found themselves clawing through a muddy saturated mass collapsing all about them. On one of his regular tunnel inspections Wings cut his knee and was soon laid up in the camp hospital with blood poisoning. In the autumn, the tunnel became flooded and by mid-October it was unworkable. It was about halfway complete. But the ground would soon be frozen, so they decided to close it down for the winter.

Work began once more on the tunnel in March 1941 and the committee decided the break-out would be on the first weekend in June, the Whitsun holiday when German supervision in the camp would be at a minimum. They calculated that the moon would not rise before midnight on that date. By then the prisoners had built up a supply of pilfered Deutschmarks and had obtained rice-paper

198

maps of various escape routes from parcels sent by relatives and friends. Their parole walks had furnished them with invaluable details about bus and train timetables and the various pathways through the Taunus forest.

Roger Bushell came up with a separate plan to break out of the camp at the same time as the 18 prisoners escaping through the tunnel. He proposed hiding in a goat shed on the recreation field outside the perimeter fence the afternoon before the tunnel break-out. He would then escape later that evening, aiming to get an early train the next morning from Frankfurt, taking him to the Swiss frontier. He hoped to pass into Switzerland at Schaffhausen where a long narrow bulge of Swiss territory projected into Germany. It was reputed to be less well guarded than the rest of the border.

That Sunday afternoon during roll-call on the sports field, Bushell managed to squirrel himself away in the goat shed. His absence went unnoticed in the general melee as about 70 prisoners milled about during the head count. He escaped later that day. That night, at nine, the other eighteen escapers began their tunnel break. A party was held in Wings' room to create a diversion. As the gramophone blared and their comrades burst into song and noisy ribaldry, the men lowered themselves one by one into the tunnel. Wings was the sixth out, Johnny followed at number seven just before Wing Commander 'Hetty' Hyde, who had arrived in Dulag Luft only a month or so beforehand. The fears about Johnny's size proved well founded. He got stuck under a cast-iron conduit pipe and had to be pulled back and re-launched down the tunnel. Not for the last time,

199

Johnny caused considerable delay in the process of escaping through a tunnel. But it was not long before he eased himself out of the tunnel exit and emerged into the ditch beneath a clear and starlit sky. He sped off into the dark.

It was the first mass escape of Allied prisoners during the war (a mass escape being loosely defined as any more than five men). But, sadly, none of the men remained free for long. Most were picked up within 20 or 30 miles of Dulag Luft. Johnny was found because he made the mistake of walking nonchalantly along an autobahn, not realising that it was strictly against the rules to walk on one of Hitler's new super motorways. Bushell nearly made it to Switzerland, but was caught seconds away from liberty by a diligent local.

Most of the escapers ended up in Frankfurt's civil prison. Theo Rumpel visited them there. His job was on the line. It turned out that the Reichsführer-SS Heinrich Himmler, no less, had complained to Hitler about the lenient treatment that 'anglophile' Rumpel had accorded his RAF prisoners. Wings Day was not to know this, but he nevertheless apologised to Rumpel. The commandant said he would have done the same if the positions had been reversed. He told them they were going to be sent to Stalag Luft I, the new purpose-built Luftwaffe camp on the coast of the far-flung Baltic at Barth. They shook hands and he departed. A Luftwaffe bus arrived to take the British prisoners to Frankfurt railway station. In it the men discovered a case of champagne with a note attached. 'With the compliments of Major Rumpel,' it read.

BALTIC INTERLUDE

It was some months later, on Saturday, 25 August 1941, that the *Daily Mail* reported, under the headline: 'ESCAPED, CAUGHT':

Colonel J. B. Dodge, handsome 6 ft. 3 in. son of the Hon. Mrs. Lionel Guest and friend of Mr. Churchill, who has found adventure in nearly every corner in the world, has escaped from the German prison camp Dulag Luft, been recaptured and taken to another camp.

By then Johnny had grown accustomed to the grey and grim surroundings of Stalag Luft I, usually known simply as 'Barth' after the small town it was nearest to in Pomerania, the ancient Baltic province of Germany.

In fact Stalag Luft was a misleading designation, '*Stalag*' being a contraction of the word '*Stammlager*', which translated literally means 'a prison for common stock' or, in military parlance, 'a prison for servicemen below officer rank'. It would have been far more appropriate to label it '*Oflag*', for *Offizierslager*: officers' camp. But for some reason the Luftwaffe called all its prison camps Stalags. It was situated some miles north of Barth on a narrow, unprotected finger of land that stretched into a lagoon on the Baltic coast. A landscape of flat sandy dunes, salt marshes and creeks, the area was fringed with pine forests and, in the winter when the weather was foul, could be a miserable and dispiriting place. Barth was just about visible to the south, but a long dark row of pine trees obscured the prisoners' view to the north and the Baltic beyond.

The officers were housed at first in two, later three, wooden barrack blocks in a cramped and dusty compound some 100 yards long by 70 wide. The enclosure was surrounded by a double row of barbed-wire fence and overlooked by guards in watchtowers with searchlights and machine guns. Sentries and dogs patrolled the perimeter at all times. (By now the guards were almost universally referred to as 'goons' and the watchtowers had become 'goon boxes'.) The facility included two small compounds, one for officers and the other for non-commissioned officers. Both were attached to a *Vorlager* (front of the prison), which contained the camp commandant's administrative offices, the sick bays and the notorious 'coolers'—solitary confinement cells for offenders.

At this place that felt like the end of the world Johnny and Wings and the other first 'Great Escapers' from Dulag Luft arrived in the summer of 1941. They could be forgiven for feeling dejected taking in the dismal setting, but worse was to come. Johnny and the new arrivals were surprised at the hostile reception awaiting them from many of the officers already in the camp. They were greeted by catcalls and booing as they were marched into the compound. Many of the onlookers shouted insults; others simply stared at the new arrivals with ill-disguised contempt. It must have been a disconcerting experience for such a cheerful and friendly soul as Johnny. Wings was initially angered by this treatment, but when he and Johnny learnt the reason for it, they could not help but have some sympathy for the protesters.

Most of the incumbent prisoners had passed through Dulag Luft and subsequently contrasted the civilised surroundings of the Frankfurt transit camp with the dire conditions they had to endure in Pomerania. In addition, unflattering stories had spread throughout the POW community of the Dulag Luft prisoners enjoying regular walks in the woods and visits to Frankfurt, not to mention convivial dinners with German officers and plentiful supplies of alcohol and tobacco. These stories were true, of course. However, when the Barth men learnt that all along their Frankfurt counterparts had been using these indulgences to facilitate escape, hostility towards the new arrivals swiftly dissipated.

It was at Barth that Johnny first became acquainted with a young flight lieutenant who would become a partner in crime with him throughout his time in German prison camps, and a friend to the end of his days. Bertram Arthur James, known universally as 'Jimmy', was born in India, the son of an English tea planter. He had been educated at King's School, Canterbury. After his father died, Jimmy James decided to see the world, took a steamer to Panama and worked his way up the length and breadth of North America before ending up in British Columbia as a bank clerk. As war loomed he joined the RAF. He was the second pilot of a Wellington bomber that was caught by heavy flak over the Dutch coast in June 1940. Jimmy was lucky to escape alive as the Wellington, fully laden with bombs, burst into flames and plunged to earth 'like a fiery comet'.

Jimmy James was one of a number of Barth prisoners who had been involved in several escape attempts, including a failed tunnel bid predating the one at Dulag Luft. These convinced escapers were naturally now delighted to discover that their new comrades, far from being lackeys of the German authorities, were actually kindred escapologists. Wings Day, as the new Senior British Officer, promptly ordered an inquiry into the escape system at Barth and found to his displeasure that everything had been conducted in a spirit of amateur enthusiasm. In future, Wings ordered, escapes would be regulated and controlled by the official escape committee, which the men soon dubbed 'the X Organisation'. Wings appointed Jimmy Buckley to be the first chairman, and the role was known thenceforth, inevitably, as 'Big X'.

Despite the difficulties posed by the harshness of the immediate environment, the RAF prisoners at Barth were able to boast prolific tunnelling operations over the forthcoming months. Less than two years after Barth's opening, forty-three tunnels had been constructed from the officer and NCO compounds. Ultimately 100 tunnels were built. There were a great many other types of escape attempt too, some marvels of simplicity, others audacious in their daring. Making a 'home run', though satisfying, was never the principal object of escape. The purpose was to create as much disruption as possible for the enemy. It was at Barth that the prisoners began to perfect their tunnelling techniques, using bed boards, for instance, to prop up the shafts; raiding their Red Cross parcels for Klim milk cans, which were attached together to make air lines; and constructing bellows for ventilation.

In the meantime, the Germans also perfected their own methods for disrupting escape attempts. In particular a new type of goon was created that was soon to be known as a 'ferret'. With dark-blue boiler suits adorned with a single leather belt, these new guards looked more like caretakers than soldiers. They were not armed, but carried long metal rods that they used to poke the ground as they looked for tunnels. Ferrets soon became a ubiquitous part of camp life: they were discovered crawling under the barrack blocks and into the rafters through the trap-doors, looking for excavated sand. Their boiler suits ensured they could scramble under floorboards and into attics yet keep their uniforms clean. A requirement of the job was perfect English and the prisoners soon became used to stumbling upon a ferret eavesdropping on their conversation. Ferrets were entitled to enter any barrack whenever they wished, and they would barge in without a moment's notice.

At Barth, Johnny became acquainted with the German security staff, some of whom would become sworn enemies; others became useful as tame goons, and friendships of sorts with some of them were not unknown. Hauptmann (Captain) Hans Pieber was a mild-mannered and conscientious Austrian who boasted that he held the Nazi Party's 49th membership card and had been awarded the Nazi Blood Medal (or Blutorden, the honour awarded to those few who had taken part in the notorious 1923 Beer Hall Putsch). Pieber, however, had refused to wear it after the Anschluss, which had aroused his indignation. An engineer in civilian life, Pieber had spent some time in South America. Studiously polite, he spoke good English, which he was always trying to improve. He became adept at sniffing out the prisoners' many tunnelling operations. He was often the butt of the prisoners' discontent and suffered much abuse from them over the years. Yet Pieber was generally liked by the prisoners.

Feldwebel (Sergeant) Hermann Glemnitz had worked in Yorkshire before the war and, as a result, not only spoke English well but also understood the British mentality, which was perhaps a more valuable asset. He, too, had been an engineer, and would earn the respect of the prisoners over the forthcoming years for his ability to find their tunnels. A shrewd and clever man, the Kriegies awarded him the ironic nickname of 'Dimwits'.

Hauptmann Gustav Simoleit, the head of the Lagerführung (the compound 'control' office, made up of four intelligence officers whose job it was to monitor prisoner escape activity) was formerly a professor of history, geography and ethnology. He was a highly erudite man who spoke English well. (After the war, Simoleit wrote a highly praised book about East Germany and its relations with Eastern Europe.) Simoleit was at first apprehensive at being taken off his anti-aircraft battery and being made a jailer but after a while he began to enjoy the company of the 'reasonable and well-educated' men in his care. He later said that 'the POW camp in Barth was one of the few places in the world where, during a merciless war, soldiers of both fighting armies could meet and establish personal contacts'.

Corporal Karl Griese did not come to have such

a comfortable rapport with the prisoners. He would become the head of the ferrets, and was nicknamed 'Rubberneck' because of his extraordinarily long neck that seemed to be able to poke its way around any corner. Rubberneck went about his duties with a psychopathic passion. He despised the Allied fliers and in turn was disliked by prisoners and German staff alike. There was another ferret known simply as Keen Type, for self-explanatory reasons, and one called 'Adolf' because of his uncanny resemblance to the Führer. Another of the ferrets, Karl Pfelz, the prisoners called 'Charlie'.

The German staff, on the whole, behaved very well towards their charges. One of the Luftwaffe officers taught a German-language class for the prisoners. There were also Russian lessons. In the hot summer, the Germans took prisoners down to the local creek for a swim and there were also walks outside the camp once a week for those prepared to give their parole. The prisoners were issued with wallpaper to brighten their cheerless barracks. And the Germans provided board games, ping-pong tables and a well-stocked library. There were occasional performances of plays and concerts in the NCOs' compound. Regular theatrical shows were held in the dining room and a thriving dramatics society developed.

As the winter approached, the Germans obtained some warm winter coats and distributed them among the prisoners. The officers constructed an ice-hockey rink between two of the barrack blocks, and soon Red Cross parcels were coming at the rate of one per man, per week. Relations improved further when the Germans introduced camp money (*Lagergeld*), which was deducted from their pay and could be used to buy cigarettes or a crude wine the inmates dubbed 'red biddy'.

In a further attempt to distract the men from boredom, Wings put Johnny in charge of organising debates, talks, educational projects and sports. It was a role he easily slipped into after his political experiences in the East End. There were many nationalities among the prisoners: Czechs, Norwegians and Poles had served in the RAF alongside Australians, Canadians and New Zealanders. Thus Johnny decided to call his discussion group 'the International Union'. Johnny was a generation older than most of the men in the camps, and the discussions proved to be an interesting contrast between his ultra-conservative views and the often more liberal outlook of the younger airmen. One prisoner, Leonard Hall, recalled, 'He took great pride in being a British Conservative, while being also proud of his part-American ancestry and he used to express his political opinions as if they were incontrovertible facts, appearing genuinely surprised if they were not always accepted.'

In his classic wartime memoir, *Moonless Night*, Jimmy James recalled the Dodger's contribution to these political debates, which embraced every subject from 'Medieval Monasticism to Marx and Metaphysics, God and the Universe'. The discussions, James writes, were sometimes enlivened when the Dodger dropped in to give some fatherly advice, or more often to provoke a political argument. Pursuing his favourite theme on the merits of capitalism, the Dodger would launch into some pseudo-Marxist who had been discoursing on the dialectical process in history.

208

'My dear fellow,' he would exclaim, jabbing his finger at the man to emphasise each point. 'I used to think like you when I was your age. When I went to the Soviet Union in 1921, I was a firm socialist and I thought it was the promised land, but I was very soon disillusioned.'

'That was because they put you in the jug.'

'Not at all,' continued the Dodger. 'I became convinced that collective socialism was inefficient as an economic system, and it has been enforced in Russia by a totalitarianism which has put 20 million into concentration camps. Competitive free enterprise means freedom for all.'

As the weather grew bitter in the autumn of 1941, Johnny grew a beard in order to keep warm. He shaved it off, apparently as a symbolic gesture of celebration, on 7 December, after the Japanese attack on Pearl Harbor. The entry of the United States into the war was not enough to prevent the prisoners getting on each other's nerves. Even the generally affable figures of Johnny and Wings were beginning to tire of each other's shortcomings. In a colourful and powerful passage in his biography of Wings Day, Sydney Smith wrote:

> He once found himself sitting at the long deal table thinking quite coldly that if Johnny persisted in buttering his bread with that careful, stroking movement, trimming off the edges, wiping the knife, smoothing the butter again, and again, he would kill him with great pleasure. Any man who buttered his bread like that deserved death . . . . At one moment or another, Wings nursed homicidal feelings about each one of his mess companions

209

although outwardly he remained his normal good-natured self. But Johnny, his best friend, roused him to berserk limits.

It was not at all unusual for the prisoners to entertain murderous views about their fellow detainees. But for Wings to harbour these thoughts towards such a good-natured companion indicates the degree to which his temper had frayed and his spirits had sunk. His mixed feelings towards Johnny were revealed on another occasion. Wings, as SBO, was compelled to sit in judgement on a young officer accused of collaboration with the enemy. He realised it would be futile to call upon his best friend's opinion because 'Johnny's angelic view of the world usually left him without any critical sense. His advice was invariably useless because he was so concerned not to hurt anyone's feelings.'

Despite the joy brought by the entry of the United States into the war at the end of 1941, that Christmas was a depressing one for most of the men. Their Russian allies were crumbling under the onslaught of Hitler's Operation Barbarossa. British forces in the Far East were suffering a similar humiliation at the hands of the Japanese, who had sunk two of the Royal Navy's most up-to-date warships, the *Prince of Wales* and the *Repulse*. Nevertheless, Johnny remained characteristically cheerful. To Minerva he wrote: 'Xmas evening we had some beers and sang songs. A Xmas present of books for the camp from King + Queen was very much appreciated.'

Johnny's letters reveal how he attempted to enliven the monotony of imprisonment and mundane matters at home with the sundry entertainments afforded by the camp and the parochial duties given to him by Wings. A fellow prisoner, John Madge, was proving to be an adept theatrical producer: 'Madge produced 3 one act plays by Noel Coward last Friday afternoon + they were a great success. Next week we are producing a pantomime.' The sergeants gave the officers regular concerts, and the officers had formed their own orchestra. Two nights a week they listened to classical gramophone records sent by the Red Cross.

The Red Cross continued to be a source of great comfort and Johnny could not praise their efforts enough. To Flora he wrote: 'The Red X parcels arriving now are beautifully packed—sugar, cheese etc + the contents are excellent. They send some food parcels direct from Canada + the Argentine + U.S.A. and the same applies to them.' The prisoners even received a consignment of 300 Ajax pyjamas, of which 200 were donated by Flora. Parcels of cigarettes, sardines and nuts and raisins arrived almost weekly, somewhat dispelling the image of Spartan frugality fostered by the film *The Great Escape*.

Johnny continued to run his international debating society and related enlightening activities. He wrote home, 'I am i/c of debates + we have some very interesting ones fortnightly + general knowledge games as well. I am also arranging lectures on different subjects of common interest Wednesday evenings at 9.' Wings had written to the Red Cross asking for an authoritative course of general study with examinations for preparing the POWs to play their part in the world after the war:

This is particularly wanted by the young ones who are uncertain as to their future careers + therefore lack a guide as to how to employ the time available for reading + studying. The examinations would provide the necessary incentive if the results were placed on their record which otherwise would be blank.

Johnny thought along similar lines to Wings: 'My comrades come from the flower of the youth of the empire + are delightful companions. I hope I may be of some use to them.'

Somewhat fitfully, Johnny used the time to expand his mind. He had started reading the Old Testament, which he was beginning to find fascinating, particularly Kings and Chronicles. ('Am appreciating O.T. as never before.') He devoured Macaulay's essays, of which the one about Gladstone on Church and State was the most interesting, alongside those on Lord Byron and Addison. ('I know you will enjoy it as I did.') He was particularly taken by Henry Ford's *My Life and Work*. ('I think that many of his ideas on business are very sound especially "Service comes before profit."') Alongside his more cerebral pursuits, Johnny maintained his good health: during that bitterly cold winter he played ice hockey daily.

The routine matters of home life clearly remained important. Johnny asked Minerva, 'Have you sold the car? Has Florida been rented?' He was pleased to learn that his stepson Peter Sherman had enlisted in the US Army, and passed on his love to his sons Tony and David. He did not forget his prospective constituency back in Britain. On 1 February 1942, he asked Minerva to be remembered to 'my old friends in Mile End . . . + our friends at Gillingham'.

News from home brought mixed reactions. 'I am delighted with what Clemy's husband has done in Washington + also with our representative there,' he wrote to Minerva. He was referring, presumably, to Churchill's meetings with Roosevelt in the Arcadia Conference that sealed the Atlantic Alliance and confirmed the 'Europe First' policy of concentrating on defeating Hitler. Later, to Flora, on the news of the death of the wife of his old Gallipoli commander Sir Ian Hamilton, he wrote: 'Sorry to hear about . . . Lady Hamilton. Please give Sir Ian my sympathy + love. I am proud to have had the privilege of serving under him.'

More than occasionally he adopted a philosophic poise:

At times like these we learn how much we can do without, which before we mistook for necessities. This afternoon we had an amusing game of cricket with a bed board made into a bat + a tennis ball. It is wise not to depend upon material things for our happiness.

He wrote: 'After the war there will be more love and unselfishness + less envy + hatred. More cooperation, respect + toleration of others.'

In March came dramatic news of an imminent change. Johnny wrote to Minerva, 'W/Cmd Day with 1/3rd of the compound have been moved to another camp + the rest of us join them next month.' He was referring to the vast new prison complex that was under construction in the depths of Silesia near Sagan, built to contain the ever-

213

increasing numbers of downed Allied aircrew. Stalag Luft III was built on Hermann Göring's direct orders and to such a specification that it would be 'escape proof'. Most of the Barth prisoners would be transferred there as soon as possible. But, as the Germans were soon to discover, there was no such phrase as 'escape proof' in the lexicon of indomitable spirits the likes of Johnny Dodge.

GÖRING'S 'ESCAPE PROOF' CAMP

Not long after arriving at Stalag Luft III, Johnny wrote to his mother, 'We are gradually settling into this new camp, which is much larger + therefore we need fewer circuits to walk any distance.' The new air force prisoner facility was much larger than anything preceding it and it would be in a constant state of expansion to cater for the huge numbers of Allied airmen being shot down over German-occupied territory. Eventually, some 90,000 Allied airmen were brought down over Europe, about half of them surviving to become prisoners of war. Stalag Luft III would eventually hold some 12,000 prisoners.

It was built on the edge of a vast Silesian pine forest, and consisted of a series of austere wooden barrack blocks in sandy compounds, with not a blade of grass in sight. The camp was surrounded by barbed-wire fences, watchtowers and a multiplicity of other security measures, including sophisticated underground listening devices. The gloomy line of trees on the outside, which stretched as far as the eye could see, obscured the flat, featureless landscape beyond. Nearby was the ancient town of Sagan, which boasted many attractive buildings and one of the busiest railway junctions in continental Europe. Sagan was about 90 miles south-east of Berlin.

In the summer at Sagan, the heat could be unbearable. In the winter the camp was battered by icy Silesian winds of up to 30 degrees below freezing. For all that, though, Sagan was an improvement on Barth, as far as most of its inmates were concerned. Hardly surprising, since the new Luftwaffe facility was intended to be the perfect camp in almost every respect: impossible to escape from, but also comfortable enough to persuade inmates that escape was not worth contemplating. Stalag Luft III was endowed with an extraordinary quantity of sports, leisure and educational facilities. Prisoners could play virtually any sport they liked, and there were classes for them to earn educational qualifications. Eventually there was even a theatre. The fire reservoir in the middle of one compound served as a swimming pool most of the time.

The Senior American Officer, Albert Patton Clark, once went as far as describing Sagan as a 'holiday camp':

> We had clean sheets practically every week and orderlies to come in and change them. The living conditions, the sanitary conditions and the food rations were good. We were probably the best-treated POWs anywhere in the world at the time.

Alan Bryett of the RAF's 58 (bomber) Squadron conceded the point. Bryett compared Stalag Luft III to the public school he was educated at in southeast London. In fact the first person he remembers meeting there was Bob Stanford Tuck, who happened to have been at the same school, Saint Dunstan's College. 'Robert was kind enough to bring me some of his spare shirts and collars and razor blades and so on. He made me feel at home.'

Bryett said of Sagan, 'It was a rather gentlemanly affair.'

A sample of Johnny's letters home bears out this view. To Flora on 10 May he wrote: 'Have been playing the mandolin with a Canadian who plays the guitar . . . we have been singing the old songs we sang together at Ferring. I wish I had some gramophone records of you playing the guitar.' Later, displaying his pride in Anglo-Saxon fellowship, fondness for physical exercise and incurable optimism, he wrote: 'There are an extraordinary fine lot of young men from all parts of the Empire + the States here now + I enjoy their companionship.' To Flora on 14 June: 'Am running ½ mile barefoot and swimming in the fire reservoir each morning before breakfasting at 7.30. Have not been so well for ages. Hope to see you by Xmas.' To Minerva on 23 June: 'I generally walk from 8.30 to 10 when I go to bed. This with my ½ mile run barefooted, followed by either a swim or a cold shower before 7.30 breakfast, is doing me a world of good.' To Flora on 21 July: 'Our band gave us a very good concert last week + we are having some very good Rugby football games. The Canadians are learning the English game. It's a splendid one.'

The privilege of parole walks continued, and Johnny enjoyed many excursions in the local countryside accompanied by German officers or men. On 26 July, he wrote to Minerva: 'Had a 2 hrs walk last week with 4 others outside. Lovely change.' And a few days later: 'Had a 2 hour walk outside, the other day, through lovely woods + had a beautiful view of a river flowing slowly along a rich valley. It seemed as peaceful + reminded me of the Thames.'

In an early letter to one of his sons (probably David), Johnny described aspects of his new life at Sagan:

Have been walking barefoot around the compound a distance of over ½ mile + throwing the medicine ball + volley-tennis stripped to the waist in the sun. Nearly every form of sports is being carried out here— cricket, fencing, boxing, tennis, quoits, 'Judo', throwing the discus + javelin + long + high jump. At 8am there is a physical exercise class. Have been digging up the roots for sports fields.

To Flora he wrote:

My room-mate + I take our meals with 6 others in their room. Among the 8 are 2 South Africans, 1 Canadian, Hardy de Forest [actually, Hardie de Forest], 1 New Zealander, 1 Anglo-Indian. I bathe by pouring basins of water over my head in the wash-house. The water is good, soft + cold + the air is good too. I feel very well + have enjoyed digging up tree stumps for a sports field.

The camp commandant who presided over this benevolent regime was a friend of Theo Rumpel. The parallels between Johnny's Dulag Luft commandant and Oberst (Colonel) Friedrich-Wilhelm von Lindeiner-Wildau were uncanny. They were both former cavalry officers who had served on Hermann Göring's personal staff. They were both married to Dutch heiresses. Von Lindeiner's

218

wife, a baroness, had an estate in Holland, and he owned the Jeschkendorf estate near Sagan. The couple divided their time between these ample land holdings and an apartment in Berlin. It is hardly surprising that von Lindeiner approached the prospect of being a 'common jailer' at Sagan with the same disdain that Rumpel did at Dulag Luft. Nor that he adopted a similarly respectful and often indulgent attitude to his prisoners, at least to the American and Western European ones.

The Russians, in contrast, were treated with abject indifference as a result of Nazi racial ideology—which von Lindeiner did not appear averse to—and their government's failure to sign the Geneva Convention. The Russian compound was next to the American one. In the winter they were left in the open to freeze to death. In the summer they boiled beneath an unrelenting sun. The Russians were often given nothing to eat. Cannibalism was rife. It is interesting that in all his letters home Johnny never mentions this unpleasant aspect of existence in Stalag Luft III, something the film *The Great Escape* also managed to obscure either purposely or by accident.

In the British compound, Johnny continued to read widely and in late April was enthusing about the works of Évariste Régis Huc, or Abbé Huc, the French missionary traveller famous for his accounts of China, what used to be called Tartary and Tibet. 'Thank you for sending me "The Dragon Book",' he wrote to Flora:

I like what Huc said about the basis of society. 'The idea of the family is the grand principle which serves as the basis of Chinese society.

219

Filial piety, the constant subject of dissertation for moralists + philosophers, + continually recommended in the proclamations of the emperors + the speeches of mandarins, has been the fundamental root of all other virtues.'

Given the amount of time on his hands, it is unsurprising that he was able to dwell at length upon the future after the war. To Flora, once more, he wrote:

I feel . . . this will teach men + nations the necessity of more unselfishness + more cooperation between nations + all sections of any community, if the whole is to be strong, healthy + happy . . . Life here teaches one to appreciate + be grateful for blessings which one too often ignores + takes for granted. Many of my comrades here are thinking of farming overseas after the war + I hope they will be encouraged to do so.

He reaffirmed the men's faith in Churchill, though, once again, he refrained from mentioning the great man's name: 'We all here admire Clemy's husband + are glad he is where he is as we have complete confidence in him. Each and every one of us say "God bless him".' The children were never far from his mind: 'To-day I picked up a volume of Hans Andersen's Fairy Tales which I expect you will have read or will do before long. His stories have taught millions yet he had very little school life + was very poor,' he wrote to David. 'Hope the Doggies, chickens + goats are well. Love, Daddy.'

220

To Minerva he wrote:

So glad David enjoys his school. He will learn there the necessity for working + pulling together with others for his own benefit + the team's. Efficiency is the test as to whether or not the best means are being employed for any desirable end. Inefficiency has to make way for efficiency. It is a law of nature . . . Read Ecclesiastes occasionally to Tony.

Flora appears to have been deciding on a school for David. Johnny wrote her: 'Eton has the reputation now of having a good system of teaching + individual attention + produces a high percentage of leaders in all spheres of activities. Westminster too, has its good points + I am sure whatever you decide will be right.'

To Tony he wrote:

Thanks for your letter. Your handwriting + spelling has improved. Practice will make perfect. I should like you to read a short passage of Shakespeare's Henry V, Act III, Scene I. King 'Once more into the breach etc' + Act IV Scene III King 'What's he that wishes so?' Perhaps you will learn by heart one of these. It will improve your memory + power of concentration. I hope the animals are all well. Especially the 'doggies'. Give Grandmother a Kiss from me on her birthday Oct 18th.

And later, 'to My Precious Tony': 'Has your mother read you the Fairy Tales of Hans Andersen or

Grimm + the stories of Jack the Giant Killer in Jack + the Beanstalk? If not, ask her to get you the books as a present from me + read them to you.'

In fact, the outward appearance of an easy-going regime at Stalag Luft III was, as it had been at Dulag Luft, a facade. Behind the wire a deadly war between captors and captives continued. By the time Johnny arrived at Sagan, his old friend Wings Day was already well settled into his familiar role as Senior British Officer in offices provided by the Germans. The move to Sagan coincided with a period of reflection on Wings' part, during which he formulated a new approach for escape. Up until then he had regarded escape, like most of the other men, almost as a game, with the International Red Cross acting as referee. Now, however, he told his men that the time had come 'to change into higher gear'. Prisoners of war should no longer regard themselves as semi-neutrals merely because they had had a brush with death and fallen into enemy hands, he explained. They were to be an extension of the Allied war effort. Their battlefront was the razor-wired fences that surrounded them on all four sides. Before arriving at Sagan, Wings thought of escape as a way to maintain the prisoners' pride and boost their flagging morale, but now escape was to be pursued mainly to impede the German war effort and there would be less concern for the effect on the men's spirits.

In putting Wings' new concept of war behind the wire into effect, Jimmy Buckley divided the escape committee into three operational sections to oversee three types of escape: under (tunnels), over (wire jobs) and through (gate escapes). All three would be attempted with varying degrees of success, but tunnelling remained the most popular form. Escape from a tunnel usually ensured a head start of at least eight hours and caused the Germans the most trouble. During the summer of 1942 alone, some 30 to 40 tunnels were begun from the barracks of the East Compound in Sagan. All but one failed. In one instance three uncoordinated tunnels ran across one another resulting in the collapse of the barrack block above them. Von Lindeiner was so amused by these escape attempts that he maintained a permanent 'Escape Museum' with photographs and diagrams of the various efforts.

Buckley went about recruiting the veterans of the hard-core escaping fraternity, mostly escape artists and troublemakers from Barth. But the steady stream of new recruits who were arriving from other camps was very much to the escape committee's advantage, as they brought their own different experiences of escape and contributed their own unique skills. In the design of Stalag Luft III they were up against a formidable obstacle. The camp incorporated dozens of the new security measures that the Luftwaffe confidently predicted would make it 'escape proof'. To start with, each barrack block was built on stilts and the only 'hidden' parts that descended into the earth were the concrete piles that supported the small area of the kitchens and washrooms above. The ferrets and their dogs would have a clear view of what was going on underneath the buildings, and if the prisoners planned to tunnel out, they would have to go through the concrete. And inside the barrack blocks all of the ceilings and the floors were lined with trapdoors that facilitated quick inspection and detection of clandestine activity. It would not be easy for the prisoners to hide much of Sagan's bright yellow sand in these rafters.

Each barrack block was a considerable distance from its neighbour, reducing the prospect of dark shadows at night disguising furtive movements around the camp. And the compound could be flooded with light from the watchtowers that ringed each compound 15 feet above ground at 100-yard intervals. At Sagan, even the nearest barracks were at least 100 feet from the wire and some 200 feet from the forest line, which had been cut back purposely to leave a great swathe of open land surrounding the compounds. Any tunnel would have to be at least 300 feet long if it was to emerge in the shelter of the woods, and deep enough to evade the new seismographs that ringed the compound, ever alert for underground noises.

The compounds themselves were surrounded by a formidable double fence, ten feet high and topped with razor wire. The space in between each fence, about seven feet wide, was layered with huge coils of more razor wire. At regular intervals along the outer perimeter wire were the goon boxes, permanently manned by guards with machine guns and powerful spotlights. Dogs patrolled the outside perimeter fence. And there was a low (18 inches high) 'trip wire' 30 feet inside the fence that prisoners were forbidden to cross without permission.

Besides these new physical security measures, the Germans had by now perfected their systems of security. The ferrets now knew what they were doing and were properly equipped. Pairs of them were likely to emerge at any second, taking the prisoners by surprise. Other ferrets patrolled in the dark shadows of the woods, surreptitiously watching the prisoners' activities through binoculars, hidden behind 'ferret fences'. Stalag Luft III was as escape proof as escape proof could be. But it did not have the daunting effect on the new inmates that the Germans had hoped. As that indomitable escaper Jimmy James once reflected: no prison camp is truly escape proof. So much depends upon human ingenuity—and human shortcomings—and less on the overcoming of physical obstacles, the challenges of which have formed mankind's evolution.

If the Germans had learnt by their mistakes, the prisoners had benefitted by theirs. Many of them were now adept in the arts of forging, map-making and tailoring. Many of them were to put their ingenuity to the test in creating all sorts of devices, mechanical and otherwise, that would aid escape. And no longer would these escape resources be produced at a whim, or willy-nilly. The X-Organisation, regrouping in Stalag Luft III, was to oversee the advent of mass production on an industrial scale.

The escape committee was immediately inundated with tunnel proposals but ruled early on that only a small number should be authorised. It was felt that if resources were concentrated on three deep tunnels (to avoid detection by the seismographs) from three barracks, the men were more likely to succeed in the more onerous circumstances they faced. However, it soon became difficult to enforce this stricture. New prisoners arriving in Stalag Luft III felt they were being excluded from a chance to get out. When one of the three deep tunnels was discovered, the policy was dramatically reversed. It was reasoned the more tunnels there were, the more likely at least one would succeed.

The Germans spent a great deal of time driving a heavy fire truck around the compound and on one occasion flooded the camp with water. The problems were obvious. Besides the sand being unstable it was difficult to hide. The prisoners hid much of it in the barrack block roofs, but when one roof collapsed the game was up. Most of the tunnels depended on air holes for ventilation, but these could easily be detected by the ferrets. The distances the tunnels needed to travel were just too intimidating. Many of the diggers were buried in falls, but surprisingly, despite scores of cave-ins, no tunnellers were ever killed in Stalag Luft III.

Throughout these frantic ongoing efforts, which continued under the noses of the Germans, none of Johnny's letters home betrayed a sign of them. The musings on life and philosophy continued, alongside the trivial, or otherwise, domestic details that, it would seem, could not escape a man behind the wire nearly 700 miles from home. It appears that Flora took up his offer of taking back Florida:

> I am glad that you have taken back 'Florida' + hope you can make use of it . . . Everything there including furniture etc., is yours. Thank you + Lionel so much for the use of it + the happiness we all have had out of it . . . Returned from sick quarters last week. The week's change did me good + I am quite well again. Am enjoying Henry VI + Aristotle's Politics.

226

He continued to read and philosophise:

As Buchan says, 'It is quite right that youth should be hostile to tradition + hot for new things, but if a fellow has any real stuff in him, he will come to see that the only freedom is that which comes from the willing + reasoned acceptance of discipline, + the only true originality that which springs from the re-birth of historical tradition in a man's soul.' Do read his essay 'The Interpreter's House'. I think Belloc is right when he says 'Truth lies in Proportion.' 'Religion is the main determining element in the foundation of any civilisation.' From the principles of reason + insight + struggle + application a community develops, not a promiscuous herd, like a flock of sheep following a bell-weather [sic], but with an order of its own in which each member has a special place to fill according to his gifts + ability. The ideal society is built up on achievements, on the principles of reason + insight, + can demand a contribution from each member, but protects each single member belonging to it.

His reading ranged from current philosophy to classical literature, and embraced an eclectic ensemble from Elizabeth Browning to Homer's *Iliad*, Thomas à Kempis and Confucius. He enjoyed the Proverbs, especially the first chapters, and Ecclesiastes.

I hope the war will soon be over and we can work for the restoration of well-divided property, upon which economic freedom + therefore the dignity + permanence of the family depend. Peace + progress is impossible where class warfare ideas exist. I hope the boys will be imbued with your idea that everyone should primarily consider how he can be of use + serve others, as the only way of being happy. In other words, think first of what he can give the community + afterwards about what he may get out of it.

Parcels of 'goodies' continued to arrive to supplement his already generous Luftwaffe rations and Red Cross offerings: a plentiful supply of pyjamas, pants, vests, pullovers, socks and hankies. 'You have sent me everything I ever needed. A parcel with 1 large bath towel 1 pr wool-lined leather mits from Uncle Poultney + vest + pants arrived a fortnight ago.' Uncle Poultney sent cigars, which Johnny gave to Wings Day, and there appeared to be a constant supply of cigarettes from divergent sources. Once more the profligacy of Johnny's presents is in stark contrast to the image of austere hardship engendered by *The Great Escape*.

Politics continued to interest him and in June he wrote a letter to Flora expressing his admiration for Neville Chamberlain. As with Churchill, it seemed it was taboo to mention the former prime minister's name in full.

My best wishes to Mrs. Neville Cham. I always admired them both so much + he will be appreciated more + more along with his predecessor as time passes. We have a drawing of Clemy's husband hung over the door of our mess. He is trusted + beloved by everyone here.

But he did not hold 'the other side' in such high esteem. Displaying the unswerving conservatism that could be so infuriating to even those who liked him, Johnny wrote:

There were too many people at home after the last war who did not realise how comparatively well off they were + were urged on to ask more from + give less to the community by misleaders like Morrison + Bevin. They did their best to disarm us mentally as well as physically. They preached class consciousness + class war. It seems strange to see them where they are today, conscientious objectors as they + so many of their friends have been. Perhaps they have reformed some of their ideas + aims. If so, good. If not, they should be put into prison, if they won't fight. It is largely due to the foolishness of men of their way of thinking in Russia, France + elsewhere that war broke out + we were so ill-equipped to meet it. In future we shall have to regard National Service more as an honour + sacrifice than as they would make it out to be, a means of getting more out of the community for less work.

To Minerva he wrote:

Long for the day when peace will reign once more. When it comes, everyone will, I hope

229

think rationally + understand that the members of every community are knit together by destiny + either perish or stand united. I hope the boys realise that daily bread cannot be had permanently except by struggle. It is an eternal truth that 'struggle is the father of all things.' Where something has to be accomplished + success achieved, action must be based on insight + reason, the knowledge that men must stand together.

And later: 'May peace come soon. We have as much to learn from the Germans as they have from us.'

Flora was the main recipient of his letters and the thoughts contained within.

So glad you have some ducks + goats as well as the chickens. Your cow + milk book, plus the one you wrote on chickens should be printed for every young person to read who goes overseas or leaves school after the war. Included in it should be some of your maxims + hints re domestic science. We must all get back to a simpler + less artificial life + the closer we are to nature + the earth the happier + more independent we shall be.

And later: 'The older I am, the more I appreciate what a wonderful Mother you have been + are to me. Thank God for you.'

POLISH INTERLUDE

With the Allied officers' appetite for escape clearly undiminished, the Luftwaffe quickly began to realise that putting all the rotten eggs in one basket might not have been such a good idea after all. It decided to send some hundred of the most accomplished escape artists to a Wehrmacht camp in Poland. Among those who were to be sent to this less lenient army camp were Jimmy Buckley; Aidan Crawley, the officer who subsequently wrote the official history of RAF escapes; Peter Fanshawe; Paddy Barthropp, an irrepressible RAF fighter pilot; and Jimmy James. 'The list of prisoners . . . read like a *Who's Who* of recidivist escapers,' observed Bill Ash, an American Spitfire pilot flying with the Royal Canadian Air Force, who was also on the list.

Johnny wasn't included, nor was Wings Day. Since most of their friends were, Wings beseeched von Lindeiner to let them both go along, and the commandant gave his assent. In November 1942 the 'deportees' left for Schubin in north-west Poland. Their new quarters at Oflag XXI B were near Posen, about 150 miles west of Warsaw. The prisoners were accompanied by some of the Sagan German security staff, notably Feldwebel Hermann Glemnitz. The men were crowded into the third-class compartments of an ancient steam train, the windows of which had been secured with closely entwined barbed wire and planks. To discourage them from escaping en route, Glemnitz made them take their boots off and they were piled in an untidy heap at the end of one of the compartments. The trip to Schubin, which was only 100 or so miles away, began to seem interminable as the train chugged slowly across bleak Polish countryside, stopping at quiet local stations for no apparent reason and sometimes remaining stationary for hours. It took a day and a half to complete the journey. Glemnitz's precautions seemed to have their desired effect. Bereft of footwear, there were no serious attempts on the part of the prisoners to alight into the cold Polish countryside—except for one instance.

As the train reached the end of its journey it crawled to an even slower pace and Johnny obtained permission to answer a call of nature. He was escorted to a lavatory at the end of one of the passenger cars. Once inside the cramped cubicle he found the small window to the outside world had been barred with planks and wires. But, flushing the toilet, he lost no time in levering the makeshift obstruction apart, the noise of the slushing water disguising the sound of his machinations. Within moments, Johnny was squeezing his bulky frame through the opening and jumping out of the slow-moving train. In no time he had hit the ground and was running across an open field. Unfortunately, and within seconds, a volley of shots rang out. Johnny put his hands up and his brief spell of freedom was at an end. When the guards led him back to the train, Johnny smiled and said, 'No harm in trying!' It was as if he'd been struck out in a baseball game rather than cheating death by a matter of seconds, recalled Bill Ash, the American

Spitfire pilot. Johnny completed the remainder of the journey under the watchful gaze of the guards.

Presently the prisoners were disembarking at a sleepy station called Altburgund. Their Luftwaffe escort then marched them through the local village toward the army camp at Schubin. When the men finally arrived they were made to wait outside the main gate while Glemnitz performed the official handover in the camp commandant's office. The wait gave the men the opportunity to cast an eye over their new surroundings. Situated on the gentle slopes over Schubin, Oflag XXI B consisted of brick-built barrack blocks, a large white house that was a former girls' school, and a chapel and other buildings interspersed with paths, small gardens and allotments.

It appeared to be quite an attractive setting for a prisoner-of-war camp. But the army regime that the men from Stalag Luft III encountered there was far from appealing. The colonel in charge was an ardent Czech fascist who did not have any time for the chivalrous code of conduct that existed between the Luftwaffe and its charges. Glemnitz emerged from the meeting with him seething. 'These Army *Dummköpfe* [blockheads]—they know nothing,' he fumed to the prisoners, 'so I tell you: escape!' He said that if he was a gambling man he would be laying bets on a mass break-out within a month. 'He did everything but wish us luck, and we assured him that we would do our best to make his dreams come true,' recorded Bill Ash.

No sooner had the men been admitted to their new quarters than Johnny was thrown in the cooler as punishment for his escape attempt from the train. He was allowed to take Pope's poems and

233

Plato's *Republic* with him into the isolation unit, and to write home to his family. To Minerva he lamented, 'Had hoped to be back home with you + the children + Mother for Christmas by jumping off the train last Friday, on the way to this new camp Oflag 21B, but my plan failed owing to a guard who saw me + stopped the train. My freedom only lasted 10 minutes.' He assured David, 'Next year we shall all be together again for Christmas, I hope.'

With Flora he was, as usual, more fulsome: 'I miss you more than I can say. Some of the happiest times I have as a prisoner is when I think of you + the happy times we have had together. Whenever I read anything good in the Bible, Shakespeare, Pope or elsewhere, it reminds me of you + what you have often said. Am doing 10 days in the cooler for my unauthorised leave of absence from the train + have brought Pope's poems + Plato's Republic to keep me company.'

His letters home give some idea of what it was like to be kept in solitary confinement. 'Each a.m. + afternoon I get an hour's walk. Lights go out at 9 pm. I feel like a monk in a cell. Yesterday I put my shirt on wrong side out, observed 2 minutes silence, read Plato's Republic + after reading the papers in the evening sang myself happily to sleep.' He wrote to Tony, 'I hope you will learn to play some musical instrument like the piano, flute or guitar. Training in music will introduce rhythm and harmony into your soul + have a socialising influence in which the whole life of man stands in need.'

When Johnny emerged from the cooler he reverted to his familiar existence as the prisoners' 'uncle'. He lobbied Minerva on behalf of the

234

increasing number of American prisoners he was mixing with. 'You may be able to do something for U.S.A. p's thru friends like E of E Club. Lt Col Clark at Stalag Luft 3 is charming,' he wrote, referring to the young Albert Patton Clark, the Senior American Officer at Sagan. Johnny once more organised an international relations group with the intention of getting different countries to know one another a little better. He wrote to his mother, 'Most of the world's troubles + misunderstandings, I feel certain, come from ignorance + anything we can do to remove this will help to promote peace, prosperity + happiness among nations after the war.' In Oflag XXI B Johnny shared a large room occupied by 96 prisoners. But far from being depressed at this loss of privacy, his new circumstances, characteristically, cheered him up. 'I am glad to see new scenery + faces. A change is good for everyone.' The countryside around Schubin, covered in snow, reminded him of Canada and 'The Island'.

He could not resist the occasional maudlin thought. 'I dreamt I was home the other night + saw Mother + David so vividly. It was a joy,' he wrote as Christmas approached. His curiosity about the outside world continued unabated. 'There is an able young man named Paget here whose grandfather was governor of the Fiji Islands. The natives there asked for a separate church because they said "the whites smelt".' The men prepared a skating ring on the football ground and played hockey and sleighed on the slopes.

That Christmas the inmates at Schubin were delighted to find themselves recipients of season's greetings from Buckingham Palace in the form of a card from the King and Queen with photographs of them and the young princesses Elizabeth and Margaret Rose. The gesture raised their morale a little and impressed the Germans who could not conceive of receiving such a wholesome family image from any of their own esteemed leaders in Berlin.

On Christmas Eve, Johnny wrote to Flora:

It makes me happy to think of you + Minerva + the children being together to-night over Christmas. The other night I dreamt that you and Lionel + I were together. We had just moved in to a new house in London. The children will have fun together over the holidays with you. I can see your lovely sitting room with the big open fire, the paintings on the wall + the sun streaming in the windows. The birds + chickens in the garden, we made so much of ourselves + the puppies. Yesterday we had a nice Xmas festival of 9 lessons + carols. An officer from each part of the camp read the lessons + the choir sang well. To-day we had a very amusing Pantomime produced by ourselves. Band, conjuring, hilly-billy songs included. Dick Whittington + his cat were splendid . . . There is a lot of talent here.

He apologised to Minerva for some of the ill-tempered remarks he had made about left-wing politicians and conscientious objectors in his earlier letters. One or two of them, he explained had been written when he was suffering from a high temperature and in a foul mood. 'Perhaps I have not taken enough time to express my ideas properly in the few words at my disposal + give you a wrong impression of what I mean . . . Of course everyone can change their minds + we must be ready to forgive + be tolerant.' He wrote nevertheless of the hope that 'genuine philosophers' would one day be elected to high office.

Escape, as ever, was never far from the prisoners' minds. The prospect was all the more enticing thanks to the odiousness of Schubin's loathsome commandant. He was of comparable rank to Wings Day, and should have treated him accordingly, but on one occasion around New Year the Czech Nazi made his British counterpart stand to attention while he addressed him. Wings was apoplectic. When he returned to his quarters he addressed his men in no uncertain terms:

> You are aware that it is everybody's duty to escape if possible. I have been accustomed to polite and correct treatment by Luftwaffe Commandants. Here I have not received that courtesy, in fact this Wehrmacht Commandant has been damned rude to me. He hopes to retire as a General. He won't. I intend to get people out in large numbers. So get busy. Happy escaping and Happy New Year.

Johnny was certainly one of those thinking of escape, but his family remained foremost in his mind. In early January he wrote to Flora:

> I am sure that David has knowledge + appreciation of a lot of worthwhile things that many other boys of his age haven't got. I think every boy before leaving school should be able

237

to milk a cow + harness + drive a team of horses. He should also know how to make butter + cheese + keep milk clean. With this knowledge, he could make himself a useful citizen anywhere in the Empire. 'The happy life should be 3 parts practical.' 'A man will love his country the better for (owning) a pig.'

Parcels continued to arrive even in the backwoods of Poland, and Johnny very generously distributed the various pyjamas, blankets, sweaters, 'lovely clothes' as well as cricket and football 'things' to his friends and comrades. 'Am wearing your lovely blue sweater from Harrods.' He wrote how he had lunch every day at noon following which he and Wing Commander Hyde enjoyed a game of backgammon. Tea was at 4 p.m. and supper at 7.30 p.m. The prisoners had made sleighs to slide down a toboggan run and they had been skating too. 'All great fun.' But he complained that the mild weather had interfered with their winter sports. Again, life for an English gentleman prisoner of the Third Reich was not quite the hardship cinema would have its audiences believe.

Wings' words of encouragement in the new year were welcome, but the prisoners needed no urging to escape. Within weeks of their arriving, half-a-dozen tunnels had been constructed, and scores of escape attempts were made. One staged by the army inmates was named Operation Forlorn Hope and was typical of the British Army's 'gung ho' approach to warfare. It involved two teams of men armed with two ladders for scaling the electrified fences. They hid in the shadows after lock-up as their comrades fused the electricity generator and plunged the entire camp into blackness. Upon this moment they sped towards the wire. Unfortunately, by the time they had successfully placed their ladders up against the wire and were about to make their vault to freedom, the ever-efficient Germans turned the lights back on and the British were compelled to flee back into the shadows. The operation was indeed forlorn of hope after all.

At least one escape attempt, however, was successful, but it did not entirely please Wings. The escape of Sergeant P. T. Wareing was an object lesson in simplicity. Sergeant Wareing slipped away from his guards on an outing to collect bread from Schubin railway station. He walked and cycled his way to Danzig and smuggled himself on a coal ship to Halmstad, Sweden, arriving Christmas 1942. 'Wings was a bit put out by Wareing's escape,' confessed Jimmy James many years after the war. 'There was a bit of the officer class about Wings and the idea that an NCO would escape with such a straightforwardly simple plan rather offended his class sensibilities!' On the other hand, of course, Wings might have been a bit sniffy about Wareing's escape because it hardly contributed to his stated policy of harassing, confounding and confusing the enemy as much as possible.

Perhaps the most audacious escape from Schubin began in the somewhat unappetising surrounds of the communal lavatory. The Abort was a black and extremely malodorous shed which housed a row of 36 holes in a wooden bench over an open sewer. It was one of the closest buildings to the perimeter fence. A French Canadian Spitfire pilot called Eddy Asselin conceived the notion of constructing a tunnel from underneath one of the toilet holes, reasoning, rightly, that the goons would not be entirely enthusiastic about searching a stinking drain of raw effluent. Asselin and his fellow Spitfire pilots, the Texan Bill Ash and Paddy Barthropp, were the most assiduous participants in this tunnelling bid.

The entrance to Asselin's tunnel was through one of the lavatory seats. The diggers began by cutting a trap in the brick wall of the foundations beneath the lavatory seat. On the other side of this trap they dug out a chamber, and this was where the digging on the tunnel began. The chamber soon contained a workshop and a ventilating pump made out of old kit bags. The tunnel was lined with bed boards taken from the prisoners' huts.

At first it was slow going, the goal they had set themselves seemingly so far distant that it was barely worth dreaming about. Each day the diggers would wriggle down through the lavatory seat metaphorically holding their noses against the steaming piles of human waste before entering the comparative cleanliness of the chamber and tunnel. Their companions would wait in the lavatory block to accept cans of soil for dispersal, putting it down through the other open seats and ramming it down into the filth with long poles. Others would keep an eye out for security patrols, chatting amiably with the men who visited the latrines on legitimate business.

One of the diggers was Robert Kee, a bomber pilot who would in civilian life become one of Britain's most prolific journalists, authors and broadcasters. He wrote an account of the escape attempt in *A Crowd is Not Company*, which captures the peculiar sensations of gruelling despair and enduring hope that these endeavours induced in the participants. The filthy work went on for months. Eventually the tunnel was 150 feet long and reached a depth of 17 feet to avoid the many seismographs ringed around the camp. The men prepared for the next moonless night to break out.

As winter turned into spring, Johnny's thoughts continued to be with his family. 'So glad Peter has joined the Air Corps,' he wrote to Minerva:

Thank Tony for his nice letter. I am so glad he is learning carpentry + likes history . . . Thank David for his well-written letter of Nov 15. I am so glad he is getting on so well at school + likes it. Have just finished Green Mansions by Hudson, which I enjoyed enormously. Reading about other people's trials + sufferings such as are described in it + Garibaldi's Defence of the Roman Republic makes one's own seem trivial.

The idiosyncrasies of Johnny's mind, his love of nature and the wider world were revealed in two letters he wrote to one of his sons, and his mother:

A Canadian—Campbell gave us a talk the other day on the Eskimos in Northern Canada where he lived for 5 years working with the Hudson Bay Co. Eskimos never cook their food + live on raw meat + fish. They do not suffer from scurvy although they never have fresh vegetables or fruits. They are great hunters + trappers + fishermen.

And to Flora:

The news of your visits to London + old friends makes me feel as if I had been there with you. Many thanks for the books from Hatchard's + games from Harrods . . . S/Ldr Barrett our bird expert saw or heard today 34 different species of migrant birds. Your music always soothed me + your singing. Aristotle says music has the power of purifying the soul.

Events eventually forced the hand of the lavatory tunnellers when, in February 1943, the prisoners heard a rumour that the air force contingent was going to be transferred back to Sagan. Not wanting to see their efforts going to waste they decided to break out on the next moonless period, which was in March. All the escapers were issued with bogus documents, small amounts of cash and rations to get them through their first days of freedom. It was decided to go out after the 9 p.m. lock-up when the German security staff closed the prisoners' barracks down for the night. The last Appell (roll-call) before lock-up was 5 p.m., which meant that the men escaping would have to be squirrelled down the tunnel shortly afterwards and wait down there for some four hours before the break-out. It was estimated that 33 could be kept down the tunnel for such a length of time without suffocating.

And that is exactly what they did: for four hours or more the thirty-three lay stretched out in their subterranean hole, finger nail to boot heel, while another twenty waited in the chamber performing sundry tasks as back-up. It was a distinguished company of men: among them, besides Jimmy Buckley, Wings Day and Danny Krol, were Robert

Kee and Anthony Barber, the future Conservative Chancellor of the Exchequer. (Some accounts have Johnny in this escape bid. But in his own post-war debriefing session he listed all his escape bids and the Asselin tunnel was not one of them so, in this author's view, it is unlikely that he took part.)

At times they were on the verge of suffocating and the men operating the ventilation pump in the chamber worked themselves into a frenzy of exhaustion. But soon after 9 p.m., the tunnel broke through to the surface outside the camp and one by one the men quietly edged their way out. Remarkably, the escape route was not discovered the next day as they had expected it would be. This omission gave a further man the opportunity to break out: a South African who was not with the original 33 decided to take a chance when he realised the Germans still had not found the empty tunnel.

The security staff at Schubin were mortified. One by one over the next two weeks almost all the escapers were returned to captivity. The one exception was Jimmy Buckley, who disappeared while attempting to escape from Denmark to Sweden in a small boat. It has always been presumed he died during the voyage. It was a sad ending for a brave man, but a fitting one for the first Big X and such a determined escapologist.

The escape attempt had had its intended effect. More than 300,000 Germans were tied up looking for the escapers. It was, at that date, the biggest 'mass escape' of the war. It was the first that attracted the protracted attention of the Sicherheitsdienst or S.D., the intelligence section of the Gestapo. Many of the Wehrmacht officers involved in camp security were court-martialled. And the Germans decided that it was time to bring the prisoners' Polish interlude to an end. In April 1943, all the 800 prisoners of Oflag XXI B were evacuated to Stalag Luft III, from whence many of them had come.

TOM, DICK AND HARRY

Back at Stalag Luft III Johnny and the other British
prisoners found themselves in a vast new North
Compound, bigger than the old East and Centre
compounds together, having a perimeter more than
a mile long.

Johnny was given a room in Hut 104, which he
shared with Bernard 'Pop' Green, an even more
elderly officer than he. Green had won an MC in
the First World War and was far too old to serve in
the Second but he lied about his age and was
enlisted as a tail gunner in the RAF. Johnny and he
had both been trained at the same school of
machine gunnery in 1916. Johnny wrote to Minerva,
'2 weeks ago we returned to the camp we were in
last summer but are in a new compound which is an
improvement + a change is good . . . I am now
sharing a double room with Capt. Green, charming,
an air gunner who was a machine gunner in the last
war . . .' Johnny was also introduced for the first
time to Murdo Macdonald, a padre of the
Parachute Regiment, from Portree, Skye: 'a great
help + a wonderful character. He is a fighting
padre.'

On his return to the Sagan camp he wrote to
Flora in reflective mood:

Spending the winter in a new camp with its
change of scenery, soil, trees + ground,
together with many different faces + a

different atmosphere was very pleasant. Now to be back among old friends again in comparatively comfortable conditions, is also a nice change. Your lovely clothes parcel sent on Jan 23rd came today with just the things I wanted. In it was ½ lb. of delicious chocolate.

Johnny found himself busy once more organising the International Union:

We are doing this by means of general interest talks, common interest discussion groups, debates + an 'Any Questions?' on B.B.C. lines. I long for the day when we all have learnt our lesson + there is peace again. Every situation in which we find ourselves is meant to teach + develop us.

In a reference to the Allies' improving hopes he wrote: 'My love to Clemy + her husband. How happy he must feel.'

Colonel von Lindeiner believed that if he made the new North Compound as comfortable as possible, the prisoners would be quite content to sit out the war in peace. Consequently he indulged them in a manner that his superiors in Berlin found irritating, but which many of his captives appreciated. Indeed the opening of the North Compound was later referred to by some as the beginning of 'the Golden Era' of Stalag Luft III's history. There was more space, more food, and more recreational and athletic activity than ever before. Against the advice of his security staff, von Lindeiner allowed some trees to remain in the space separating the compound and the

Kommandantur. And he gave the prisoners permission to build their own theatre, which they did using excess timber donated by the Germans, and old Red Cross boxes.

Johnny threw himself back into the turmoil of camp life and helping to build the new theatre. To Flora he wrote:

> Have been doing some brick laying + work as a general labourer helping to build a theatre + general social centre. It has been great fun doing it + has reminded me of the building Lionel + I have done together in Canada + at Ferring. I often think of him + feel he is with us. What fun we used to have at Ferring and on The Island in Canada with Lucy before the last war . . . There are growing numbers of Americans here + I am glad to be able to do here a little of the kind of work Minerva is doing for them at home. If they can get into the houses of representative people + make friends it will do more good than anything else . . . I love hearing from you about the singing of the black birds + thrushes. I always associate them with your lovely house + garden. The birds, the doggies, the chickens, the cows, the garden + the fields.

He heard from Minerva, presumably, about black American troops in Britain, and replied, betraying the disgraceful prejudice of his age, 'I hope the Negroes are behaving themselves in Wales + are being treated properly. They require knowing, like everyone else.' Social life continued as normal: 'I have started community singing Sunday evenings accompanied by guitar, violins, accordions, etc + interspersed with Shakespeare + other poetry. The music from each nation is beautiful + all produce harmony.' And his observations about life continued to be educational: 'The father of one of our batmen use [*sic*] to suffer before the war from diabetes + could hardly walk 100 yards with help. Since the war he has had to live on vegetables + fruits without meat or sugar + can now walk 10–15 miles daily. He is 72 + lives in the Channel Islands.'

Johnny's philosophy remained obdurate:

My belief is that without Christianity, we live in a state of chaos, wherein we lose not only our peace of mind, but also the gifts of distinguishing things + appreciating them at their true value. Nothing attracts us, nor does anything suit our taste. We know not what to do nor what to decide upon. By Christianity, I mean the truth, which bridges the gulf between rich + poor, social ranks, nations + races.

In another letter he wrote:

Am reading Buchan's Cromwell. It points out how issues in the strife of the early 17th century in England lay at the root of all democracy—the right to personal liberty, the denial of any power to dispense with the law which normally protected a subject's life + property, the hostility to special tribunals which usurped the duties of common courts of justice. A settled law + the equality of all men before it were claims which survived the wreckage, for behind them was the spirit of England.

Occasionally, Johnny was struck by glimpses of normality. 'From my window I could look down a lovely path through a pine wood. It reminds me of Freudenstadt [a German resort popular with the wealthy, which Johnny and his family had often visited]. A woman on a bicycle, with a small child sitting behind, occasionally passes by + reminds me of the world outside . . .' Over the forthcoming year, the theatre was to stage everything from *Hamlet* and *A Midsummer Night's Dream* to *The Importance of Being Earnest* and *The Man Who Came to Dinner*.

If the recreational facilities at Stalag Luft III were now more extensive, so were the prisoners' escape activities. The escape committee was now under the direction of Roger Bushell, the South African-born Hurricane pilot. Under Bushell, the X Organisation struck upon the idea of building not one but three tunnels, each of which would be minor feats of engineering genius. Each would be sunk 25 feet down to evade the ring of seismographs planted around the compound. They would be built to the standards of industrial mining shafts with ventilation pipes, air pumps, trolleys and electricity diverted from the compound supply.

The tunnels would be code-named 'Tom', 'Dick' and 'Harry'. But Bushell was unconcerned by the possibility that this frenetic activity might arouse the security staff's interest. If one of the tunnels were to be found, the Germans would be so impressed that they wouldn't conceivably believe two identical structures existed elsewhere. The plan

249

was for two of the tunnels to go west, the most direct route out of the camp. One would start in Hut 123 close to the wire, another from Hut 122. The third tunnel would go north out of Hut 104, directly under the parcel store and cooler. The tunnel entrance would be in the room directly next to the one shared by Johnny Dodge and Pop Green.

The story of 'the Great Escape' has been well documented. But, for the uninitiated, it is perhaps helpful to offer a quick summary of the famous break-out of Stalag Luft III. The three tunnels were extraordinary achievements of engineering prowess constructed by many men, who braved the dangers and suffocating claustrophobia of the job day in, day out. But the escape committee also established an enormous production line employing some 600 people, which created escape tools (such as compasses and food pellets), as well as civilian disguises and a panoply of bogus documents, pass books, railway tickets and so forth. They called the forgery department Dean & Dawson after a well-known London travel agency. The prisoners developed a security system based upon an elaborate network of watchers (called stooges), who deployed a complex semaphore system to warn their comrades of enemy intrusion whenever a ferret entered the compound.

Johnny's role in the new escape plan was crucial though not particularly glamorous. Owing to his advanced years (he was almost 47, and in the services that made him practically pensionable), tunnelling was out of the question. It was felt he played a better part in distracting the goons. At Bushell's suggestion, Johnny and Pop Green regularly entertained a German ferret called Picken to tea in their room in an attempt to allay any suspicions about what might be going on in the room directly next door. Johnny also performed another crucial distracting role. A big problem for the escapers was the infernal racket made by the engineers as they were smashing up the concrete foundation stone to create the tunnel entrances. To disguise this noise Johnny held choir-singing practices when work was underway. (A role recreated in the movie *The Great Escape* by 'Cavendish', whose character bore a close resemblance to Johnny's.) With his love of singing and music, this important function would have been a joy to Johnny.

Tunnelling started on 11 April and it took the best part of the following six weeks to construct the three vertical shafts descending into the Silesian soil. By the end of May, all three shafts and their base chambers were finished and much of both Tom and Dick's horizontal excavation was underway. The omens were not promising. By early 1943 there had been as many as 30 tunnel escape attempts from the camp. None had succeeded. More depressing still, most had been detected long before they had reached anywhere near the wire. The stamina, both physical and mental, required to build a tunnel more than 300 feet long was beyond most of the prisoners. Many were beginning to be depressed by seeing their efforts go to waste. Worse still, the German authorities were beginning to take an increasingly harsh attitude towards escape attempts. That April, the High Command issued an order that stated:

Each POW has to be informed that by

escaping in civilian clothing or German uniform he is not only liable to disciplinary punishment but runs the risk of being court-martialled and committed for trial on suspicion of espionage and partisanship, in the affirmative he may even be sentenced to death.

Later that year, von Lindeiner felt compelled to write to the senior officers in all the compounds, clarifying the grounds on which a POW might be court-martialled by the German authorities. They included wearing civilian clothes or a German uniform. (Although the Geneva Convention did not forbid officers escaping disguised in the enemy's uniform.) Von Lindeiner wrote that even the theft of bed boards for tunnel making would be regarded as damaging to the German war effort and therefore liable to court martial. Indeed, so all encompassing was the order that virtually everybody engaged in any form of escape activity could be dragged before a German court martial.

That July there was a happy interlude in the North Compound. There were now some 500 Americans in the camp and they had decided to celebrate Independence Day. On the morning of 4 July the other inmates of the North Compound awoke to the sound of banging drums and blowing bugles as a party of 'Red Indians' and 'Colonialists' marched around the camp. They were quickly joined by the British and other RAF officers of different nationalities. Soon the whole camp was heaving with thousands of noisy prisoners. They shared tin mugs of an illicit and fiery alcoholic concoction especially brewed by the Americans to celebrate the occasion. The prisoners became increasingly inebriated as the day progressed, and at one stage Johnny and Wings Day were unceremoniously thrown into the fire pool by the American 'rebels'. The Germans watched on, at first bewildered but soon quietly amused. Pieber could not resist a good-natured chuckle at evening Appell (roll-call) as the prisoners tried to stand up straight for the count. The day ended in good spirits all around.

Digging on the three tunnels continued apace into the late summer of 1943 with Tom and Dick (heading westerly out of Huts 123 and 122 respectively) getting priority over Harry because they were nearer to the wire. The by now familiar camp distractions continued as well. The prisoners cultivated vegetable plots outside their barrack blocks (an activity that also helped disperse the soil from tunnel digging). There were theatre productions every month. The men exercised on a regular basis to keep their spirits up and took part in competitive games. Others signed up to language, art and drawing classes.

Irritated at Johnny's unswerving conservative views, some of the other inmates established a rival to his International Union. They staged a mock parliament every so often, casting one another in the roles of post-war politicians. On one occasion Roger Bushell played the deputy leader of the Labour Party and proposed a motion that all industry should be nationalised. Another colourful character was Tom Kirby-Green who had grown up in colonial climes and had developed an endearing fondness for native music and dress—both of which he indulged in to the bemusement of the Germans.

In one 'parliament', Kirby-Green argued that it was time the British recognised the prevalence of the black majority in much of their empire. Johnny's reaction to this outrageous suggestion is not recorded.

Even if he disagreed violently with the motion, it would not have been possible to dislike Johnny. On 29 July 1943, Wing Commander Tony Eyre wrote to Mr E. Cornwall of National Provincial Bank, 'We have moved a mile or so into a new compound which is more spacious and better equipped. Major Dodge has to our joy returned to the fold and as of old charms away many an hour. He is very fit and wishes to be remembered to you.' And on Wednesday, 4 August 1943, the (London) *Evening Standard* reported:

In a recent letter from the prison camp to Mr. Claude E. T. Rogers, chairman of Gillingham Conservative and Unionist Association, Colonel Dodge says he has started an International Union to promote closer understanding among the men of many nationalities in the camp. He continued, 'After the war I hope we shall see a development of rural industry in England. The industry must be able to afford good wages and conditions of life for those employed in it.'

Johnny continued to be a prolific writer of letters. To Minerva he wrote: 'Give Tony my love + congratulate him from me for winning the 80 yards run + doing so well in geography + history. The war has taught Kriegies geography as most of us have maps of the world pinned up in our rooms.'

254

And to David, 'Congratulations on reciting Julius Caesar so well . . . The boys have been playing cricket + water sports lately + we have had some good races, high jumping, throwing the discus + putting the shot. How are you getting on with Botany? Knowledge is Power.'

Some days later, he wrote to Flora:

I long to see you again + the animals + garden . . . So pleased David is such a good shot + that you are putting him down for Eton. Thanks for the uniform + 2 clothing parcels. Also the Benson + Hedges cigarettes. Thank Miss Roberts for hers and Mrs Morton for the lovely socks + Mrs Dawes, Montreal, for cigarettes, books + puzzle. Our orchestra of 26 gave an excellent classical concert recently. Roy Wilkins a South African is conductor.

No sooner had the men arrived in the North Compound than rumours began to spread that the Germans were going to be adding yet another compound to Stalag Luft III—directly to the south of the North Compound. When von Lindeiner's men started clearing the forest to the south it was apparent the rumours were true. The men soon discovered that the new South Compound was going to be reserved entirely for American prisoners. There was a flurry of disquiet. The Americans had worked as hard on Tom, Dick and Harry as anyone else had, but it now looked as if they would be removed from the North Compound before any of the tunnels were due to break through. Roger Bushell held an emergency meeting of the escape committee.

He proposed speeding up the break-out by concentrating all their resources on Tom—which was nearest the wire—to give the Americans a chance to escape. But worryingly, Block 123, the barrack from which Tom was being built, had already attracted the suspicions of the ferrets. Selflessly, the Senior American Officer Albert Patton 'Bub' Clark objected to Bushell's plan, observing that Tom was the most vulnerable of the tunnels and working intensively on it would arouse the interest of the ferrets. But Bushell overruled him and the prisoners threw all their efforts into Tom, closing down Harry in the meantime, and using Dick to store sand. Ultimately, the Americans were to be proved right. Within weeks the Germans had discovered Tom. Despondency spread throughout the camp. But not for long.

The Germans were astonished by the ingenuity of Tom. So amazed, indeed, that dignitaries from Berlin visited Stalag Luft III to see what an incredible piece of engineering the tunnel had been. Colonel von Lindeiner took great pleasure in showing off the engineering masterpiece that his prisoners had so painstakingly constructed. Newspaper photographers came to take pictures. Indeed, it was such a beautiful work of engineering that the Germans had difficulty in working out how to destroy it. Eventually a sapper was brought in from a nearby army unit and Tom disappeared under 100 pounds of high explosives. A good part of Hut 123 was damaged, too, provoking catcalls and whistles from the prisoners watching. The remnants of the tunnel were displayed in von Lindeiner's Escape Museum, and the commandants took great pleasure in showing guests around the small room.

The prisoners now had one tremendous advantage. The Germans could not possibly believe that another two tunnels of equal complexity existed beneath their feet. They were lulled into a false sense of security. The prisoners reopened Harry, now determined more than ever to make their escape good. Late that autumn, the Americans were marched out of the North Compound and into their new South Compound. Johnny did not dwell on the matter.

To David, he wrote: 'Congratulations on shooting that rabbit from the roof. I once shot a pigeon in Burma with a .22. What fun you must have had with Aura harvesting, driving a tractor + riding. You will soon learn how to look after a farm on your own.' He wrote to Flora asking her to thank his cousin Olive and her husband Bertie in Portugal for 'a parcel of delicious nuts, raisins + prunes'. Adding, 'Thanks for another clothing parcel which came three days ago, with 2 shirts, tooth brush, socks, pullover, chocolate, all of which I needed . . . 5 books have arrived including the Cherry Orchard + Eminent Victorians.'

The dream of escape remained no more than that, until, that is, the winter of 1943 when, in an audacious effort unconnected to Tom, Dick or Harry, three officers actually managed to get back to Britain. The 'wooden horse escape' is another epochal tale of Second World War POW existence that was turned into celluloid drama. It was the idea of an army officer, Lieutenant Michael Codner, and his friend Flight Lieutenant Eric Williams. Inspired by the Trojan Horse of ancient

Greek legend they wondered whether it would be possible to build a short tunnel from underneath a wooden athletics horse of the sort used in schools. The charm of this idea was that the tunnel would not have to be very long.

The difficulties were twofold. Firstly, that of persuading the Germans to allow the prisoners to build and position such a contraption in the compound. Secondly, the logistical problem of constructing a tunnel from such a confined space under the noses of the German watchtowers. Nevertheless, and much to the escape committee's surprise, neither obstacle proved insurmountable. The Germans readily agreed to the prisoners constructing their own wooden horse and had no objection to where they decided to place it. Codner and Williams were subsequently joined by a third companion, Oliver Philpot, and they broke out of the camp on 29 October 1943. All three made it home to England by early November. When the news reached the inmates of Stalag Luft III, the effect on their morale was incalculable. Despite all the dire predictions of the cynics, it really was possible to make a 'home run'.

LAST LETTERS HOME

As Christmas approached, Johnny's thoughts returned to home. To Minerva he wrote: 'best wishes for a Merry Christmas + happy new year, which I hope + pray will see an end to hostilities + a peace dictated by truth + justice. Have enjoyed reading Pope Pious XIII's [*sic*] Encyclical written in 1893 . . .' To David:

A very Merry Christmas to you + best wishes for a happy new year. I wonder if you ever exercise on the horizontal bar + the parallel bars. They are good for developing balance, coordination + confidence + I should like to see expert instructors in every school. Some of the men here are splendid with them. Take care of the family, till my return next year. Keep up your shooting + riding.

With Flora he was in philosophic mood:

Speaking generally, the landed gentry are enduring witnesses of past worth + good work done + until they forfeit our esteem . . . they deserve to be respected + honoured. High place is lost as easily that when a family has been of long continuance we may be sure that it has survived by exceptional merit. Nature rapidly finds out when the wrong sort have stolen into promotion. When a Knave makes a fortune his son spends it—one generation sees an end to him. Even among the best there is quick succession. Warriors, lawyers, politicians, press perpetually to the front . . . material is for ever being replaced. Each family thus raised is for ever on its trial. Those who survive remain as links between the present + the past, + carry on unbroken the continuity of our national existence.' Frocade. Thanks to you + Mrs Roberts for the books + your parcel. The Red X is doing wonderful work. Casson gave us a splendid production of Macbeth. Best wishes for 1944.

And later:

The Theatre Club put on 3 very good 1 act plays the other night + a few days before that, an amusing variety show was produced. Last summer a number of model sail boats were made + sailed on the fire pool. Now model aeroplanes are being flown. They have been made most ingeniously + fly beautifully. The other day I saw 2 little girls walking along the road with a goat, which behaved first like a dog, + it reminded me of the goats you have kept. I am sure boys + girls can do important auxiliary work suited to their years + having a definite value for the young people themselves as it builds them up physically + enlarges their outlook. I am so glad David has done farm work.

In November, the son of the United States ambassador to England, John Winant, turned up in camp. 'Winant's son is in an adjoining compound,' Johnny wrote to Minerva. 'My love to your mother and mine. I appreciate more + more, the importance of the home + family life + wish we had at least 5 children. We need bigger + better families.' To Flora, speculating about how the world would work after the war, Johnny told her how he was convinced that:

reciprocal aid is the basis of the solution of both international + social problems. 'Those who, in the past, took up the notion that nation or class is naturally hostile to nation or class, + that the wealthy + the working men are intended by nature to live in mutual conflict, made a great mistake. So irrational + so false is this view, that the direct contrary is the truth. Just as the symmetry of the human frame is the result of the suitable arrangement of the different parts of the body, so in the society of nations or in a State, it is ordained by nature that all nations + both classes should dwell in harmony + agreement so as to maintain the balance of the body politic. Each needs the other: nation cannot do without nation; capital cannot do without labour, nor labour without capital. Mutual agreement results in the beauty of good order.'

In deepest Silesia the 'escape season' was effectively over. The winter in central Europe was so cold that few prisoners wanted to endure the prospect of life outside the wire at that time of the year. Most of them battened down the hatches to enjoy a quiet Christmas, perhaps dreaming of the escape plans that would become live once more in the spring, or simply settling down to reading and attending classes and staging theatrical and musical productions. German classes were the most popular, with so many officers preparing themselves for escape.

It was generally agreed that October's *Macbeth* had been one of the theatre's most accomplished productions, which few subsequently could hope to match. Roger Bushell was immersing himself in rehearsals for his role as Professor Higgins in the forthcoming production of George Bernard Shaw's *Pygmalion*. But his interest in the production was less to do with a new found enthusiasm for treading the boards than a desire to convince the Germans that the ever-unruly Big X had wisely given up on escaping. An added joy for the prisoners that winter was the arrival of British and American feature films, which were shown at a makeshift cinema. Among their favourites were the Ginger Rogers and Fred Astaire classic *Shall We Dance*, and *Bringing Up Baby* starring Katharine Hepburn and Cary Grant.

November brought the first fluttering of snow, which turned into a near blizzard when December arrived, covering the camp in a thick blanket of white. On the night before Christmas the camp listened in total silence as a bugler played 'Silent Night'. It can have been of little comfort to the men, who would have preferred to be with their families sitting by the glowing embers of a coal fire in their own homes. Many of the prisoners tried to create some sort of festive distraction, organising Christmas dinners and so forth. Most of the men had been saving up supplies to splurge out on

Christmas Day. When on New Year's Eve they toasted the arrival of 1944 with illicit whisky, the mood might have been lightened somewhat by the forthcoming thaw and re-opening of the 'escape season'.

The various forgery and bogus-papers 'factories', such as Dean & Dawson, were still in the process of producing an impressive armoury of escape accessories. They would soon have 250 compasses and 4,000 maps, as well as more than 100 handmade civilian suits practically indistinguishable from those lovingly made by the tailors of Hamburg or Dresden, and 12 German military uniforms. One tame ferret had provided the escape committee with a typewriter and another had given them a Contax camera, which, along with the prisoners' own dark room, greatly assisted production of the false passes. Tommy Guest kept his suits and other completed clothing in the attic of the toilet block. The rest of the escape resources—compasses, maps, high-energy food, and so on—were hidden behind false walls. They had constructed a small printing press that operated from the bottom of the entry shaft to 'Dick'.

In fact, by January 1944, Dick was no longer seen as a viable escape tunnel. Partly because it was becoming so clogged up with various escape supplies, but also because of the Germans' construction of a new West Compound that meant the tunnel would have to be extended another 600 feet or so to ensure it emerged outside the camp. Instead, every effort was now poured into Harry, the tunnel in Hut 104 beginning in the room next to the one shared by Johnny and Pop Green.

Harry had already extended some 100 feet

northwards underneath the Vorlager (and directly under the cooler). The escape committee calculated that it would only need to be extended a further 220 feet for it to emerge safely behind the tree line. Bushell decided to take the Germans by surprise by breaking out before the onset of spring. To meet this pressing deadline, work began on 10 January.

Johnny's letters home give away no clue to the exciting developments underground. To Flora:

> Gave a talk yesterday for the E.S.U. [the English Speaking Union] on Chamberlain whom I admire very much. The political life of man finds an analogy in the organism of the animal or plant + change is a slow process in the one as in the other. The State is a natural product, which stands, as Burke said, 'in a just correspondence + symmetry with the order of the world.' Not decades but centuries must be allowed for each stage of its development.

Later, Johnny wrote a letter that dispels the myth that all POWs were on starvation rations: 'Please thank Olive + Bertie for the delicious parcels of nuts, raisins + sardines they sent me + others here . . . for Xmas. Please ask her not to send us anymore, as the Red X give us all we need.' It transpired that his cousin and her husband's generosity had come at some personal cost. 'I am sorry to hear that they are hard up + that we have been a burden on them,' he wrote, thanking his mother for sending them £50, a considerable sum of money for the time.

The camp distractions continued.

We are holding a 'Kriegie parliament' soon +
I have been asked to form a government. It
should be fun . . . Saw a wonderful variety
show here recently produced by the theatre
club. Most amusing . . . Cold shower every
morning + exercises am + pm have kept us
splendidly all winter. Have given up eating
meat. Your blue sweater + brown blankets
have been a blessing + I use them + all the
other things you sent me.

The digging proceeded at a hectic pace, as did the
ancillary preparations for escape. In the tunnel,
two staging posts were constructed—they became
known as 'Leicester Square' and 'Piccadilly
Circus'—and above ground the 'penguins' found
ever more ingenious ways to disperse the growing
mounds of sand dug up. But in February the men
received a shock. Suddenly, and without warning,
the ferrets barged into Hut 104 turning everything
upside down—including Johnny and Pop Green's
room—obviously aware that there was a tunnel
somewhere. Thankfully they discovered nothing.
But it was apparent to the escape committee it was
only a matter of time before the Germans would
stumble upon their secret. The decision was made
to break out on the night of 23 March, the next
moonless night.

After this decision was made, the escape
committee set about working out who would be the
lucky 200 to take part in the escape. In the end the
510 names were put in a hat for a draw to be held
on 20 February. A priority system was established.
The first 30 places in the tunnel went to those who
had the best chances of escaping, almost all of

whom would have to be fluent in German or other foreign languages familiar in the Reich. The first 30 would be provided with the very best documentation and disguises that the forgery department and tailors could supply. They would all travel by train and it was vital that they got the chance to get to Sagan railway station first, preferably before midnight, after which time there were very few trains until the morning. The following 20 places would be reserved for the prisoners who had done most work on the tunnel itself. Again, their names would be drawn out of a hat. The next 20 would be selected in the same way from the prisoners who had worked above ground as stooges and penguins, and in the forgery, tailoring and compass-making departments. The next 30 would also be drawn out of a hat, this time taken from the ranks of those who had failed to get a place in the earlier draws. Finally, the last 100 places were drawn from the remaining names on the list. When the names were drawn out of the hat, Johnny Dodge found that he was number 30.

The next letters that Johnny wrote to Flora and Minerva betrayed nothing of the adventure that was about to begin. 'There is a delightful officer here, named Fl/Lt Ferry, from Western Australia, who runs the Australian group of the International Union,' he wrote to Minerva:

His brother is a Sergeant in England + I would be glad if you could help to give him a good time . . . Have enjoyed reading J.S. Mills' essay on 'Liberty' . . . 'The individual is not accountable to society for his actions, in as far as these concern the interests of no person but himself. For such actions as are prejudicial to the interests of others, the individual is accountable + may be subjected either to social or legal punishment, if society is of the opinion that one or the other is requisite for its protection. It is their remarkable diversity of character + culture, not any superior excellence in them, which has made the European family of nations an improving, instead of a stationary, portion of human kind. The unlikeness of a person to another is generally the first thing which draws the attention of either to the imperfection of his own type, + the superiority of another, or the possibility, by combining the advantages of both, of producing something better than either.'

To Flora he wrote:

It has been snowing the last few days and there is still snow on the ground which has reminded me of Spring on The Island in Canada. Have given up smoking for Lent + feel much better for it. Many of us smoke much too much + I did for one . . . The South Africans here are a remarkably fine lot . . . They gave an interesting talk on their country for our International Union last week . . . Have been taking a cold shower every morning this winter + walk 3 hours a day + feel very well.

The dates of these last two letters are confusing as they imply they were written on the night of the

Great Escape, when we might expect Johnny would have had other things on his mind. But perhaps they were written in the long hours while the men waited in Hut 104 to go down the tunnel. They were the final letters that Johnny wrote home, and after receiving them his family would have no idea of his fate until a few days before the end of the war.

PER ARDUA AD ASTRA

The appointed night of the escape was 23 March. Before the break-out, the lucky 200 were compelled to thoroughly rehearse their escape strategy and cover stories. Some took this rather rigorous process seriously but it is hard to imagine that Johnny was among their number. There can be no doubt, however, that he would have relished the adventure ahead. Johnny's lot was to be part of a group of 12 who were aiming to travel southwards to try and cross the border with Czechoslovakia. They would pose as foreign workers from a local wood mill taking a few days' leave, a not unlikely cover story in a Third Reich which was host to several million foreign labourers. The plan was for the 12 men to catch an early morning train from Tschiebsdorf (now Trzebow), a country station not far from Sagan. They were aiming to travel about 70 miles south to a little town called Boberöhrsdorf (now Siedlecin) near Hirschberg on the Czechoslovakian frontier. The party would include, among others, Johnny's great friends Pop Green and Jimmy James.

Once they had broken out of the tunnel, an Australian, Squadron Leader John Williams, was going to lead the party through the woods and guide them to Tschiebsdorf. Williams had already been out on parole walks with the Germans and knew the area better than the rest. At Tschiebsdorf station a Polish officer called Jerzy Mondschein would take the lead. Mondschein spoke fluent German. He would buy the train tickets and it was hoped his fluency would see them through any sticky situations that might arise on their hoped-for journey to Czechoslovakia. They would travel on the train in pairs but once at the frontier some individual officers chose to be left to their individual devices. Johnny's partner was Flight Lieutenant Jimmy Wernham of the Royal Canadian Air Force, who was born in Scotland but had moved with his parents to their native Winnipeg. They were going to masquerade as Serbo-Croat labourers. The fact that neither of them spoke a word of the language gave them no pause for thought.

The plan for what became known as the 'Great Escape' had always been to get 200 men out. But there was never any realistic hope that this target would be achieved. On the moonless night in question, dusk came at about 9 p.m., and the sun rose around 5.30 a.m. That gave the men eight-and-a-half hours of darkness. Past experience had shown that one man could be got out of a tunnel every two to three minutes at the very most. That meant they could aim for between 170 and 255 escapers—but only under the most ideal of circumstances.

The escape committee had sensibly factored in all the unexpected delays and hitches that were inevitable in such an ambitious enterprise. Many of the would-be escapers would never have been in a tunnel before. Some might be overcome by claustrophobia and panic. Many would be carrying suitcases and other elaborate baggage and were bound to take a little longer. There might be tunnel collapses that would take valuable time to shore up. If they accepted a realistic figure of one man every four or five minutes, then between 102 and 128 men might stand a realistic chance of getting out. Even this figure was optimistic, wildly so, the more cynical would have said.

The escapers were going to make their way across Germany in a variety of disguises ranging from smart lawyers, accountants and doctors in petite bourgeoisie business suits, to foreign labourers and seamen in worn rags. As 23 March approached, they each rehearsed their cover stories, studied maps and brushed up on their foreign languages. (Johnny had attempted to learn German intermittently during the years of his captivity, but could barely master more than a few incoherent phrases.) Some, perhaps, revised their plans. 'There was a fever of excitement about the place,' recalls Jimmy James in his memoir *Moonless Night*. 'None of the escapers seriously gave any thought to the consequences of recapture after a mass escape on this scale. In the same way that a pilot doesn't think about whether he's going to be shot down before he climbs into his cockpit.' Perhaps that was a credible state of mind for an English officer, but some of the other nationalities flying with the RAF had had many sleepless nights wondering what their fates might be if the Gestapo got its hands on them.

The escapers had been given dozens of talks about the various escape routes out of the camp, details of which were provided by those who had been out on parole, or by tame ferrets, or prisoners who had escaped. They knew that there was some sort of heavily guarded lighted compound near the camp that it would be preferable to avoid. There were several large and small towns near Sagan that would be best steered clear of: urban areas were far more extensively patrolled by the ever-vigilant Hitler Youth and the elderly Home Guard, and it was difficult to evade the unpredictable security checks at street corners. The escapers knew that the Oder River was to the north of Sagan, and might provide a valuable means of escape; the Berlin-to-Breslau autobahn was to the south. Anyone planning to go to Switzerland was given a pep talk by Roger Bushell, drawing upon the unhappy experiences of his ill-fated escape bid in 1941.

As the date of the break-out approached, a palpable sense of excitement filled the air and spread to the surrounding compounds. The Senior American Officer, Albert 'Bub' Clark, remembered there was a 'buzz' about the camp for several days before the actual escape. This, surely, could not have escaped the notice of the German security staff, who were intimately familiar with every aspect of camp life.

Unfortunately, when the morning of 23 March dawned, a thick blanket of snow covered the compound. One of the prisoners, Leonard Hall, a member of the RAF meteorological branch, advised the escape committee to postpone the break-out for another day. He said that the next few days would be very cold but cloud cover would make the evenings very dark. That night, there was a heavy snowfall during a rehearsal of *Pygmalion* in the theatre. Roger Bushell was playing Professor Henry Higgins. The following morning the escape committee met at 11.30 a.m., and the decision to go was made. The forging department promptly began stamping the correct dates on scores of bogus papers.

In the South Compound, Senior American Officer Bub Clark received a message that Bushell wanted to see him on the other side of the wire. Shortly afterwards the two officers exchanged greetings through the 12-foot-high fence dividing their compounds. 'We go out tonight,' said Bushell. 'Please don't do anything to screw us up.' Clark assured Bushell that the Americans were not planning to do anything that would compromise the British break-out. He then wished Bushell luck. 'And that was the last I ever saw of Roger Bushell,' said Clark 60 years later, in an interview given to this author for an American documentary on the subject. 'And some of the finest men I have ever known in my entire life.'

The following hours are familiar to everyone who has watched the enduringly popular 1963 Hollywood movie that tells this incredible story— one of the most celebrated episodes of the Second World War. Over the course of the night, more than 200 men slipped into Hut 104. So many men were squeezed into the confined space that steam began streaming out of the shuttered windows into the freezing Silesian night. They waited there patiently, and sometimes not so patiently, for many hours. After many frustrating delays, the tunnelling men dug through to the surface but, much to the prisoners' dismay, they were several yards short of the cover of the tree line. The camp lights seemed fearsomely bright and the watchtowers loomed over the tunnel's exit. To compensate, the men strung a rope between the tunnel exit and the darkness of the forest. Each man would give two tugs on the

273

rope to indicate it was all clear for the next man to make his escape.

Other points when the escape did not go according to plan can mainly be ascribed to failures on the part of individual escapers. In extreme cases some panicked, overcome by claustrophobia and fear. They had to be removed, often involving the removal of several others in line behind them. It was a laborious process that wasted valuable time and produced frayed tempers. The main cause of delay was that almost all of the escapers carried more baggage than they had been told they were allowed, and wrapped themselves in too much thick winter clothing. The temperature outside was minus 30 degrees, and no one wanted to freeze within moments of achieving their liberty.

Johnny was one of these reprobates. He went down the escape hatch wrapped in heavy blankets and wearing so many thick woollen sweaters that the tunnel could not accommodate his bulky form. He got stuck and had to be pulled out. To his dismay, Johnny was forcibly persuaded to discard much of his excess outerwear. The delay meant that another half a dozen or more would-be escapers did not even get into the tunnel.

Eventually, Johnny emerged into the night, his first taste of real freedom since his capture in 1940. Like the others he must have been exhilarated by the sensation and, no doubt, a little confused as he fumbled about in the thick pine forest looking for his escape partners among the many shadowy figures lurking between the trees. He found his own partner, the Canadian Jimmy Wernham, and the other ten in the 'wood mill leave party', as they had become known. It was about 1.30 a.m. on the 25th that the 12 of them finally set off for the tiny country station of Tschiebsdorf.

They walked in single file led by the Australian airman John Williams. Occasionally they ventured onto quiet roads and country trails, but mainly they stuck to the forest through which they stumbled quietly like a silent procession of spectral creatures. By the time it was 4 a.m., to their consternation, they still had not found Tschiebsdorf and were fearful that they would miss their local commuter train, which they knew from intelligence was due at the station at 5 a.m. Presently, however, they emerged from the thickets onto the railway line. On turning south they were delighted a few minutes later to arrive at the country station. A single light illuminated the little ticket office. Fortunately, it was manned at even that ungodly hour.

At this moment it was the task of Flight Lieutenant Mondschein, the fluent German speaker, to purchase the tickets. Johnny and the others stood somewhat self-consciously in the waiting room as Mondschein approached the little window behind which the ticket master sat. Mondschein carried with him their bogus leave passes and requested 12 tickets to Boberöhrsdorf. In Jimmy James' peerless memoir, *Moonless Night*, he recounts the nail-biting moments that followed:

'*Zwölf?*' asked the booking clerk somewhat incredulously.

'*Ja, zwölf,*' Mondschein repeated.

The man disappeared from his counter into a back room. It is not hard to imagine the trepidation in the minds of the 12 escapers. After what seemed an eternity, the booking clerk returned and asked once more if Mondschein was sure he wanted

275

12 tickets.

'*Ja, zwölf,*' said Mondschein, impatiently.

If the German clerk had any doubts about the strange party of men who had suddenly turned up at his station in the early hours of the morning, they must have been allayed because presently he issued them with 12 third-class tickets to Boberöhrsdorf.

The wait for the train was tense, as the men fully expected the Gestapo to descend upon the station at any moment. They tried to look as unconcerned as they possibly could in the circumstances. In the event, only an elderly farmer and his wife came in, and they, on seeing the gathering of ruffians, quickly turned on their heels and left the ticket hall without a word. Thankfully the train arrived on time, and the men got on, practically skipping on board in their relief to be finally on their way from Sagan. They found themselves in an old-fashioned carriage devoid of passengers except for the elderly couple they had seen at the station.

The train trundled on to its destination through the snowy Silesian landscape, stopping, tortuously, at every station en route as more and more people crowded on board. But nobody paid the 'wood mill leave party' the slightest attention, except for a woman who remonstrated about one of them smoking in a 'non-smoking' compartment.

It was shortly after 9 a.m. on the morning of 25 March that they arrived at their destination. To their relief there was not even a ticket check, let alone Gestapo agents awaiting them. As planned, the men split up, mostly in pairs, quietly nodding farewell to one another while trying not to draw attention to themselves. Johnny and his partner, the Scottish-Canadian airman Jimmy Wernham, walked along the river towards Hirschberg. Presently, on arriving at a small country station on the outskirts of the city, Wernham attempted to buy two tickets to a destination on the Czech frontier. He was refused the tickets and was unable to understand the reason why.

After discussing the situation with Johnny they decided to try again just as the next train arrived, hoping that in the confusion the ticket office would this time grant their request. They were wrong. No tickets were forthcoming, and the train left without them. Johnny and Wernham left the station empty-handed and headed along the main road covered in thick snow toward Hirschberg. This time Johnny was successful in buying two tickets at the main railway terminus. They had desperately hoped to avoid this option, believing the station would be teeming with Gestapo.

Nobody, however, challenged them as they boarded their next train, which was due to leave at 4 o'clock that afternoon. It was only some minutes later, however, after they had settled in their seats, that a civilian official entered the compartment and began demanding where they were going and who they were. Johnny and Jimmy babbled away in what they thought was a good impression of two Yugoslav workers who didn't speak a word of German. They might very well have got away with it had it not been for the unfortunate fact that there was a Yugoslav citizen nearby who could speak German. The stranger confirmed for the official that Johnny and Wernham could not speak a word of Serbo-Croat. They were promptly arrested and ordered off the train.

At the station police office, Johnny and Jimmy

Wernham continued to try to bluff their way through, but soon realised that their attempts were falling on deaf ears. They finally admitted they were escaped Allied prisoners from Stalag Luft III. They were dispatched to the local criminal police (the Kripo) headquarters in Hirschberg. On arrival there they found Jimmy James and his escape partner Nick Skanziklas, a Greek flier, as well as Pop Green, Johnny's roommate at Stalag Luft III. As the day progressed, one after the other the remnants of the 'wood mill leave party' arrived at the Kripo station. One by one they were dragged before Gestapo agents for interrogation. While they waited for their turn, the others attempted to destroy the maps, money and other illicit resources they had on them by stuffing them down the back of a filing cabinet that stood against the wall behind the long bench where they were seated.

Johnny recorded that he was asked where the photographs in his false identity card had come from, how he had reached Hirschberg and who had travelled with him. He refused to answer any of these questions and according to his own account was not threatened or interrogated further. It was different for his friend Jimmy James who, at midnight that night, was dragged before a group of Gestapo and SS men for further interrogation, and found their manner frightening. After questioning, all of the recaptured escapees were thrown back into cells, where most of them fell into a deep sleep after their exhausting ordeal.

In the early hours of the morning, eight of the 'wood mill leave party' were aroused from their slumber and ordered into the snow-covered street outside. Each was manacled to a policeman and, formed into a line, they were ordered to shuffle their way through the night like a chain gang to the local civil prison, a gloomy old building in which they were all crammed into a dank dark cell. Despite the cold and their damp clothes, they all fell asleep immediately.

The prisoners were awoken the following morning to the sound of the barked order, 'Aufstehen, aufstehen!' (Get up, get up!) An attractive Polish girl came in with meagre fare of barely palatable ersatz coffee, and black bread with a scrape of jam. The same woman came back at midday to give them a Sunday lunch of a morsel of meat, cabbage and potatoes. Johnny kept up his comrades' spirits by leading them in a sing-along. Jimmy James recalled, 'He had been singing when he was arrested by the OGPU in south Russia in 1921 . . . Now he was singing in another repressive regime.' Some French prisoners in a nearby cell responded by singing their own uplifting songs. And for a few minutes the prison resounded to a cacophony of Anglo-French songs such as 'The White Cliffs of Dover', 'La mer', 'Alouette' and 'Son et Lumière'. They all hoped the four members of the 'wood mill leave party' who had remained at the police headquarters were safe.

The next day two civilians in a car came to take Johnny away. He was taken to a prison in a bombed-out and devastated Berlin, the sight of which at least afforded him some cheer. The prison was probably the headquarters of the Gestapo on the Prinzalbrechtstrasse, but in his post-war recollections Johnny showed no sign of recognising the notorious surroundings of the feared secret state police. Johnny remained there until the afternoon of the following day. Then he was taken by car through the rubble of Berlin's suburbs and into countryside of sparse pinewoods. After a short while the car arrived at a long narrow road with thick forest on one side and a forbidding brick wall on the other. The wall was camouflaged in dull black and green, and what looked like electrified wire ran along the top. As Johnny stepped out of the car he could see watchtowers at either end with sentries and heavy machine guns. It appeared to be a monstrous prison complex, far more ominous and menacing than anything he had experienced in his four years of German captivity. Inside he was greeted by the impassive faces of young men in jet-black uniforms bearing the insignia of a skull and crossbones, the Death's Head symbol of the Allgemeinen or Totenkopf SS, which ran concentration camps. Johnny had arrived at Sachsenhausen concentration camp near Oranienberg, one of the most notorious places in the Third Reich. For Johnny, the Great Escape was over.

What Johnny didn't realise then, but would soon come to know, was that 76 officers had managed to make it out of the tunnel. It wasn't the 200 or so that Roger Bushell had hoped for, but it was enough to make it the biggest mass break-out of the war. It tied up hundreds of thousands, if not millions, of ordinary Germans, Home Guard, policemen and soldiers looking for the escapers for many weeks, diverting valuable human resources from the war effort. Hitler was incensed and even suspected that the escape was part of a plot coordinated with British intelligence to create havoc in the run-up to the long-awaited 'second front' offensive that the

Allies were expected to launch in Normandy any day.

Unfortunately, all but three of the escapers were recaptured within a comparatively short time. Sadly, too, the escape had had even more appalling consequences for many of Johnny's friends and comrades. The Führer demanded bloody retribution. He wanted every last one of the Allied officers shot out of hand. Even the SS chief Heinrich Himmler, the evil-eyed architect of the Final Solution, blanched at this murderous demand. Air Reichsmarschall Hermann Göring feared the unblemished record of the Luftwaffe would be besmirched, and that he would join the Allies' rogues' gallery of German war criminals. Hitler was persuaded to restrain his demands. It was eventually agreed that more than half of the 76 airmen would die. The final figure settled on was 50. Included in their number was Roger Bushell.

There followed a macabre ritual in which the recaptured escapers were taken away either singly or in pairs from the Gestapo jails where they were being held. They were escorted to a quiet and discreet location where, without a word of warning, Gestapo agents would shoot them in the back of the neck—the Genickschuss—their favoured form of execution. It would take some weeks and months for the full truth to emerge. When it did, there was outrage.

DEATH POSTPONED

Sachsenhausen was a vast complex that towards the end of the war housed some 40,000 political and criminal prisoners of every nationality. The main camp was a malevolent place where prisoners were driven to their deaths through merciless work routines, or left to die through bad nourishment or medical neglect. They were often compelled to work ten- or twelve-hour shifts, given as little as four hours' sleep, and were fed on a starvation-inducing 350 grams of foul bread and watery soup a day. Brutal beatings and random killings were a feature of everyday life for the unfortunate souls who found themselves in the murderous grasp of those who ran Sachsenhausen with such medieval cruelty. Prisoners who proved incapable of work were made to stand to attention all day in the freezing snow or blazing heat, depending upon the season, without receiving so much as a morsel of bread to eat. Many were murdered in the execution area for a variety of imagined transgressions against their oppressors. Others were sadistically tortured to death. One of the most tortuous ordeals was to make malfeasants lie face down in the sandy parade ground and roll backwards and forwards for hours on end. Many decided to put an end to their misery by running into the electrified perimeter wire, which carried a 1,000-volt current.

The screams from the victims of the SS's brutality would become a constant reminder to

Johnny of the vile nature of the regime he was fighting. But mercifully the compound into which he was shown at Sachsenhausen was a comparatively benign affair, attached to but separate from the main complex. Sonderlager A (special compound A) was some 80 yards long by 40 wide, separated from the main camp by a 12-foot-high electrified fence. It contained just two long wooden huts parallel to this wire. The other three sides of the compound were guarded by two electrified wires, between which SS guards patrolled with their vicious hounds.

The sandy soil sparsely covered by grass and interspersed with a dozen fir trees gave the impression, one inmate observed, of the wolves' enclosure at Whipsnade Zoo. In fact it was a compound for VIP prisoners held for a variety of reasons, not least as potential hostages in the event of the Reich collapsing. Next door to Sonderlager A was the slightly bigger Sonderlager B, another special VIP prison compound, which even boasted small villas for some of its more distinguished prisoners. Among them were the former Austrian chancellor Kurt von Schuschnigg and the German plutocrat Fritz Thyssen who had bankrolled Hitler's regime before falling foul of the dictator. These two Sonderlagers were an oasis of civility compared to the hell on earth that existed on the other side of the fence in the main Sachsenhausen camp.

When Johnny was shown into 'Sonderlager A' he found himself among an intriguing collection of casualties of war. There were two Russian generals—the colourful and crude Ivan Georgio Bessanov and the elegant and refined Piotr Privalov, a Russian lieutenant colonel by the name of Viktor Brodnikov, and their orderly, a cheerful Red Army private, Fiodr Ceridilin. There were two Polish RAF pilots shot down dropping agents and supplies over Poland, and their orderlies—two Italian regular army soldiers, Bartoli and Amichi, who had once worked in their country's Berlin Embassy. (The latter was a cousin of the Hollywood actor Don Ameche.)

There were also four British soldiers of Irish origin, Thomas Cushing, Patrick O'Brien, John Spence and Andy Walsh. These four men were a curious bunch. Spence had worked in Berlin for the Nazi's Irish-language wireless station broadcasting propaganda. He was treated as a stool-pigeon by the others. The other three had also volunteered to work for the Germans and had spent some time in Berlin being trained in sabotage warfare. The plan to drop them back in Britain on various missions was, however, dropped for one reason or another. The men insisted they had been ordered to take up this work by their commanding officer, who envisaged it as a cunning way of double-crossing the Germans. It would appear that after the war the authorities accepted their version of events, not least because their commanding officer confirmed it. But during their stay in Sachsenhausen it led to their being treated, understandably, with a modicum of suspicion by the British officers.

Johnny found that the most senior British member of Sonderlager A was Captain Peter Churchill, an agent of the Special Operations Executive. Churchill had been caught at Annecy with his courier, known as Odette, on his fourth mission into occupied France. They pretended to be a married couple and he claimed to be related to

284

Winston Churchill, hoping to save both of them from torture or death. The ruse had half-worked. Despite being confined in Paris's dreadful Fresnes prison and interrogated several times by the Gestapo, Churchill was never tortured. Odette fared less well, however. She too was sent to Fresnes, but was tortured, and subsequently she was sent to Ravensbrück concentration camp where the ill-treatment was intensified. She did, however, survive the war and probably would not have done so had it not been for Churchill's actions.

Johnny shared a room with Churchill in the hut alongside the foreign contingent. It must have been a joy for him to share his accommodation with such a refined Englishman. He must nevertheless have felt a somewhat isolated figure, adrift from the old friends he had spent so much of the war with. However, he did not have to wait long before some more familiar faces began turning up at Sachsenhausen. The first, to his joy, was Wings Day. Johnny learnt that his old friend had managed to get as far as the Baltic port of Stettin with his escape partner, a dashing young Polish Spitfire pilot called Peter Tobolski. The two men were comfortably ensconced in a relatively open French prisoner-of-war barracks and awaiting a ship to Sweden and freedom when they were betrayed to the local police by an informer.

They had both been brought to Berlin but separated, before Wings was sent for interrogation at the Gestapo's Prinzalbrechtstrasse head-quarters—probably the same place Johnny had been taken to. Wings said he had felt uneasy when 'Tob' saluted him 'goodbye'. Perhaps Tobolski, wearily familiar with Nazi racial dogma, had more than an inkling of what might lie in store for him. But Wings seems to have been completely oblivious to the fate that awaited the youthful Polish flier. In the Gestapo's feared Prinzalbrechtstrasse building, Wings was ushered into the presence of one of the most curious figures of Hitler's Nazi Reich. SS Gruppenführer Artur Nebe is a character who will be encountered later, briefly, in this narrative. He had already played a murderous part in the events surrounding the Great Escape, though Wings was not to know it on the cold October day he arrived at the Prinzalbrechtstrasse to be introduced to him. Nebe might not have been an unsympathetic personality, but in the shadows and fog of Hitler's Third Reich it is difficult to say.

An early supporter of National Socialism, and a passionate advocate of effective policing (he implemented pioneering and imaginative initiatives), Nebe had enjoyed swift promotion in the Berlin police force under Hitler's regime. He was an early member of the party and of the SS. However, it is said that Nebe rapidly became disillusioned with Nazism when he was ordered to take part in some of the more unsavoury aspects of Hitler's reign of terror. These include early bloodletting campaigns to 'liquidate' Hitler's rivals, and the subsequent mass Einsatzgruppen killings in the east during the onslaught upon Soviet Russia.

Nebe, like so many functionaries of totalitarian states, was adept at playing it both ways. He is said to have come to loathe his superiors Reinhard Heydrich and Heinrich Himmler, yet he continued to have lunch with them and be outwardly deferential to them. It is not surprising that when he met Wings Day at the Gestapo's

286

Prinzalbrechtstrasse headquarters he did not mention his role in the recent killing of 50 of the RAF wing commander's comrades. The order had come direct from Himmler standing next to Hitler at his Berchtesgaden alpine retreat. Of the 76 escapees, 50 were to be summarily executed. Nebe had been responsible for deciding which of the 76 would die. It had been an unsettling task, totally against the strictures of the Geneva Convention. But Nebe could not possibly let Day know exactly where his sympathies lay in the unfolding drama of the Third Reich: that he, Nebe, was actually actively assisting the German resistance movement. He was implicated in the 20 July plot to assassinate Hitler. Instead, Nebe warned Day that he had been a perpetual troublemaker during his captivity in the Reich, and he was finally being sent to a place from which there would be no escape.

Shortly after Wings arrived in Sachsenhausen, Johnny and he were joined by two more Sagan escapers, first Jimmy James and then Sydney Dowse. James had almost made it to Czechoslovakia with his companion, a Greek flier called Sortiros 'Nick' Skanziklas. They had been defeated by the extreme cold when attempting to cross the appropriately named Riesengebirge, the giant mountain range that separated Czechoslovakia from Germany. Sydney Dowse had almost made it to Poland with his partner Stanislaw 'Danny' Krol (one of the architects of the 'Tom', 'Dick' and 'Harry' tunnels). But Dowse and Krol were discovered and handed over to the Gestapo. Both James and Dowse had been separated from their escape partners under spurious pretexts. It would be some weeks before they would discover the fate of their companions.

The new arrivals were given rooms in the empty second hut in Sonderlager A, but they messed in Peter Churchill's room, served by the Italian orderlies Bartoli and Amichi. In Sachsenhausen the British were classed as political prisoners and were not allowed to receive or send letters. Neither Johnny's wife Minerva nor his mother Flora received any news of what happened to him after the escape. The War Office, however, in an attempt to cheer Minerva up suggested that 'no news was good news'.

The new captives had each separately been assured by their jailers that the only way out of Sachsenhausen was up the crematorium chimney that belched out its foul smoke night and day. Yet this served more to strengthen their resolve than weaken it. Sydney Dowse was the first new prisoner to be caught in a supreme act of subordination. The compound was ringed with warning posts bearing the SS's Death's Head emblem of the skull and cross bones. One day Dowse had cheekily turned these symbols around. This act provoked the fury of the camp commandant Standartenführer Anton Kaindl who demanded the presence of Dowse's commanding officer. It was Wings' first encounter with Kaindl who warned him in no uncertain terms that to attempt to escape from SS captivity in Sachsenhausen was futile. The guards could not be bribed, the barbed wire was thick and electrified and patrolled by vicious dogs, and there were sensors deep beneath the ground that would set off alarm lights in the guard room at the slightest indication of tunnelling. Wings sympathised with Kaindl, believing that Dowse's action had been an infantile act of insubordination that the young lieutenant should not have perpetrated. Subsequently, Wings attested, 'The Death's Head is the SS Crest & should not be fiddled with with impunity,' noting that one of Britain's Hussar regiments had the Death's Head as its insignia.

However, Wings took offence at the tenor of Kaindl's remarks. It was after this interview with Sachsenhausen's commandant that Wings told his men, 'I feel very strongly that we as RAF are being insulted, defamed or what have you by these SS types.' He added, curiously, 'I also include the Luftwaffe with us.' (It was an odd comment to make and reinforces the view that the Luftwaffe and RAF saw themselves as very much part of a superior caste above the hoi polloi of ordinary servicemen and, certainly, Nazis.) He continued, even more curiously, 'We & the Luftwaffe have been struggling together for 5 years. They certainly know their job. Therefore for the honour of the RAF & Luftwaffe let's see if we can make a break.' He told Dowse and the other flight lieutenant, Jimmy James, to go off and explore the possibility of excavating a tunnel. The two had returned within the hour to present their report.

It did not take James and Dowse long to plot a course for their putative endeavour. An empty compound stood between the Sonderlager and the road outside Sachsenhausen. It was strewn with the evidence of an abandoned building site including, incredibly, a ladder lying discarded close to the wall that separated the camp from the outside world. The plan was to build a simple tunnel into this compound and use the ladder to climb over the wall.

The tunnel they proposed would be 2 feet square and 115 feet long. It would be built 10 feet down, and it would have to do without the security of wooden boards to prop it up. It would be tunnelled out using nothing more than knives and spoons, the only tools available to the men. The soil to be dispersed would be packed into an S-shaped trench dug beneath the barrack block. It would be an extraordinary accomplishment if they could do it. But the arrogance of their SS guards proved to be one of their greatest assets. Heinrich Himmler's villainous foot soldiers paid little attention to their British and other VIP prisoners, convinced, no doubt, that the fear the SS struck into other men's hearts would be sufficient to deter any escape attempt.

THE SACHSENHAUSEN TUNNEL

Construction of the tunnel began around about May 1944. Jimmy James and Sydney Dowse, the youngest men among the British prisoners, and the smallest and nimblest, did the digging. Wings organised the security and gathered intelligence about conditions outside, railway timetables, possible underground contact and so on. Johnny was quite happy to help with the digging, but the others feared he was too large and bulky to be efficient. And he was such a larger-than-life character with the foreign prisoners that his absence would not go unnoticed. Johnny's task, therefore, was to be as conspicuous as possible above the surface to allay any suspicions of the SS guards. He did this mainly by playing deck tennis with Captain Churchill and two of the Irishmen, Sergeant Thomas Cushing and Private Patrick O'Brien, outside the hut where the tunnel was being dug.

The tunnel was still in its infancy when the camp heard the electrifying news of the D-Day landings. It was on 7 June that Wings read in the *Völkischer Beobachter* (*The People's Observer*—the Nazi party newspaper) about the opening of the long-awaited second front, the Allied assault on Hitler's 'impregnable' Fortress Europe. A frisson of excitement shot through the camp. The British prisoners celebrated with a feast of grilled sparrows, caught and cooked by their Italian orderlies. It was some time later that Wings picked up another copy of the *Völkischer Beobachter* and read less happy news. The report was of a speech made by Anthony Eden in the House of Commons. The Foreign Secretary had condemned the Germans for the murders of Allied airmen in the escape from Stalag Luft III. The slant of the report was somewhat sarcastic, comparing the deaths of the airmen 'while escaping' with the many thousands of German civilians slaughtered daily in Allied bombing raids. It was the first inkling the prisoners had had of the fate of their escape companions.

Johnny and the others were separated from one of the Nazi regime's most notorious death camps by nothing more than a wire fence. They could see and hear odious atrocities being committed every day. Yet the death of their erstwhile companions still came as a dreadful jolt to them. They might have been comforted somewhat had they seen a story in the *London Evening Standard* from the previous month. It reported that on 20 June 1944, a service of remembrance was held at St Martin-in-the-Fields church in Trafalgar Square for the 50 escapees murdered by the Gestapo. Sir Charles Portal, Marshal of the RAF, read the lesson from the flower-decked pulpit. The organ was played by an RAF sergeant, and there was a massed choir of RAF men and WAAFs. The RAF string band played on the altar steps. All the Allied and Dominion governments were represented, and parents, wives, children and sweethearts of the dead filed into the church past an RAF guard of honour. Sir Charles said, 'In the sight of the unwise they seemed to die and their departure is taken for misery, and their going from us to be utter destruction; but they are in peace.'

The *London Evening Standard* reported:

There was a note of calm, proud triumph throughout the ceremony. The relatives, grey-haired women, young widows, schoolgirls with plaited hair and schoolboys in flannel shirts, all looked proud. They held their heads high. There was triumph in the swelling music of Elgar. Triumph in the shrill of the violins. Triumph in the voices of the choir as they sang, 'For all their Saints who from their labours rest'.

The Reverend J.A. Jagoe, Chaplain-in-Chief of the RAF, was quoted as saying, 'It has been truly said of them that they did their duty twice over. They strove to be masters of their fate, captains of their destiny.'

It would be years before the full truth about the murders was known. Hitler ordered that every last one of the seventy-six escapers should be shot the moment they were recaptured. Hermann Göring, however, feared that such an outrage might produce a reciprocal action from the British. Thus the compromise was reached whereby a random 50 would be killed. The so-called Sagan Order was issued by SS Chief Obergruppenführer Dr Ernst Kaltenbrunner and stated that circumstances should be arranged to make it appear that the 50 had been shot while resisting arrest. General Arthur Nebe, the SS general who had interrogated Wings at the Gestapo's Albrechtstrasse head-quarters, was charged with deciding which of the

76 should live or die. Johnny and his companions found themselves alive and well in Sachsenhausen because the Sagan Order stipulated that 'prominent personalities will be excepted: their names will be reported to me and a decision awaited'.

Wings had presumably been saved because he was the Senior British Officer, and Johnny because of his distant kinship with Churchill. Dowse speculated that some of his ancestors came from a prominent German dynasty and maybe that was why he was not shot. But Jimmy James, until his dying day, had no idea why he was included on the list of *Prominenten*. The fact that he had already escaped 12 times from German captivity might have qualified him to be classified as some sort of special prisoner.

There was a curious twist to the murders of the 50, which would be enacted in Sachsenhausen in the forthcoming weeks—though Johnny and his comrades were probably not aware of it. It happened after the 20 July plot to assassinate Hitler, when Colonel Claus von Stauffenberg planted a bomb near the Führer in the conference room of his eastern headquarters. Among the plotters who were rounded up after the plan failed was Artur Nebe. Nebe was sent for his sins to Sachsenhausen, where he was strung up by piano wire. Artur Nebe's story is a complicated and intriguing one, and illustrates that not all was black and white in the dreadful totalitarian regime that was Hitler's Germany.

On reading the news of the murders, Wings summoned the other British officers and advised them that if they escaped and were recaptured they would almost certainly be shot this time. They decided to press on regardless. In his own unpublished memoir, Peter Churchill commented:

> Instead of thanking their lucky stars that the mad rage of Hitler had somehow passed them by, or perhaps because they felt that this new lease of life had been unaccountably given them for a special purpose, it was precisely at this moment that they unanimously decided to show their captors to what extent they were cowed by this vile inhuman example of butchery, by escaping.

They were assisted immeasurably in their resolve by the arrival in mid July of a fearless British commando in Sonderlager A. Lieutenant Colonel Jack Churchill had been captured on an island off the Dalmatian coast. Mistaken by the SS for Randolph Churchill, the prime minister's son, 'Mad' Jack had been kept for some weeks in the elite VIP compound of Sonderlager B next door to Sonderlager A. He had lived in a villa next to those of Kurt von Schuschnigg and Fritz Thyssen and their retinues. 'Mad' Jack had trenchantly insisted that he had nothing to do with the more famous Churchill. Eventually the SS believed him and he was 'demoted' to Sonderlager A. No sooner had he arrived than he was on the digging team with James and Dowse. Remarkably, and luckily, the almost constant Allied bombing raids on Berlin and its environs, which shook the earth every time they happened, failed to have the slightest effect on the tunnel. It was completed by the middle of September. The plan was to go out on the next moonless night.

It would not be entirely true to say that the men went ahead with their plans without hesitation. For in September 1944 the Allied successes in France made it perfectly plausible that the war would be over by Christmas. The thought that it might, just possibly, be folly to risk almost certain death when victory was barely weeks away certainly crossed Johnny's mind, according to Peter Churchill:

> The Major who was a man of balanced views with a first class position awaiting his return to England not to mention a lovely family and house, was in quite a dilemma. If he stayed he would miss the unique opportunity of cocking a snoot at the S.S. There was much of the truant in the Major's make-up and this spirit had not been damped in the least . . .

Johnny might have wavered in his determination to escape, but not for long.

There remained one obstacle to overcome, and one arrangement to be made. The first problem was to get Johnny removed from the hut he shared with Peter Churchill and the foreign VIPs so that he could be in the hut occupied by his friends Wings and James et al from which the tunnel led out to the wire. The prisoners were locked up in their respective huts after supper and it would be impossible for Johnny to get between the two after lights out. Thus he wrote to the camp commander, Kaindl, asking whether he could be transferred. He pointed out that as an 'old' man of 50, he enjoyed the peace and quiet. He found it difficult to sleep in his own hut and noted that the other had far more space so he should be able to find a quiet corner.

Luckily, Kaindl gave his assent.

The next task was to arrange the escape to time, if at all possible, with 'Jim's' night on duty. 'Jim' was a guard commander who was heartily loathed by everyone in the compound. A loud-mouthed sergeant, he was a typical product of the Nazi regime, whereas the other guard commander, 'George' (whose real name was Hans-Peter Raffel), was a pleasant-spoken man who spent his time on duty seeing that the inmates were given every comfort to which they were entitled. 'If there was anything that would add flavour to this already spicy enterprise it was the idea of Jim . . . being court-martialled for negligence while on duty.' By a stroke of good fortune the next moonless night was 23 September, which happened to be Jim's night on duty. It was also Jack Churchill's birthday. The five escapers and Peter Churchill planned to hold a party to celebrate Jack's birthday.

The men had hoped that the night of their escape would be a rainy one. The noise of hard rain would mask the unavoidable sounds made by breaking out of the tunnel, and would have the equally fortuitous effect of dampening the spirits of the goons exposed to the elements in the watchtowers. They were disappointed, therefore, when for three weeks before their break-out date, the weather had been fine. And they were delighted when, as they settled down to Jack's birthday supper, the roof of their hut began drubbing to the sound of driving rain. Their Italian cooks laid on a special feast in honour of the occasion and it was a 'gay party', recorded Peter Churchill. At around 10 p.m., Jim turned up to take the Italians and Peter back to their own quarters, and the latter shook each man's hand more firmly than he would normally have done as he bade them farewell.

That night in his hut, Peter Churchill lay in bed listening to the familiar noises that always disturbed the night air in Sachsenhausen.

All the sounds that night being made were well known: allied bombers overhead, exploding bombs, anti aircraft fire, dogs barking, the shouting of German guards, the burst of machine gun fire aimed at some unhappy wretch outside the huts in the Concentration Camp, the screams of men electrocuted on the wire and other ghastly noises.

He prayed he would not hear the sounds of shooting before midnight when his friends were due to break out.

31

ESCAPE FROM THE SS

As soon as 'Jim' had departed, locking the hut behind him, Jimmy James and Sydney Dowse disappeared down the tunnel to open the exit hatch at its far end. In those last moments of so many months of hard work, each man had a chance to review his escape plans. Wings Day was going to team up with Sydney Dowse and try to link up with a member of the Todt organisation in Berlin. The Todt organisation was the giant private conglomerate that had constructed much of the infrastructure of Hitler's 1,000-year Reich, from the new autobahns that spread across Germany, to the concrete defences along the coast of France that protected 'Fortress Europe'. Todt lorries and buses carrying raw materials and workers were endlessly criss-crossing the continent. Wings and Dowse had heard from one of the Irishmen that it was possible to bribe the drivers to take illicit passengers. Andy Walsh supplied them with an address in a pleasant suburb of Berlin where a contact with links to the Todt organisation might arrange for them to be smuggled aboard one such transport, and driven closer to where the Allied armies were advancing in the west. They were hoping to get the last S-Bahn train from the local station near the camp, which left just before midnight. Jimmy James was going out with Jack Churchill and they were to head for a Baltic port, preferably Rostock, or possibly one in Denmark, and try to stow away on board a ship bound for neutral Sweden. Johnny had the simplest plan. He was going to 'hard-arse' it, travelling in a westerly direction, probably along railway routes, trying to find a quiet place to lie low until the Allies arrived.

There was a reason why Johnny found himself without a partner—besides the awkward arithmetic of having the odd number of five escapers. The unspoken truth was that none of the others wanted to risk pairing up with such a well-known liability. Because of his physical bulk, Johnny was an easily identifiable target. And he didn't do much to help ameliorate the situation. He could not speak a word of German despite many months of trying and, more recently, much patient tutoring on the part of Peter Churchill. He was blithely indifferent to the risks he faced, making no serious plans nor constructing a realistic cover story. He relied too much on his natural charm and lady luck. As Wings Day confided, a little wistfully, many years later to his biographer Sydney Smith, 'Not even among themselves did the others put their feelings into words, but they all felt that the Dodger, with his earnest simplicity, his radiant faith in things good, right and just, was a bad escape risk. He believed so profoundly in his right to succeed in doing the decent and proper thing that his planning was somewhat left to the gods.' Nobody wanted to hazard being jinxed by Johnny's happy-go-lucky approach to life.

Jimmy James and Sydney Dowse were down the tunnel for more time than was comfortable for those left waiting in the hut. The three others were beginning to imagine that something was awry when, much to their relief, the two young lieutenants finally emerged from the black hole, their faces and clothes covered in dirt. They blamed a last-minute hiccup for the delay. Quickly, they washed the filth off their naked bodies and donned clean clothes. All the men had civilian disguises and some cash but none of the panoply of bogus papers that the X Organisation had provided them with in Sagan. They each had fashioned satchels out of old cloth and in them carried a modest supply of food and odds and ends planned to see them through three weeks. When they were ready, all five of the escapers lowered themselves one by one into the narrow opening of the tunnel. James and Dowse went first, followed by Churchill and Wings. Johnny was last, pulling the trap door behind him as he squeezed his bulky form down into the gloom. Each of the men pulled his satchel behind him.

Their progress along the impossibly narrow tunnel was far from easy. The last three men found the going considerably more claustrophobic and suffocating than the two younger men who had preceded them and who had left a trail of fallen sand in their wake. It was a terrifying experience, Wings admitted later. Much to his relief and after what seemed an interminable journey, he and Churchill finally scrambled out of the exit hatch into the open and the refreshing September breeze.

For Johnny the experience was even worse. He was half as big again as any of the other men and so the tunnel seemed even more tortuously constricting. His progress was slow and laborious. Finally, in a reprise of his Dulag Luft and Sagan experiences, he became stuck, this time halfway out of the exit hole. He could only manage to get his head out and one hand while his other hand trailed

301

behind him clinging on to his bag of provisions. Above ground Wings Day and Jack Churchill desperately pulled on Johnny's free arm in an attempt to yank him out of the ground. For a few grim minutes they achieved no success whatsoever. They began to think that perhaps it would not be possible to get their friend out of the hole. Johnny was caught like a squashed mole. After ten minutes of pulling, they finally dragged him out of the mouth of the tunnel. 'Ah! Free at last!' he blurted out in a stage whisper, typical of his sangfroid. The other two were appalled and ducked instinctively. They were convinced that a cackle of machine-gun fire in their direction would be the only reply to Johnny's incautious cry of triumph. But miraculously the expected burst of ordnance did not come. The watchtower looming over them in the near distance appeared oblivious to their presence.

Wings and Churchill were utterly relieved. Quickly they pulled Johnny to his feet and all three of them dashed across the unoccupied compound. In the gloom they found the discarded ladder, which had been left by James and Dowse propped against the wall. They were quickly over the top and joined the other two men on the other side. Dropping to the ground they were elated to find themselves at last out of the bleak surroundings of Sachsenhausen. After the last few minutes of fear and the near-disaster of Johnny's getting stuck, the escape had turned out to be spectacular in its sheer simplicity. But none of the men was deceived about the ease of the task ahead of each of them. They were anxious to put as many miles as possible between them and the camp, hoping, if everything went according to plan, that their absence would not be discovered until 7 a.m. the next day.

Churchill and James set off first, heading in one direction; the others wished them luck. The remaining three stayed together for a while, skirting along the side of the camp walls until they reached the end. Wings' and Dowse's route to the S-Bahn suburban train station was to the south; Johnny planned to head westwards to the main railway line at Oranienburg. They turned to one another to say their goodbyes. 'Take care of yourself, Major,' said Wings to Johnny. 'The main railway line should be about a mile straight ahead.' It was with a pang of remorse and, perhaps, guilt that Wings watched his friend disappear into the night. Wings knew he had deserted him. Johnny vanished into the darkness. Wings and Dowse continued to walk along the perimeter fence, huddled against the night cold, only to find themselves following in the footsteps of two SS soldiers obviously patrolling the outer wall. The four men were abreast of one another when the unfortunate coincidence dawned upon all of them. 'I noticed out of the corner of my eye that they woke up to our presence,' wrote Day. 'Before they entangled [*sic*] any of their armament from their capes etc., we were well away in the rain sodden darkness.' Day speculated that the two SS soldiers would be disinclined to report the encounter, especially once the escape became known the next morning.

In the meantime, Johnny made his way to Oranienburg station and the main railway line to Rostock. It must have been a disconcerting experience to be alone for the first time after many years of being surrounded by so many other prisoners and friends. His principal concern during his escape was to avoid any contact at all, and particularly verbal contact, with Germans. Despite many months of earnestly inspecting various German language and phrase books, Johnny had found he simply had no facility for languages. He carried in his pocket a small German phrase book that he would have to depend upon in emergencies. Fortunately, he had barely arrived at the railway line at the station when a train came into sight. He saw the lights of a level crossing, slipped underneath it and walked by the side of the slowly moving train. By the time it had passed him, Johnny had passed Oranienburg, using the train for cover, and he breathed a sigh of relief having overcome a small but important obstacle. He headed north towards a distant Rostock.

Johnny walked at a reasonably brisk pace for two hours when, presently, he came to another station. Weighing up in his mind whether to bypass it by some circuitous route or go straight through, laziness got the better of him and he unwisely chose the latter course of action. His mistake was brought home to him when the silence of the night was suddenly broken by a German voice challenging him. Johnny was crestfallen. Vainly trying to articulate one of the scores of German phrases he had spent months learning by heart, he failed to utter anything but unintelligible gibberish. Luck, as ever, was on his side. When the German challenger in the darkness before him next spoke, Johnny could just about understand that he was directing him to a French labour camp. He must have presumed Johnny was a foreign worker. Mumbling another selection of unintelligible phrases Johnny

304

made off in the correct direction. He soon found himself in some beautiful wooded country with lakes either side of him. Thankfully, at that moment, the rain stopped.

He bided his time for a few hours. Some two hours before dawn he had found the railway line again and to his delight saw the red tail-light of a stationary goods train. He approached the red lights, this time cautiously. There was not a soul in sight. Sauntering past the rear truck he scrambled aboard the next one along. Within moments the train began to move forward. It was almost too good to be true. Soon he was trundling along at a fair pace. It must have been some 30 miles later and just before dawn that the train came to a halt. Johnny waited to make sure the coast was clear before jumping off and making his getaway into the surrounding countryside. His plan was to lie low during daylight hours and resume his escape at dusk.

Fortunately for him he soon found an ideal hideout in marshland surrounded by trees where he was sure no interloper would venture and disturb him. Johnny was completely hidden from view by the reeds. He was soaked to the bone and cold but far from miserable. Far from it. He counted himself lucky to have put so much distance between himself and Sachsenhausen on his first night. That day he managed to sleep a little and eat some of his provisions, admiring as he did so the many varieties of birds and cows that shared his countryside idyll.

When nightfall came, Johnny headed back to the station where he had left the goods train that morning. He hoped he would enjoy similar luck to the night before and find another train conveniently

305

waiting for him with no observers around. But luck had abandoned him. As he approached the station a German voice cried out. Johnny slipped into some nearby bushes, crouching and keeping perfectly still. But the German continued to shout at him and a powerful light was shone in Johnny's direction. Feeling its inquisitive ray fall upon him, Johnny took to his heels and ran as fast as his feet would take him. He headed back for the sanctuary of the marsh and reeds, a cacophony of shouting voices following behind him in hot pursuit. Thankfully, the darkness seemed to confuse his pursuers and their voices grew ever more distant. Nevertheless, for peace of mind, Johnny continued to run for another mile and a half or so. By then it had begun to pour down with rain again, and worse, was blowing a gale. Johnny spent the rest of the night sheltering under a hedge soaked to the skin and a little chastened.

When daylight came once more, Johnny could see the railway in the far distance. He decided to take a chance and began warily walking along it. His pursuers of the night before were nowhere to be seen. The morning turned out to be bright and sunny and Johnny thought it wise to take the opportunity to dry his sopping clothes. Finding a suitably discreet location, he stripped off and spread them over a hedge. Naked, he lay down in the grass and basked in the unseasonably warm sunshine for three hours or so until his clothes were as dry as they could be in the circumstances.

At about 6 p.m. he decided to move on and when walking along a road encountered a lone individual coming in the opposite direction. To his relief the man turned out to be a French prisoner of war.

A weekly walk with the enemy. The Luftwaffe's chief interrogator at Dulag Luft, Sonderführer Heinrich Eberhardt, sharing a convivial drink with unidentified officers, 1940. (courtesy of Alice Berkeley)

Johnny and Wings on an outing near Dulag
Luft. Johnny's handwritten note on the back of
the photograph reads: 'At a restaurant on one
of our weekly walks. I am next Wing
Commander Day with my back to the camera.'
(courtesy of Alice Berkeley)

Another lazy restaurant jaunt in 1940. (courtesy
of Alice Berkeley)

A convivial lunch on one of their weekly walks, Johnny in beard and smoking pipe. (courtesy of Alice Berkeley)

Johnny in expansive mood on a weekly walk. (courtesy of Alice Berkeley)

Sonderführer
Heinrich
Eberhardt strikes
a friendly pose.
(courtesy of
Alice Berkeley)

Eberhardt and
Feldwebel
Hermann
Glemnitz pose
for the camera.
(courtesy of
Alice Berkeley)

Christmas dinner, 1940, at Dulag Luft. They could almost be at home in England. (courtesy of Alice Berkeley)

Johnny (far left) with (l–r) Wing Commander Williams, his best friend Wings Day and Wing Commander 'Hetty' Hyde at Stalag Luft III. (courtesy of Alice Berkeley)

Johnny at Stalag Luft III with Pop Green, with whom he shared a room in Hut 104 next to the room from which the tunnel 'Harry' was constructed. (courtesy of Alice Berkeley)

Johnny outside his room in Hut 104, with Roger Bushell, the South African RAF officer who became 'Big X' and masterminded the Great Escape. (courtesy of Alice Berkeley)

Ploughing the snow at Stalag Luft III.
(courtesy of Alice Berkeley)

With Flora and family in quieter times.
(courtesy of Jane Aitken)

Johnny in skipper's outfit. (courtesy of Jane
Aitken)

They greeted one another warmly. In his schoolboy French Johnny explained who he was, and the Frenchman said he would like to help him. He directed Johnny to a barn on the other side of a quiet village and told him to wait there until the Frenchman could arrange help. Some time later the Frenchman turned up with two others bearing a haversack of food and bottles of milk and coffee. They told him to hide in the loft and stay well out of sight. This was the beginning of a remarkable four weeks that Johnny would spend free, thanks on the whole to the Frenchman and his friends.

By then all hell had been let loose in the Sonderlager at Sachsenhausen. The morning guard in Sonderlager A had opened the huts at the usual time of 7 a.m. When it was discovered that the prisoners were missing, pandemonium broke out. The guards of the new shift thanked their lucky stars that they had not been on duty the previous night, presuming—rightly—that the punishment for their negligent predecessors would be a swift dispatch to the Eastern Front. Cheers rippled around the camp, and the Russian officers in particular roared with laughter. The news reached the other side of the fence into the main Sachsenhausen camp, and even there some inmates did not disguise the joy they felt. The Gestapo were quickly on the scene and interrogating everyone they could lay their hands on.

When news of the escape reached the authorities, the head of the Criminal Police issued a 'wanted' bulletin that was distributed all over the Reich. It described the five men. Johnny was said to be 185 centimetres tall, with 'brown hair, broad face, egg-shaped head, hooked nose, healthy complexion, dirty slightly coloured teeth'. The bulletin warned, 'The apprehension of these escapees is of the greatest importance . . . Search is to be made of the whole of the Reich and all countries occupied by Germany. A sharp watch is to be kept at all frontier controls.'

Oblivious to the furore he had left behind him, Johnny was sheltering in the warm and comfortable surrounds of his new home. He had learnt that the little village nearby was called Beilershof. Johnny supplied a full report of his escape to Peter Churchill who, in an unpublished account entitled 'Escape from the SS', describes an almost idyllic sojourn that Johnny enjoyed for the next few weeks. Churchill wrote:

> It was a delightful spot in which to await the arrival of the allied armies. At night, under the moon, the deer would come out and browse under the barn. In the daytime, through slits in the beams, he could contemplate a splendid herd of Holstein cattle which pastured in a beautiful open meadow close by. Further off a flock of geese waddled around the farm buildings. People passed to and fro all day long and the changing scene was a constant delight to the Major. His French companions had taken a liking to him and looked after his needs with unfailing regularity and kindness. He called them the Three Musketeers.

Sadly, Johnny's peaceful reverie came to an abrupt end when a Polish worker happened upon him in an unexpected moment. Johnny tried to hide but it was too late. The Pole was as surprised by the encounter as he was. He promised Johnny that he would not tell a soul about his presence in the barn. However, when the Three Musketeers turned up some hours later their good humour had abandoned them and this time they were angry with Johnny. They told him that the Pole had promptly told his wife about the Englishman sheltering in the barn and by now the whole village was aware of his hiding place. With no time to spare the three Frenchmen moved Johnny to a different location— another barn in another village—some five kilometres away. But sadly, the Pole's indiscretion was the beginning of the end for Johnny, who had only himself to blame.

That night his French protectors took him to a local *estaminet*. There, he enjoyed the company of 15 or so other Frenchmen crammed into the tiny café-bar. The German bartender, fortunately, was stone deaf and appeared completely indifferent to the English escaped prisoner in his midst. Over the next few hours they drank a great deal of beer and became increasingly noisy and boisterous. After years of living in the dim and dark surroundings of various prison camps, Johnny was amazed by the bright lights blazing away in the little hostelry. They listened to the BBC on a wireless and enlisted Johnny's help in attempting to translate the news for them. At the news of each Allied advance they cheered ecstatically. Unfortunately, the news did not bode well for Johnny, because soon virtually everyone in the surrounding vicinity knew about him: including the local police chief.

Yet inexplicably he remained unmolested by the authorities in his new barn for several more days. Every day some local Russian prisoners of war would arrive at his new hiding place and leave him some fresh milk and food, and warm water with which he could wash and shave. Soon, however, after another incautious episode on Johnny's part, another local began talking too much. The Three Musketeers moved him back to his previous hiding place in the barn near Beilershof. Johnny was comfortably ensconced there—studying his German phrase book—when he heard an unmistakably German voice shout, '*Kommen Sie mit!*' He peered out and saw a farmer holding a Luger pointed at him.

The farmer was courteous enough to Johnny but was standing for no nonsense. He marched his prisoner out into the open and eventually the chief of police turned up on his bicycle. The policeman, Pierre Risch, who came from Luxembourg, sympathised with Johnny and told him that he had known of his presence in the vicinity for three weeks. Risch showed Johnny the Police Gazette leaflet that gave his description. He didn't handcuff Johnny, but asked him, 'Is there anything I can do for you while you wait in the local cells for the Sachsenhausen guards to arrive?' Johnny replied, 'Yes.' He asked if the policeman would let the Red Cross know the names of the Allied officers imprisoned in Sachsenhausen. Risch agreed to do so. Shortly afterwards, the Sachsenhausen officials arrived to take Johnny back. It was 23 October, and Johnny, though handcuffed all the way, enjoyed the beautiful views of the countryside basking in autumn weather as he was driven back to the camp.

MISSION TO DOWNING STREET

If Johnny's first impression of Sachsenhausen had
been depressing, his return to its grim environs was
even less encouraging. He was taken straight to
solitary confinement in a formidable concrete
compound called the Zellenbau. The Zellenbau
was within the perimeters of the main part of the
concentration camp—the part where inmates were
treated abominably and worked to death if not
executed outright—not in the more comfortable
surroundings of one of the two Sonderlagers
reserved for 'VIP' prisoners of Himmler's SS. The
Zellenbau—or 'cell block'—of Sachsenhausen had
something of a mixed reputation. There are those
who have portrayed it as a veritable torture
chamber known as the 'death block' because so few
who entered it ever emerged alive. Others have
painted a more rosy picture in which 'the Bunker'—
as it was also called—was more akin to a boarding
house than a prison block in one of Nazi Germany's
most notorious concentration camps. In fact, in the
early days of the war, the Zellenbau appears to
have witnessed its fair share of beatings and
murders. But towards the end of 1944 when Johnny
was incarcerated there, it had become a more
civilised place.

A high-security, single-storey, T-shaped structure
next to the punishment blocks and Kommandantura,
the Zellenbau contained eighty cells along three long
corridors. Some were more like the well-appointed

rooms that a monk might occupy in a monastery or such as might be found in a modest hotel. Many were positively luxurious—by wartime standards—and a few had been knocked into two or three rooms to make suites with separate toilets and living rooms for their distinguished occupants. These occupants ranged from high-ranking German generals who had defied Hitler's orders to foreign dignitaries of countries allied to, or overrun by, the Germans; relatives of Hungarian, Italian and Russian leaders; and British spies. One of the Zellenbau's longest residents was Sigismund Payne Best, the British intelligence officer who had been kidnapped by the Germans in the notorious 'Venlo Incident' on the Dutch frontier orchestrated by SS Brigadeführer Dr Walter Schellenberg. Best—to illustrate how the better half lived—had his own electric cooker and shelves of books made especially for him (by his alleged co-conspirator Georg Elser, the Munich Bürgerbraukeller bomber who lived down the corridor). Best was also provided with a magnificent wardrobe for his collection of beautifully tailored suits, which the SS had thoughtfully rescued for him from his home in the Netherlands, and a wireless set on which he frequently listened to the BBC without the slightest interference from his guards. Rooms like his were referred to as 'VIP' accommodation.

Best lived on double SS rations, which were more than sufficient for his modest appetite, and was allowed to purchase beer, spirits or wine from the SS canteen. (It all had to be signed for and deducted from his salary of ten marks a week which the Germans awarded him assuming it would be retrieved from his British employers at the end of hostilities.) He regularly visited the SS dentist in the main camp to have his teeth fixed, and was full of praise for the first-class treatment he received (which he subsequently compared to the post-war National Health Service). And he enjoyed daily walks of an hour or longer in the garden outside the Zellenbau, where he was allowed to grow his own vegetables and flowers. His warders attended upon him more like obsequious servants in an English country house than prison guards in Nazi Germany. In his memoir of the five years he spent in German captivity, *The Venlo Incident*, Best described the Zellenbau, unsurprisingly, as something akin to a boarding house.

However, he did not deny that some of the cells in the Zellenbau were less comfortably appointed than his own and those of equally distinguished individuals. Many were bare of furniture and they often had nothing more than concrete slabs or wooden planks for beds. Usually their inmates were chained to the walls or the floor. Often they were kept in complete darkness all day long, and fed morsels of indigestible food at intervals of three days or more.

Johnny's accommodation fell somewhere nearer this end of the spectrum of institutional incivility. In his new lodgings there was no furniture, blank concrete walls, a heap of dirty bedding strewn on the floor and a foul-smelling bucket for ablutions in the corner. Johnny would not have recognised Payne Best's rosy description of his sometimes luxurious days in Sachsenhausen. His cell was in every meaning of the word a cell.

Johnny was kept in solitary confinement in these unappealing surroundings for 24 hours. He was handcuffed, quite unnecessarily, to a heavy chain

313

anchored in the concrete floor. It was a relief a day later when the heavy iron door swung open and he was escorted from his cell. It was equally encouraging to discover that he was not destined for the hangman's noose, which he had half expected, but a small exercise yard in the Zellenbau compound containing grass and neat paths lined with flowers and other plants (mostly laid by Payne Best). In these slightly pastoral surroundings, and greatly to his pleasure, Johnny found his four old companions Wings Day, Jack Churchill, Sydney Dowse and Jimmy James also taking a ritual daily exercise. None, thankfully, looked the worse for wear physically, and all appeared as cheerful as they could despite the disappointment of their recapture and re-incarceration.

Unfortunately for Johnny, who was craving human company, Day, Churchill, Dowse and James were not allowed to communicate with him (or with one another for that matter). After a while everyone except Johnny was marched back to his own individual cell without a word being passed between them. Johnny was taken back to the Zellenbau to a small room where he was interrogated by three men from the Kripo. Present, in addition, was an interpreter who appeared to speak perfect English as only an Englishman could. Before this panel of inquisitors Johnny spent the next three hours or so answering a series of questions about his escape and activities outside the wire. It was a tiresome ordeal but not, he later attested, a particularly menacing experience. When it was over it was perhaps natural that Johnny should strike up a conversation with the only other person in the room who spoke perfect English: the interpreter. It was fortunate that he did so because Dr Hans Wilhelm Thost was to prove his salvation.

Thost was a part-time employee of the foreign intelligence branch of the Sicherheitsdienst (the SD), the intelligence service of the SS. A linguist, he was employed as an interpreter for the Reichssicherheitshauptamt (the Reich Security Main Office)—the umbrella organisation for the myriad of German state security and police services. Thost reported directly back to Walter Schellenberg, an infamous figure in Nazi mythology who, as discussed, had been behind Payne Best's capture at Venlo. Johnny and Dr Thost were to strike up something of a friendship, beginning with their first encounter in Sachsenhausen. Fortunately, both were to leave written documentation of this first meeting, and of their subsequent adventures together. Johnny gave his account to MI9, the intelligence service concerned with escaped POWs, after his liberation. Thost wrote an account that was serialised in 1952 by *Der Mittag*, the Düsseldorf daily newspaper. Broadly the two accounts agree with each other, though there are nuanced differences. This narrative draws upon both versions of events.

According to Thost, at the end of the interrogation Johnny said, 'I say, you speak English like an Englishman and you seem to understand British mentality. Is it possible to talk to you sensibly—quite privately?' Thost replied that it certainly was, and explained that before the war he had lived in Britain for seven years. 'It was not the worst part of my life,' he said. In fact Thost had been London correspondent of the Nazi newspaper, the *Völkischer Beobachter*. Wounded in

315

the Great War, he had been an early member of the National Socialist German Workers Party and was an unapologetic admirer of Adolf Hitler. He was considered an Alter Kämpfer (old fighter), an honour reserved for the most dedicated party members. He was the first officially sponsored Nazi party member to be sent to Britain and, as the London correspondent of the *Beobachter*, reported back directly to the newspaper's editor-in-chief, Alfred Rosenberg. Rosenberg, the influential philosopher and thinker of the Nazi movement, was one of a dozen or so men in Hitler's immediate entourage. Thus Thost was a highly placed Nazi indeed. Besides his role as a journalist, Thost had visited Britain many times as a youth with his parents, and he had grown up with an English governess of whom he was inordinately fond.

But while in England as a newspaper correspondent, Thost had gained some notoriety as a political troublemaker. This was hardly surprising, since his brief from Berlin was to both foster Anglo-German relations—and to secure 'justice' for Germany from the restraints of the Treaty of Versailles. Both these issues divided the London political elite, half of whom remained wary of Germany while the other half liked and sympathised with the Germans. When in 1935 the British security services discovered that Thost was also informing on émigrés from Nazi Germany and members of the overseas German community in London, it provided them with the ideal excuse to pressure for him to be ejected from the country, which is what happened. He was expelled. In Berlin, however, Thost's star continued to be in the ascendant, and after September 1939 he became a 'political warfare'

316

specialist in the British department of the German Intelligence Service (the Geheimer Nachrichtendienst, Britische Abteilung).

In Sachsenhausen in the private tête-à-tête that followed Johnny's interrogation, according to Thost, Johnny said, 'The present position is quite simple. Your country has lost the war. The Russians will soon be in Germany. I know the Russians; your country will suffer terribly.' Johnny then gave him a brief précis of his own experience of trading in Russia between the wars and being imprisoned by the Cheka. He then stated his own credentials as an American-born British subject who was a member of the London County Council. 'I love Germany,' he said. Johnny then made a proposal. If the Germans freed him and allowed him to return to Britain, he would attempt to persuade the Western Allies to make a separate peace with Germany to prevent further incursion of the Russians into their territory. Thost was intrigued.

As Thost had not dined that day, and Johnny was famished after a month on the run, the German interpreter asked for a meal to be prepared. Shortly afterwards, prisoners in white tunics from the SS officers' canteen came into the interrogation room and laid the table for lunch with napkins and cutlery. Johnny and Thost continued their conversation over goulash and beer. ('The old boy was so hungry. He had been living on potato peelings for a month. It was amazing to see how much he put away,' wrote Thost in *Der Mittag*.)

As they were served, Johnny asked Thost:

What use is it to keep me a prisoner? . . . If I were freed and could go back to England—I know Churchill well; we are even connected. I am not without influence in England. We must try to prevent the Communists from penetrating further into Germany. If an armistice on all fronts is impossible, an armistice must be made immediately in any case between Germany and the Western Allies.

Johnny added that since he was old and useless as a fighting man, Germany would have little to lose by unconditionally releasing him and letting him go home to see Churchill.

Johnny's own account of this meeting is opaque about who came up with the suggestion in the first place. He merely states that it was raised by one or other of the parties present. He said that Thost said he could assist him back to England if he would agree to not taking up arms again against Germany. In Johnny's version of events, he replied that while he was anxious to return to England, he could not possibly make a separate peace with his country's enemies. Thost attempted to nuance his offer by implying that Johnny could always go back into battle against the Japanese. But Johnny suggested that to earn his liberty he was prepared to carry the terms of an Armistice to the British Government. Neither account differs from the other in its essentials, merely in the nuance of who came up with the suggestion in the first place. (This is important, because according to Sydney Dowse, in his own MI9 debrief, he was approached before by Johnny with a similar suggestion. He immediately rejected it because he regarded the idea as akin to treachery.)

An air raid interrupted their conversation. Oranienburg was far enough away from Berlin to be safe from the bombing and the men remained in their seats while the bangs and crashes echoed in their ears. Thost found Johnny a 'sympathetic' figure. What he proposed was exactly what many Germans hoped for. But according to Johnny's own account, Thost said at the end of their encounter, 'I do not think your connections in England may be sufficiently important.' Thost returned to his SD quarters south of Berlin, and Johnny was taken back to his cell in the Zellenbau.

33

BERLIN DAYS

Thost's discussion with Johnny, while sympathetic, had ended on an apparently dismissive note. However, on his return to his Sicherheitsdienst barracks Thost sent a memo to his superior SS Brigadeführer Walter Schellenberg recommending that they send Johnny to Britain on the proposed mission to Downing Street, no matter how wildly speculative the undertaking might have been. Johnny was not to know this as he returned to his cell in the Zellenbau.

Nor was he to know that he and Thost had a great deal more in common than the ability to speak the same tongue and a mutual admiration of England, though neither of them was aware of it at the time. Thost's father had been a friend of Lord Curzon, a relative of Johnny by marriage. It was undoubtedly through this connection that Thost met many of his contacts in London when he was sent there to represent the *Völkischer Beobachter*. Among the influential friends Thost made was Bernard Rickatson-Hatt, editor-in-chief of the news agency Reuters. Rickatson-Hatt was one of (Wallis Simpson's cuckolded husband) Ernest Simpson's closest friends and, it is said, one of several lovers that Johnny's wife Minerva took during her husband's absence in Germany.

Johnny was to remain in solitary confinement for another 28 days. It was only after his punishment period was over that he was allowed to exercise for one hour daily with the other captured escapers. It was in these brief moments together, in the course of snatched, illicit conversations, that Johnny learnt what had happened to the others during his absence.

The efforts of Wings Day and Sydney Dowse to link up with the Todt organisation had been futile. When they arrived at the address that Andy Walsh had given them in the suburbs of Berlin, they discovered it had been seriously damaged by bombing and the occupants had abandoned their home. They attempted to hide in the ruins but were given away by a suspicious neighbour. They were the first of the five escapers to arrive back at Sachsenhausen. Jimmy James and Jack Churchill were next. They had managed to put more distance between themselves and the Sonderlager and evaded capture for two weeks. However, they were stumbled upon while sleeping in a field and their flight to freedom was abruptly over.

After the five escapers had been returned to Sachsenhausen, they feared the worst. They were right to do so. Unknown to them, the chief of the RHSA (the Reich Security Main Office), Obergruppenführer Ernst Kaltenbrunner, had ordered that they were all dangerous escapers and must be tried by a special court. The word 'special' had a particular meaning in Nazi terminology. There was no doubt what verdict Kaltenbrunner was hoping would be delivered, given his predilection for having troublesome prisoners of war shot. Thus a special court was convened. However, the escapers soon discovered that they had an ally, of sorts, in the form of the Berlin Kripo and, more particularly, one of the criminal police's more punctilious officers, Inspector Peter Mohr. Of the myriad of spying and policing organisations that enforced the Nazi totalitarian state, the Kripo was possibly the most harmless and certainly the least sinister. The Kripo was still furious at the way it had been implicated by the Gestapo in the murder of the 50 escapers from Sagan. The Gestapo had compelled the Kripo to send out on its extensive teleprinter network various bogus messages that were intended to imply each of the 50 had been killed while attempting to re-escape. The ruse was aimed at misleading an independent Swiss commission of inquiry into the controversy.

Peter Mohr was one of those officers infuriated by the ruse. Mohr was a solid, orthodox police officer, who had a profound dislike of the Gestapo. The first that Mohr had learnt of the Sagan murders was when a fellow police officer showed him, in his office, the rows of urns containing the ashes of the murdered men. He had been sickened at the sight. Mohr was determined that the investigation into the Sachsenhausen escape would be rigorous and above board, and the Kripo would not once more have its hands soiled doing the dirty work of its less scrupulous counterpart.

Mohr was determined that the 'special court' would give the escapers a fair and just hearing. It was before this tribunal of five men and an official prosecutor, from the Kripo and the SD, that Wing Commander Day was summoned to appear. 'Summoned' is, perhaps, too gentle a word, for he was marched before them from his cell five times, usually at some ungodly hour in the early morning. Otherwise, however, the proceedings were conducted like any other legitimate court of inquiry.

The prosecutor had levelled all manner of accusations at the defendant. The escapers were nothing more than common saboteurs, he claimed. They were guilty of the criminal offence of bribery. They had subverted German civilians. They acted like spies and were in communication with British secret intelligence networks. In the latter months of the war, the Germans had routinely attempted to smear escapers as spies and saboteurs. But the intensity with which these accusations were made this time meant Wings sensed a greater peril than in the past. The Wing Commander realised that if he did not take them seriously his men's lives might be on the line. He countered them by quoting appropriate clauses from the Geneva Convention relating to the treatment of enemy combatants. He said that his men were officers who were only fulfilling their sworn duty, which was to escape. And he protested that the German authorities had no legal right to treat them as criminals. Wings played for time by pretending not to understand German phrases and indulging in lengthy and time-consuming discussions with his court-appointed interpreter.

The effort wore Wings down. In the end he could do no more than appeal to the better nature of his inquisitors. 'I am a Royal Air Force officer,' he said. 'Do you not understand what that means? I am not a spy, nor a partisan, nor a saboteur. My professional honour as well as my pride, my ambition, too, if you like, has always forced me to return to the fight. Your own forces contain men of similar spirit, men we know and respect for their fighting qualities. They would not have sat passively in captivity any more than I was prepared to do. Surely even you can understand that?' The investigating team must have been almost as exhausted by the process as the defendant. After a pensive silence, the president of the tribunal said with a quiet sigh, 'We understand, Wing Commander.'

From that moment onwards the threat of execution receded. Wings was moved to a more comfortable cell. By the time Johnny was returned to Sachsenhausen the conditions in which his five captured comrades were held had improved markedly. They were given some books to read, and rationed to two thirds of a Red Cross parcel each per fortnight. Johnny's return raised their spirits even more. Jimmy James was confined in a cell on the same row as Johnny and became used to hearing his friend walking along the corridor in his clogs whenever he was let out to exercise. Invariably Johnny's voice was raised in song, which greatly irritated the guards. But Johnny was not to be there for long.

On 15 November 1944, Johnny was taken from his cell and found himself in the commandant's office where he encountered the pleasant and accommodating Hans Thost once more. This time Thost was accompanied by another civilian whom he introduced as 'Dr Sommers' of the Ministry of Propaganda. Johnny subsequently learnt that 'Dr Sommers' was actually Dr Theodor Paeffgen (or 'Peskin', as Johnny spelt it), the Chief of Amt. VI, the section of the SD that was the foreign intelligence service. Thost opened the conversation by asking Johnny, 'How do you think the German and British people can get closer together?' Johnny replied that:

> the British people are offended most by the
> fact that Germany has overrun small nations
> and that Austria, Czechoslovakia and Poland
> must be freed. Also that the Rhineland would
> have to be demilitarised. That all countries at
> present occupied by German forces would
> have to be evacuated of those forces . . . [T]he
> persecution of the Jews would have to cease
> and that the German government would have
> to be reconstructed.

He expressed the opinion that the Western Allies
would not sign an armistice with a German
politician, and that an armistice could only be
brought by a German general.

It is hardly surprising that 'Dr Sommers', or
Paeffgen as he was, should say that none of the
points raised by Johnny presented 'unsurmountable
[*sic*]' difficulties. In reality they did. Johnny's
insurmountable optimism was getting the better of
him. He had unwittingly understated the Allies'
deep detestation of the Nazi regime, and their
utter determination to bring Germany to her
knees. Roosevelt had declared the doctrine of
unconditional surrender and there was no
indication that the Allies intended to soften their
approach. Yet Thost appeared to be encouraged by
Johnny's sanguine assessment of the situation. He
told him that, 'Germany wished to conclude an
Armistice with the Western Allies and to be
allowed a free hand to continue the fight against
the Russians.' Johnny replied that he thought the
British Government would only be interested in a

general armistice, to which Paeffgen responded, 'The guns are now speaking. It is out of the hands of the diplomats.'

Johnny asked whether it was likely he could be exchanged for a German officer in British hands. Paeffgen told him that his return to the United Kingdom could only be accomplished in this way. Johnny reiterated that he would convey any message they wished to the British Government. And after the exchange drew to a close, he was escorted back to his cell. A week or so later, he was permitted to exercise with the other prisoners in the yard and he informed Wings Day about what had passed between the Germans and himself.

No further developments took place until 2 February 1945. On that day, Johnny was taken from his cell once more. Jimmy James recalled, 'I remember hearing his clogs clatter past my door and die away at the end of the passage—but he never came back. Nobody knew where he had gone, and we were worried about him.' It transpired that Johnny had been taken once more to the commandant's office where he was told, to his surprise, that he was to leave the camp. Without further ado, two SS officers took him by car to Berlin, which by then resembled a moonscape. At a large faceless building in the centre of the city he was handed over to a naval lieutenant whose father, he informed Johnny proudly, had been the manager of the Hamburg–America passenger shipping line in New York for many years. The naval officer subsequently took Johnny to a large department store in a shopping district of the city. There, Johnny was presented with a civilian suit and overcoat. Afterwards, he was taken to an army depot on the outskirts of Berlin where he was issued with fresh shirts, underwear, socks and shoes.

If Johnny was surprised by these developments, he was even more taken aback when he found himself being taken to the apartment of the 'elegant' widow of an SS Major. He was delighted to have his first warm bath in over four years. After luxuriating in it for the best part of an hour the naval lieutenant re-emerged to ask Johnny to dress in the civilian clothes. In his MI9 debrief, Johnny stated: 'I objected to this and asked the reason for it. He told me that these were his orders. I asked for his assurance as an officer that this was honourable. He insisted that it was quite honourable and that I was to meet a high personage.' Johnny then complied with the request and dressed in his new clothes.

Soon afterwards Johnny's 'old friend' Hans Thost arrived. Thost informed Johnny that he was to be exchanged for a German officer in Allied captivity. Until the necessary paperwork was arranged, Thost was to be his guardian and guide in Berlin. He had been given ration books and money for both of them. Johnny was then presented with a welcome snack of sandwiches and wine provided by the naval lieutenant, who took his leave. After he had sated his hunger, Johnny was taken on the first of many expeditions he was to share with Hans Thost, a short excursion into the heart of Adolf Hitler's Third Reich and to the Hotel Adlon, Berlin's most prestigious hotel.

Next to the Brandenberg Gate, the Adlon had long been a magnet for celebrity visitors to the city, and during the days of the Reich became a home

327

from home for foreign visitors and a hotbed of intrigue. The German Foreign Ministry occupied two entire floors during most of the war. When Johnny and Thost arrived at the hotel they were escorted to a private room where they found three civilians in the middle of supper. One among them stood up to apologise for starting to eat before their guest arrived. Thost introduced him as Dr Paul Schmidt, one of the most senior officials of the German Foreign Ministry, and best known as the one-time interpreter to the Führer, most notably at the 1938 Munich Conference. Schmidt apologised and explained that they had expected Johnny an hour and a half earlier. He invited Johnny to join him and his supper companions at the table. (They were, according to Johnny, a Dr Hesst and Dr Weber of the Foreign Ministry.) Thost and Johnny sat down to enjoy a repast of lobster salad, fresh fish and Rhine wine. For Johnny, after four years on a starvation diet, the meal must have been a very welcome feast indeed.

Schmidt informed Johnny that he was to be returned to England. He asked Johnny for his views on how an Armistice could be effected. Johnny reiterated the sentiments he had expressed four months previously in Sachsenhausen to Thost and Paeffgen (alias Sommers). 'I stressed that Great Britain could have no confidence in the present German Government.' For their part, Schmidt and his fellow foreign office officials elaborated upon their own wishes. No unconditional surrender was their uppermost concern, and an equitable balance of power remaining between Western Europe and Communist Russia. Shortly before midnight, Schmidt apologised once more, and explained he had to go. According to Phyllis Dodge's account, Schmidt told Thost and Johnny that they would both be flying the next day to Stockholm where the former would put the latter on a plane to London. He promised to see Johnny again before he left for England. Afterwards, Thost took Johnny back to the flat of the elegant SS Major's widow and the most comfortable bed he had slept in since he could remember.

The following morning, when Thost called to arrange the tickets and papers for Stockholm, he was told there had been an unexpected delay. Thus Johnny and Thost remained in Berlin for another week. While they waited for travel arrangements to be made, Thost took Johnny on a sightseeing tour of Berlin. They travelled on trains and buses packed with passengers and though they spoke English to one another quite freely nobody batted an eyelid. In a series of articles he wrote for the *Der Mittag* newspaper in 1952, Thost observed: 'No one raised objection to our conversation in English, though possibly some people may have been surprised to hear English spoken in the worst bombed city in the world.'

Thost suggested to Johnny at one stage that Hitler was behind his release from captivity, though there is no evidence at all that the Führer would have known anything about Johnny Dodge. Throughout their subsequent travels together, Thost would repeatedly allude to Heinrich Himmler's direct involvement in the escapade. It is certainly true that the SS Reichsführer was at that stage of Germany's ignominy desperately attempting to grasp any straw within his reach to save his own skin. But, again, there is no evidence he knew specific details of the situation regarding Johnny, and it is unlikely he would have become personally involved with such 'small fry'. As for Schmidt, who undoubtedly had his own reasons for currying favour with the Allies, it appears that Johnny never met him again. Instead, on 9 February, he was taken away from Berlin by Thost in the opposite direction to the way he had been led to believe he would be travelling.

TRAVELS WITH DR THOST

Why Johnny was dispatched south to Dresden rather than north to Sweden is a mystery. Nevertheless he and Thost set off from Berlin in the company of an SS officer, travelling by car, and eventually arriving in the baroque and blissfully unscathed capital of Saxony. They checked into the Schiller Hotel, all three occupying the same room. Later, Johnny was introduced to the city's Chief of Police and Chief of Gestapo, who entertained him and Thost to lunch. He observed: 'It was obvious that every endeavour was being made to create a formidable impression on my mind of the German police and Gestapo.'

That evening, Johnny was taken to the office of the Chief of Regional Police. SS Obergruppenführer Werner von Alvensleben told Johnny that he was being sent to England at once. Von Alvensleben was not at all subtle in his overtures to Johnny. After some preliminary niceties he said, 'English people are much better diplomats than Germans. For example, a generous peace was made with the Boers with the result that they became your friends.'

Johnny reported, 'My impression was that he realised that Germany was finished and was appealing for generous peace terms.' It was not a particularly insightful observation. There were probably many such conversations going on between intermediaries at that stage of the war.

After accepting von Alvensleben's invitation to lunch a few days later, Thost and Johnny returned to the Schiller Hotel that night.

It is not entirely clear, from Johnny's own account, why his return to Britain was being delayed. But it was quite apparent that the Germans were seizing every conceivable opportunity to ingratiate themselves with him and, by extension, anybody who he could influence in Britain. It is a sign of their desperation that they seriously believed these efforts might bear fruit. Johnny's political leanings would have made him favourably disposed toward any advances remotely anti-Bolshevik. But having seen the devastation wrought by the Allies on Germany's cities, even he must have known that a pact between these two bitterly warring opponents was not at all likely.

On 12 February, Thost took Johnny to the Gestapo Headquarters in Dresden where they met another 'high personage' in civilian clothes. This man, whose name Johnny could not recall, recounted how he had worked as a merchant in the Dutch East Indies before the war. Johnny noted that the 'high personage' spoke at some length on the theme of, 'Why are the Germans and British at war?' In the meantime, Johnny reported, 'I noticed that all documents from the Gestapo Headquarters were being loaded into lorries.' Later, he and Thost were taken to 'Police Headquarters'—possibly the city's Kripo offices—which were also being hastily evacuated. It appeared that the whole of Nazi high officialdom was in flight from Hitler's fast-disappearing Reich. But still, some of them had time to pause for lunch. The following day, Johnny had his date with Werner von Alvensleben. Before giving him lunch at a local restaurant, Johnny's host first took him for a walk in Dresden Zoo.

That night, Thost took Johnny to the city's Zircus Sarasani. They were enjoying the performance when air raid sirens began wailing outside and the disappointed audience reluctantly began to file out of the circus. It was 13 February and in the black skies above, the first wave of Allied bombers was about to begin its devastating attack on Dresden. Thost was aware that von Alvensleben's headquarters, some three kilometres out of town, boasted a bombproof underground chamber. As soon as he realised just how intense the attack was, Thost took Johnny there. They found themselves in distinguished company. Among those who had sought shelter there were Field Marshal Paul Ludwig Ewald von Kleist and his wife. Johnny told von Kleist it was madness for Germany to keep on fighting and that they should get rid of Hitler. Von Kleist replied that though he understood the Allied point of view, Germany was not in the hands of the military. Army chiefs were powerless to do anything. It was a refrain Johnny was to hear repeatedly.

After the first night of carnage, and when it became obvious that the raids were to continue, Johnny was moved for safety to the home of a Wehrmacht army officer. Major Fritz von Alten was proud of his English connections. 'One of his ancestors was a German general who had cooperated with Wellington at Waterloo, and I think an ancestor of his was English.' (He was probably referring to Carl von Alten, a famous Anglo-Hanoverian statesman and general.) The Wehrmacht major, who insisted he had always been anti-Nazi, also told Johnny that the military no longer exerted any power over German policy. Johnny stayed at von Alten's home until 18 February.

It appears that the initial plan had been for Johnny to take a flight out of Dresden to Sweden. But the Allied devastation of the city had put paid to that scheme, either because air routes had been disrupted or, more likely, because Johnny might have been in serious danger of being lynched had he stayed in the city. It might have been in view of this latter risk that von Alvensleben charged his adjutant August Exter with giving Johnny 'every consideration' and to escort him safely out of the city. Exter did as he was ordered and during their brief time together he found time to discuss politics and the military situation with Johnny. Exter appeared genuinely appalled at the depredations of the Nazi regime in whose name he had served.

That night Johnny and Thost joined a party of female refugees in a bus to Weimar. Among the women crowded on board were Princess Margarethe zu Waldeck, the daughter of SS district leader Prince Josias zu Waldeck, whose area included Buchenwald where the notorious concentration camp was situated; and an aristocrat, Maria Arendt, and her daughter Edith Elizabeth Graffin Schweinitz. All five, including Johnny and Thost, were to spend a considerable amount of time together during the following weeks. In Weimar Princess Margarethe found Johnny and Thost comfortable lodgings at the Haus Elefant, the best hotel in Weimar. There, the head waiter and assistant manager Robert Hedecke supplied his guests with a good meal and bottle of wine every evening. Almost every night he and Johnny would settle down in a corner of the restaurant and discuss politics. Another functionary, Clifford Ach, enjoyed tea with Johnny on many afternoons.

Johnny and Thost were to be at the Haus Elefant until 7 April. What happened during those seven or so weeks is largely shrouded in mystery. Johnny revealed little in his debrief with MI9 to explain why he remained there so long. However, Phyllis Dodge's card index indicates that Johnny fell ill while staying at the Elefant and was poorly enough to be confined to bed. He was attended there '2 or 3 times' by a Lieutenant Colonel C. Stichforth, a Luftwaffe doctor. Johnny was also visited by the Princess and her daughter who brought him brandy, and Prince zu Waldeck, the SS leader, who apparently saw Johnny several times before he left.

On 7 April, Thost informed him that the Russians were approaching Weimar fast. 'It looks as if they will be here any day,' he said, adding, no doubt hopefully, 'I shall then be your prisoner.' Then Thost claimed that Heinrich Himmler himself had ordered that Johnny be taken to Regensburg. As has been noted above, it is unlikely Himmler had anything at all to do with the operation to send Johnny to England. It is more than likely that Thost was exaggerating his own importance to Johnny, who was not in a position to judge the correct situation. It is certainly a fact that as Thost spoke, other VIP prisoners being held as hostages by the Nazis were being moved southwards down the length of Germany in an operation being orchestrated by Himmler's underlings like Brigadeführer Dr Walter Schellenberg. In fact, among the VIP

335

hostages, or *Prominenten*, were Johnny's Great Escaping friends, Wings Day, Sydney Dowse and Jimmy James, who would follow a similar route to him accompanied by SS guards.

In the chaos of the collapse of the Third Reich, Johnny and Thost found themselves hustled from one place to the next without any real control over where they were going. At one stage somebody overhearing them talking in English suspected they were British spies. They were both thrown in jail and remained there for three days, despite Thost's furious objections that he was a loyal servant of the Reich. They were released only after a Gestapo official verified his papers. That day they found a room at a hotel in Regenstauf where they shared a bedroom.

One evening during their stay in Regenstauf, Thost told Johnny, 'I must telephone Himmler. I have got you out of prison, now I must get you out of Germany.' He showed Johnny a copy of the telegram he had sent to the SS Reichsführer. The gist of it was, recalled Johnny, 'Have Dodge here. He is well connected and it is important that he should get to England. He is an admirer of Hitler.' According to Johnny, when he protested that this was untrue, Thost replied, 'We must not be too punctilious.' It seems certain that Thost himself was not being at all punctilious. Subsequently he told Johnny that they were going to Munich the following day, 16 April, to meet Himmler. Johnny was alarmed. 'I stated that I had no desire to meet Himmler,' he recalled in his MI9 debrief.

In fact there wasn't the slightest possibility of Johnny meeting Himmler because by then the Reichsführer was in Berlin—and was shortly to

336

move to Lübeck in the north of Germany. Himmler's thoughts were entirely engrossed in negotiating some sort of settlement with the Allies via Swedish intermediaries. Johnny, however, could not conceivably have known this. Thus the following morning he fled the Regenstauf hotel room that he was sharing with Thost while the latter was asleep. Johnny hoped to hide in the woods until American forces arrived. But by 5 p.m. of that day he had thought better of his situation and returned to the Regenstauf hotel. He discovered a note from Thost asking where on earth he had gone and what did he think he was doing? The two men were eventually reunited and they did, that evening, travel to Munich. But not to see Himmler. Instead they received instructions to continue to Bad Tolz to meet Dr Theodor Paeffgen, the Chief of Amt. VI whom Johnny had last seen in Sachsenhausen.

They were at Bad Tolz on 18 April when Paeffgen arrived at the hotel Johnny and Thost had found. There was another discussion about the perilous position that Germany now found herself in. Johnny told Paeffgen that the only hope for Germany now was to surrender to the Allies. 'We will never surrender to the Russians,' replied Paeffgen. In that case, Johnny implored him, surrender to the British and Americans.

Paeffgen had no answer other than to indicate arrangements had been made to get Johnny out of Germany soon. He then departed for a village some seven kilometres distant where he was living at the time. Around about this time Johnny met a major in the Wehrmacht, Oskar Adami, who claimed to be anti-Nazi and desirous of peace. He too emphasised that the military had no control over

337

the political situation. Johnny also had an intriguing conversation with a Baron von Hahn whom he met with his wife at a 'quaint little inn'. The Baron told Johnny that after the war he would tell him something about the attempt on Hitler's life in the summer of 1944.

Less than a week later, on 23 April, Thost received instructions for Johnny to be immediately put across the frontier. On the following morning, of 24 April, the two men hitchhiked to Kemten before continuing in what Johnny later described quaintly as a 'charabanc' and arriving at Bregenz in the very early hours of 25 April. They went to a hotel for a few hours before seeking out the local police headquarters and the chief of the Gestapo to discuss the route to be followed across the border into Switzerland. After receiving their instructions and briefly returning to the hotel, they set off on the last leg of their journey, arriving at the Swiss frontier at about 10.30 on the night of 25 April.

They were met by two Gestapo agents who immediately recognised the name 'Dr Paeffgen' on Thost's order papers. Without further ado they introduced Johnny to a guide who would show him across the border into neutral Switzerland. 'Great care was taken to ensure that I should not be able to recognise him at a later date,' Johnny later reported in his MI9 debrief. Some time between then and the very early hours of the next morning Johnny said 'Goodbye' to Thost. (According to Thost, in his account given to *Der Mittag*, Johnny urged him to accompany him across the border. Thost said Johnny assured him he knew people in high places who would extend him every consideration, but Thost was compelled by duty to decline.) Johnny then accompanied his guide across the frontier. Johnny was finally a free man. It was four years, ten months and twelve days since he was first captured by the Germans in northern France on 14 June 1940.

Within the hour, he and his guide presented themselves at the Swiss Customs Office on the outskirts of St Margarethen. The guide spoke to a Swiss official before departing into the night, his identity to this day a mystery. Presently, in fact Johnny later stated 'within a few minutes', he was examined by a doctor before being interviewed by a lieutenant of the Swiss Intelligence Service. Two newspaper reporters acted as interpreters for the lieutenant. One was 'an Egyptian-born British subject writing for an American newspaper'; the other was a local man representing a Lausanne publication. It is unlikely that either of these men just happened to be at the customs post when Johnny appeared, so it is to be presumed that they lived locally and were summoned by officials to assist them. Johnny provided no further details about them in his MI9 report. He mentioned that a colonel of the Swiss Army also arrived at the customs post but, strangely, 'No attempt was made to interrogate me about the circumstances of my arrival in Switzerland.'

Subsequently, according to Johnny's report, the lieutenant and two newspaper representatives took Johnny to supper at a local restaurant where he enjoyed his first meal as a free man. There he was introduced to the head of the Swiss Mission in Germany, whose job it was to look after the welfare of Allied prisoners of war. Apparently, he had come by car with an assistant from Germany. Presently the two men returned to Germany leaving

Johnny to accompany the lieutenant to the home of a Swiss clothing manufacturer where he spent what remained of the night. All these details are derived from the ten pages of Johnny's MI9 report. No explanation is given as to how such a collection of individuals could find themselves at a sleepy Swiss border town in the early hours of a spring morning.

On the morning of 26 April, the lieutenant, the two newspaper men and Johnny were driven to the headquarters of the Swiss Intelligence Service in Bern. There, he met the head of Swiss Intelligence and the British Military Attaché, a Brigadier Cartwright, who made arrangements for Johnny to be sent to the UK. Thenceforth, Cartwright took him to the British Legation where he made a statement and was supplied with an army battledress and British passport. That night, he was taken to the home of a member of the legation staff. But Johnny did not have long there. At four on the morning of 27 April, he was taken to Bern railway station where the member of the legation purchased him a first-class ticket to Lyons. In Lyons, at RAF Transport Command, Johnny presented officials with a letter Cartwright had given him requesting his immediate air transport to Great Britain. On the morning of 28 April, he boarded a flight back to Britain.

Johnny's mother Flora was staying at her Dorchester suite when he arrived back in London after his enforced absence. (Minerva was living with Tony in Wales.) At 10.45 on the evening of 28 April, the Dorchester hall porter sent a 'Telephone Caller's Message' to her room. 'Madam, Major Dodge has returned to London by air and will get in touch with you in the morning.' He was finally home.

HOME

There is no record of whether Johnny ever
attempted to pass on his secret diplomatic message
to Churchill. It is unlikely he did so, or even
thought he had any serious prospect of influencing
the prime minister. The war was practically over.
The same day that Johnny arrived home, Hitler
discovered Himmler had been attempting to make
a separate peace with the Allies. The Führer
promptly ordered the arrest of the man whose
loyalty he had rarely doubted. In Italy, Benito
Mussolini was trying to escape to Switzerland when
he was caught by Italian partisans, executed and
hung upside down with his mistress on the
forecourt of a Milan petrol station. It was only two
days later, on 30 April, that Hitler committed
suicide in his Berlin bunker with the mistress who
had belatedly become his wife. The next day Joseph
Goebbels succumbed to the same fate along with
his wife Magda after having disposed of their six
children by means of lethal injection. On 8 May,
Germany surrendered to the Allies and the worst
conflict in human history came to an end.

It is a testament to Johnny's stamina and
trenchant idealism that within weeks of returning
from the war that had sapped his physical energy
and strained his nerves, he was returning to the
fray—this time in the political arena. He had been
selected as the Conservative candidate for the Kent
seat of Gillingham before the war, and when the

government called the first election after the war in Europe, Johnny was quick to take up the cudgels. It was a tired and weary looking figure who took to the streets of Gillingham that summer in the run-up to the 'Khaki Election' of July 1945. He stood as the National Conservative and Churchill Government Candidate, and his election leaflets featured a prominent photograph of Churchill next to Johnny. Under the heading 'A Personal Recommendation to the Electors of Gillingham Division from Britain's War Leader', Churchill wrote: 'Major Dodge reached, at a very early age, a position of marked and high executive responsibility. I cannot think of a more fitting candidate. We need men of strong character and proved capacity in the House of Commons.'

Johnny's Labour opponent was Joseph Binns. According to contemporary newspaper accounts, the voting was going to be 'close' in the Gillingham Division, but so popular was Johnny with the local electorate that the betting odds were slightly in his favour. Declaration Night was some time after polling day because it took a long time to count the votes of servicemen and women stationed in far-flung corners of the world. In the meantime, a dinner was held at the Trocadero in Piccadilly to welcome Johnny back home. Giving the tribute, his friend the Canadian journalist and politician Beverley Baxter said Johnny was the spiritual descendant of the Three Musketeers. He was a Porthos in build and a d'Artagnan in temperament, said Baxter. Referring to the election, he thought Johnny had probably won it and if returned he would be a 'stalwart back-bencher' because he was no 'mincer of words'.

Johnny did not win the seat. Joseph Binns squeezed in by a slim margin. But given the size of the massive Labour landslide nationwide, which surprised and shocked many people, Johnny's narrow defeat in Gillingham reflected well upon him and the campaign he had run. Characteristically, after his defeat when he addressed some 200 of his election workers at a social evening in the town's Central Hotel, he was generous to the man who had won. Johnny wished the victor 'all the best of luck' and told his supporters, 'We must all pull together behind him.' He continued, however:

Although we have not been successful today, the ideals for which we stand—humanity, progress and freedom for the individual—have not, and will never be defeated . . . Carry on your work for our cause and recruit everyone under its banner, for make no mistake, we'll be back again, and if you wish it, I shall be happy to be your candidate.

His words produced uproarious applause among the assembly of loyal party workers and friends. The local newspaper observed: 'It was good to note that Major Dodge was looking much better than when, as a recently released prisoner of war, he commenced his campaign.'

However, perhaps he was not really better. Shortly afterwards Johnny had second thoughts about running for office again. His defeat in Gillingham appears to have brought home to him how weak and exhausted he was and, perhaps, how mentally scarred. He announced that he would not,

343

after all, contest Gillingham at the next election. He was reported as saying, 'It is taking myself longer to adjust to a free society than I had expected. I feel a strong desire to simplify my life and enjoy as much freedom of action as possible by reducing my commitments.' For someone who for so long had craved a public role, it must have been a heart-wrenching decision. Johnny returned to his work as a stockbroker at Nathan & Rosselli, and divided his time between a new home in London and his beloved Ferring with Flora, Minerva and the growing children.

Johnny continued to have contact with the many friends he had made during his years of captivity. Leonard Hall, the RAF meteorologist responsible for changing the date of the 'Great Escape' worked for the Clerical, Medical and General Life Assurance Society in St. James's Square. One day he was expecting a call from two partners at Nathan & Rosselli. He knew the firm but had had no previous contact with it. He was delighted when Johnny Dodge walked through the door with a colleague. He had not seen Johnny since his escape from Stalag Luft III in March 1944.

Commenting on his old friend's ability as a stockbroker, Hall later wrote:

> Johnny's capacity for friendship was unique, and it stood him in good stead as a stockbroker in the early post-war years in London. He was not, and never would have been, the sophisticated, intellectual, academic investment analyst who came to the fore as the post-war era developed. He was a salesman, if that is not too abrasive a word for one so

344

urbane, who, on the basis of his deep knowledge of the City and its people, sought to persuade his many friends of the rightness of a particular investment.

There followed many years of friendship between the two men.

From then on Hall was often invited to lunch at the offices of Nathan & Rosselli at 7 Adams Court with their senior partner Reggie Rosselli, Johnny and other partners and senior staff. One day Johnny phoned Hall to invite him to a dinner to meet the American ambassador. It was July 1951 and the event would be Hall's introduction to The Ends of the Earth Club. Subsequently, Johnny asked Hall to become a member of the Anglo-American dining fraternity. The guests over the years included several US ambassadors, American and British military commanders including Field Marshal Montgomery, and Prince Charles, among others. Hall attested, 'Johnny was not only the prime mover in the Club, he was the Club, and presided over all its dinners with his usual incomparable style. The membership consisted of his personal friends, hundreds of them, all looking to him as the Club's inspiration.'

Johnny exchanged letters with many of his old comrades, but mainly those who had endured the most intimate experiences of captivity. Jimmy James and Wings Day, in particular, became regular correspondents and lifelong friends. In 1954, Peter Churchill wrote to Johnny from the Montana Hotel in Cannes, where he was a real estate agent. He told him how thrilled he had been to learn of Johnny's adventures with Dr Thost at

345

the end of the war. 'What bad luck that your attempt and all those of the German Resistance failed to bring about a situation that would have kept the Russians further back east and given the world a better chance of lasting peace.' But life for Johnny would never again capture those adventurous days of war and exploration. Instead he settled into the banal everyday routine of civilian existence in peacetime.

It was inevitable, given Johnny's interest in politics and international affairs, that he would become embroiled in one of the pivotal political issues of the post-war years. Apartheid in Rhodesia and South Africa was a subject that divided nations in every corner of the globe, and provoked as much violence around dinner tables in Britain as it did in the festering townships on the outskirts of Johannesburg and Pretoria. Given Johnny's unswerving conservative convictions, there was never any serious question as to which side he would align with. He unhesitatingly sided with the prime minister of South Africa, Dr Daniel François Malan, the champion of Afrikaner nationalism and supporter of comprehensive segregation. Malan had been the subject of repeated attacks by British bishops and other clergymen who described him as a 'cruel, obstinate reactionary'. The *Daily Mirror* called him a 'second Hitler' who preached the same evil creed of racial discrimination. But Johnny had no doubt in his mind that the white race was superior to the black race. Typically, however, his views, which would have been regarded as repellent in many quarters, then as now, elicited a sympathetic response from some liberal commentators.

346

Johnny visited South Africa for the first time in his life in the early weeks of 1955. He returned unchanged in his opinion about the country, impressed by the manner in which the 'Natives' were well housed and well fed and, on the whole, gainfully employed. Shortly after his return, he visited the home of his friend, the Canadian journalist and British MP Beverley Baxter, for dinner. Baxter was a conservative politician who had been condemned as an appeaser by Michael Foot before the war. However, he was a far more open-minded man than Johnny who held some liberal views (he opposed capital punishment) and he believed the black race should be encouraged to aspire for equality with whites. He was intrigued to get to the bottom of the Apartheid conundrum over dinner with his guest. He later wrote an amusing article for the *Cape Times* about their conversation that night. First of all, Baxter paid tribute to the bravery, patriotism and charisma of Johnny. 'His spirit is dauntless, his adventures endless, his faith in humanity deep and indestructible.' But then he cautioned, 'Colonel Dodge is an enthusiast who is inclined to champion a cause without conceding anything to the other side.' To try and find out the truth about Apartheid Baxter decided to put Johnny in an imaginary witness box. His report of the result went thus:

Is it not a fact that in South Africa there are districts where no Coloured man can own or occupy a house?—Certainly. Malan feels that it is better that way.

Do the Coloured people object?—Only the professional agitators. The people prefer it.

347

What are the conditions in the mines?—
First rate. There are showers, canteens, rest
rooms and the pay is high.

Why are the Coloured people denied the
franchise?—They can vote for their own
representative, but if they had a complete
franchise then absolute power would pass
completely to them. And they are not ready
for that . . .

Do you believe in segregation?—If you are
against inter-marriage between Black and
White—and I am—then there must be
segregation. One of the causes of the trouble
in Kenya, which I visited on my trip, is that the
huts of the Natives and the plantations of the
Whites are all mixed up together . . .

Then you do not agree with the visiting
British bishops who denounce Malan a cruel,
obstinate reactionary?—I am sorry to say that
Dodge's opinion of the said bishops cannot be
quoted in a family newspaper.

In the *Cape Times* article, Baxter continued by
reinforcing his own opinion of Johnny: 'let me say
that he is by nature the kindliest of creatures who
could not hate even the Germans or the Russians
when he was their prisoner'. His views, therefore,
could not be ignored out of hand. But Baxter made
it clear that he favoured means of advancing the
ambitions of black people and not continuing to
subjugate them in servile, manual employment.

The late 1950s brought happiness to Minerva
and Johnny with the marriages of both their
children within a year or so of each other. Their
eldest son, David, was married in Kensington in

348

1956. David's bride, Elizabeth Incledon-Webber, came from a distinguished West Country family. Their marriage was to be an enduring one. David's younger brother, Tony (who had been christened Lionel Arrington in honour of his grandmother Flora's family and her second husband, Lionel Guest), married on 28 September 1957. This marriage must have brought Johnny particular joy, as Tony's new wife, Jane Aitken, was a niece of his great friend Lord Beaverbrook. Jane was the daughter of one of Beaverbrook's younger brothers who, as a major on the headquarters staff of the 4th Canadian Division in 1915, had served alongside Johnny at Gallipoli. Major Allan Anderson Aitken had, like Johnny, been wounded in the conflict. He subsequently became a stockbroker. In that capacity he dealt in securities for his older brother and represented his newspaper empire in Canada. Sadly, Jane and Tony's marriage foundered. After their divorce, Jane returned to her native Canada. In 1986 Tony married once more, this time to an old friend, Camilla Fothergill, and they lived in a rambling old post house in Hampshire.

Otherwise the years following the excitement of the war held little prospect of great excitement. There were some efforts to obtain monetary compensation for the many prisoners of war who had returned from Germany, and the negotiations between them and their seemingly ungrateful government sometimes became tawdry. It was a long-held convention that officer prisoners—not other ranks—would be paid their salaries by the detaining power, that is, in Johnny's case, the Germans. The British, likewise, paid German prisoners of war their pay. The understanding was that these sums would be reimbursed after hostilities had ceased. But often both the German and English detaining powers subtracted amounts for supposed expenditure on their prisoners' behalf (accommodation, food, mess bills and clothing, for instance, which they had supplied). And after the war both sides' governments, rather than reimbursing their opposite numbers in full, also subtracted sums for exactly the same reason.

Officers in Barth and Sagan voluntarily donated a third of their pay for communal activities, which they felt should be reimbursed because they were for the common good of sustaining morale. In addition some of the British officers in Barth and Stalag Luft III had contributed to a communal escape fund. Considering this had contributed effectively to the war effort they felt justified in claiming it back from the War Office. However, Johnny received an apologetic letter of October 1946 from the Air Ministry informing him that it was unlikely the full amount could be reimbursed. The writer said it looked like something less than £10,000 could be found to reimburse British officers only (not Polish and Czechoslovakian RAF officers for instance). Johnny wrote back and said that he thought it only fair that any prisoner of war who had contributed more than £1 to the fund should be reimbursed in full.

The matter of compensation for the Sachsenhausen inmates was another episode. This went all the way to the House of Commons, where it was debated at length. The former prisoners claimed compensation for being held under inhumane conditions. But, unfortunately for them, all of them in their post-war intelligence debriefings had attested that they had not been mistreated, and that the conditions had been relatively benign. Their case was not helped by Sigismund Payne Best, the British intelligence agent, publishing a memoir in which he described his own treatment at the hands of the SS in the Zellenbau. The picture he painted was one of positive luxury compared to the vision of hell conjured in the public mind by the words 'concentration camp'.

After much wrangling, however, the government agreed to compensate all the Sonderlager prisoners for their time in captivity as 'victims of Nazi persecution'. When the matter was finally settled, it came too late for Johnny. He had finally passed away when Minerva received a cheque for £917 10s 0d in 1968 (a considerable sum of money at the time).

Much of Johnny's time was also taken up with replying to letters from Germans beseeching his assistance, not least Hans Thost (see subsequent chapters), and War Office officials attempting to sift through the shadows and fog of Nazi Germany's murky recent past.

Uncharacteristically, it took Johnny a long time to write a letter of condolence to the mother of Jimmy Wernham, the Canadian flight lieutenant who had escaped from Stalag Luft III with him. It was 13 January 1947 when he wrote: 'Your son was an ideal companion to be with on an escape or any other adventure. He was always cheerful and had a wonderful sense of humour. Everyone who knew him amongst his fellow prisoners had a real affection as well as respect for him.' Then Johnny offered an apology: 'Please forgive the delay in writing this letter, which is due partly to my only now beginning to adjust myself to civilization again.'

SHADOWS AND FOG

For many years after the war, Johnny was preoccupied with criminal and military investigations into the roles various dramatis personae of the Nazi regime had played in the conflict. Given the voluminous correspondence in his private papers, it must have taken up an extraordinary amount of his time. Johnny himself could not escape the inquisitions of the British authorities. The way prisoners responded to their plight was of great interest. Johnny was contacted by Squadron Leader Bruce Flockhart of MI9, the intelligence department responsible for prisoners of war and their escape activities. Flockhart was investigating prisoners' 'underground activities'. In an exchange of correspondence Johnny told him that during his time in captivity he continually attempted to counter German propaganda. In Dulag Luft he had told one German officer that he believed Hitler would be killed by a German officer.

In the last six months of 1943, he told four German officers that it was useless to continue fighting because Germany could not possibly win, and if they continued to resist every German city would eventually be razed to the ground. He told them Hitler was the one obstacle to peace and that he should resign or be removed by force.

The attempt on Hitler's life, in the summer of

1944, was in accordance with my prediction. I do not claim it was a result of anything I did or said, but it was what I was aiming at, and working for. I was simply carrying out the policy inaugurated by Wing Commander Day, of doing everything possible to break down German morale and sabotage the war effort.

Johnny wrote that he continued these efforts until the very last day he spent in Germany during his escapades with Hans Thost. He said that he continually emphasised to the senior officers he met en route that continuing the war was useless, and that the Allies would never consider making peace with Germany while Hitler was her leader. He singled out several German officers for special commendation: Major Fritz von Alten of the Wehrmacht in Dresden, Lieutenant Colonel C. Stichforth of the Luftwaffe in Weimar, Field Marshal Von Kleist in Dresden and Major Oskar Adami in Bad Tolz. All said they understood the Allied point of view but were powerless to do anything.

Johnny said the International Union that he set up in Schubin, and later the International Relations Group in Sagan, both had broadly the same aims: to keep up the morale of the men, and to counter German propaganda. They were also intended to maintain good relations between the 15 Allied nations represented in Sagan. He pointed out that he was 'had up' by the Camp Security Officer on one occasion because one of his lectures on modern history had provoked an anti-Italian and anti-German riot. He was instructed to refrain from such subjects in future. 'Needless to say, this order

354

was ignored.' On 10 January 1946, Johnny wrote to Flockhart with the names and addresses of three of the four Frenchmen who had helped him hide in the barn after he escaped from Sachsenhausen, recommending them for British decorations. They were A. Calonne, the leader, Barbier and Pierre Delahaye.

Johnny also spent a great deal of time over the forthcoming months and years trying to help many of the Germans of whom he had formed a favourable impression. He was inundated with letters from people in Germany enduring various levels of distress. He stayed in touch with Theo Rumpel who became a friend of all the Dodge family. Rumpel ended up living in the same little hillside bungalow at Oberursel near Dulag Luft where he had entertained Johnny during the war. In one of his many letters to Johnny after the war, Rumpel writes that the American prisoners of war had held a reunion with their German counterparts in September and wonders whether it is time for the British to do the same.

Frau Erika Paeffgen wrote on behalf of her husband Dr Theodor Paeffgen, head of VI B, under whom Hans Thost had served. She said that her husband had hoped to send Johnny home to see how peace terms could be arranged. But he had learnt that Ernst Kaltenbrunner, chief of the RSHA, had already decided that the prisoners were to be tried by a special court as dangerous escapers. 'Considering this state of affairs you may easily understand how difficult it was for my husband to change the mind of police headquarters.'

She continued:

According to his conviction, it was entirely due to his tireless activity that you were taken out of the camp and the lives of the others were spared too. When he finally managed to release you and send you off under the guidance of Dr Thost of his department, it was on his own responsibility and with the greatest risks for himself because the permission to release you had been revoked by strict orders at that time.

Johnny wrote to the British Control Commission in Berlin, 'Dr Paeffgen struck me as being a very decent human being and a patriotic German.' Dr Paeffgen was released from Allied captivity, and sent his grateful thanks to Johnny.

Johnny was probably pleased to hear from Heinz Dörrfus who had been the young medical orderly who had treated his feet at Dulag Luft. Dörrfus had subsequently taken part in the gruelling German retreat from Greece and endured great hardship at the hands of the enemy. 'We had a hell of a time . . . it was not fair fighting anymore.' He spent 13 months in foul conditions in a cage outside Zagreb. 'I don't want to complain about the treatment we received after all the harm Germany has done to the rest of the world, but I can assure you I have never seen any British, American or French P.o.W. who was as badly treated as we were down there.'

Dörrfus asked no favours and appeared to be writing out of genuine friendship. He told how he frequently met Theo Rumpel who was still living in the little house on the hillside and how they talked about old times. They had recently been talking about the prisoners' escape from Dulag Luft, 'and we were laughing about . . . how you got stuck in the tunnel'. Expressing the wish that they one day meet again, he signed the letter 'Henry'.

It transpired that Pierre Risch, the Luxembourg policeman who arrested Johnny after he was betrayed in the barn at Beilershof, was being accused of collaboration with the Germans. Risch was facing dire retribution. He was desperate for Johnny to confirm that far from collaborating with the Germans, he had deliberately kept him from harm as long as he could. He managed to contact Johnny via the British Embassy in Luxembourg pleading for his help. For some reason he thought that the embassy would be able to contact Johnny at 34 Downing Street. The embassy did finally track Johnny down, and he was pleased to send a letter confirming Risch's story.

Herbert Schollmerer, a Wehrmacht officer who met Johnny in a refugee column to Munich, also wrote, though there appeared to be no ulterior motive in his words beyond hoping he was well and sending him best wishes. August Exter, whom Johnny recalled as being the adjutant to the head of police in Dresden, wrote from Regensburg on 27 October 1946 to say that he had been a prisoner since the end of the war. He was relieved to discover Johnny was alive and well. Exter was one of the many Germans whom Johnny had talked with about the impending end of the war and the danger of Communist domination of Europe. He wrote in bad, but amusing, English, 'We see now that all has happened such as we discussed it for many days after the catastrophe of Dresden. Your uncle, Mrs. Churchill has discerned the problem in the clearest manner. I read his speeches of Fulton

357

and Zurich with greatest interest.'

Johnny received a letter from Hans-Peter Raffel, the 'nice' night officer at Sonderlager A whom the British nicknamed 'George' (as opposed to 'Jim' the despicable Nazi). Raffel's family had been thrown in a Russian prison camp and were now living in freedom but abject poverty. He wondered if Johnny had any old clothes to spare? Johnny replied, 'If I can be of any help in seeing that justice is done, please let me know.'

A veritable horde of letters was received from people who had met Johnny during his long convalescence at the Haus Elefant. Margarethe Prinzessin zu Waleck wrote from her Schloss to remind Johnny of 'my girls' and how she had found him a room in the best hotel in Weimar. Her father Prince Josias zu Waldeck had visited Johnny there on several occasions. But he was now in a house of correction in Kassel. The Princess wondered if Johnny would very much mind writing a letter that might secure his release. (It is not known what Johnny's reply was, but Prince Josias was later tried for war crimes.)

Clifford Ach remembered their fine teas together in the Elefant and asked Johnny if he knew anybody in the English or US zones who could help him. Robert Hedecke recalled the many evenings they spent in the Haus Elefant drinking a good bottle of wine together in a corner of the restaurant. He was the hotel manager and Johnny gave him a letter certifying that he had been of help to him during that time. When the Americans came into town, Hedecke presented the letter to their commander-in-chief who happened to stay at the Elefant. Unfortunately, the US officer had not returned it and now Hedecke wondered whether Johnny would be kind enough to write another one. Johnny forwarded a note to the Control Commission for Germany confirming the man's story: 'he seemed a decent fellow'.

Maria Arendt wrote Johnny a florid letter saying how pleased she was to hear that he had survived and 'how grateful I remember your chivalrous protection during the days at Weimar in the hôtel "Elephant"'. Johnny forwarded the letter to the British Control Commission with a recommendation: 'I met her and her daughter, Edith Elizabeth Countess Schweinitz, in a bus on my way from Dresden in February 1945, while I was awaiting repatriation. Both these two ladies seemed decent types and were kind to me.' It is not quite clear from Johnny's papers what act of chivalry he performed for Maria Arendt. But from the long list of noble names he seemed prepared to absolve of any involvement in the Nazi regime, it can be concluded that Johnny had a rather benign view of the titled classes.

A letter arrived on behalf of Frau von Alvensleben complaining that within two to three hours of the Russians arriving in Dresden they had thrown her out of their centuries-old house. She was now living in abject poverty with her three children in a wooden hut dependent on public charity, which was not enough to put food on the table. The writer hoped that Johnny would confirm in writing that her husband, the former General of the SS and police chief of Dresden, had 'behaved politically decently, and humanely, and by his actions proved this subsequently'. By this she meant that in the aftermath of the bombings when public rage at the British was rife, von Alvensleben ordered his ordnance officer to make sure Johnny came to no harm, and arranged for him to leave for Weimar as soon as possible.

Johnny was happy to oblige:

He received me, a prisoner of war on route to England, with every courtesy and invited me and my escort to lunch with him . . . During the Allied raid on Dresden . . . my escort and I made our way to General von Alvensleben's Headquarters, about 3 kilometres outside the City. He gave me shelter and showed us every kindness, putting me in charge of his Adjutant with instructions that I should be given every consideration. These instructions were faithfully carried out, and some two or three days later, he arranged for me to be sent to Weimar by motor bus. I wish Frau von Alvensleben and her children nothing but well, and hope their living conditions will improve as soon as possible and that it may be possible for the family to be re-united once again in the near future.

Wings Day, as noted in an earlier chapter dealing with Stalag Luft I at Barth, had not been impressed by Johnny's objectivity. When presiding over a court of inquiry into a young officer accused of collaboration, Wings had expressed the opinion that 'Johnny's angelic view of the world usually left him without any critical sense. His advice was invariably useless because he was so concerned not to hurt anyone's feelings.' But not every one of

Johnny's letters in reply to German post-war entreaties provided the comfort it had presumably been hoped it would elicit. Prinzessin Stephan zu Schaumburg-Lippe wrote pleading on behalf of Walter Schmidt, the police–president of Weimar, who was now in an American detention camp. Johnny's response was far from solicitous.

In a brief note to the Control Commission he wrote: 'I do not remember this lady, although I may have met her, as she states in her letter.' But he said he thought he recalled Schmidt whom he had to visit two or three times in his office in order to register with him and have his rations assigned. 'I know nothing about this man but believe that he could give some information to you as to who was the head of the Gestapo in Weimar as well as some information about the Concentration Camp, near Weimar, which I think was the Buchenwald Camp.'

He heard from Frau Kresz Kemmetex, whom he had met in Regenstauf and whose life had fallen apart since then. Her eldest son had lung trouble, she hadn't heard a word of her youngest son and the family home had been badly damaged. 'The poverty and misery here is indescribable.' On 6 August, Johnny wrote a somewhat non-committal reply. 'I am sorry to hear that your eldest son is ill and you have heard nothing from your youngest one. Also that you have been ill and bed-ridden. I do hope that you will soon be better and that you will have good news on your sons before long.'

By far the greatest amount of correspondence concerned Hans Thost. Thost was arrested shortly after leaving Johnny at the Swiss frontier and ended up being at Dachau concentration camp. At Dachau he was summoned as a witness in the war crimes trial of a Mauthausen concentration camp case in which, it appeared, Thost had been an unwilling accomplice. The incident occurred in between his first meeting with Johnny in Sachsenhausen in October 1944 and their journey together across Germany commencing in February 1945. Interestingly Thost made no mention of it to Johnny during their travels, though it must have left a terrible impression upon his mind.

The crimes in question involved the torture and murder at Mauthausen of several American and British POWs who had been captured after their involvement in commando activity in Slovenia. Thost was there in his capacity as an interpreter and did not like what he witnessed. Indeed the men's suffering at the hands of their sadistic torturers made him sick. Thost, however, was found not to have been directly implicated in the atrocity. He wrote to Johnny from Dachau to say he was shortly to be released and hoped to see Johnny by the end of the year. Unfortunately for Thost, his release was delayed for one reason or another and he spent many months more in captivity—much of them at a British POW camp at Watten, Caithness in Scotland.

Johnny embarked upon a lively correspondence with Thost and regularly sent him cigarettes, as did Bernard Rickatson-Hatt. In one letter to the latter Thost complained, 'We Germans set too much trust in one man who then seemed to be the only alternative to Bolshevism.' To Johnny he wrote: 'I am neither a War Criminal nor have I been a member of the SS or the SD, nor did I join the Intelligence as a civil employee knowing that that office could be classified as criminal. What I have

362

done is serve my country as millions of others did all over the world.' On 9 January 1948, Johnny wrote to the War Office that he would like to do anything he could to extricate Thost from his captivity as he was convinced that the German had saved the lives of Day, Dowse and James, and had accompanied him to safety in Switzerland.

Eventually Thost was released and returned to Germany where he turned to novel-writing: an endeavour, apparently, he had pursued with some success before the war. He sent Johnny one of his books, *Doppelmord im Hypnosegebiet*, set in the Cambridge of 1948. He wondered whether any of Johnny's publishing friends might care to translate it. He said his financial position was somewhat improved and he thought he was over the worst of it. He thought he might be able to rescue his property in the Russian zone. A friend of his had plans to produce the best and cheapest flashlight in the world. Subsequently Thost wrote two detective novels, which he sent to Rickatson-Hatt.

In 1952, Thost wrote a 20-page account of Johnny's and his journey through the Third Reich for *Der Mittag*. He was still hard up and Johnny's mother Flora sent him £50. Johnny, thinking more of his old friend's spiritual health, sent him a *Book of Common Prayer*. 'I am using it every day and the prayers are absolutely the same as they are here and everywhere in the world, the only way and hope that the different nations can come together again.' The last that was heard of Thost was in 1956 when he was working as a sales manager in Cologne.

Johnny also heard from Dr Paul Schmidt. On 26 August 1950, Schmidt wrote: 'If ever you should come by any chance to this part of Germany, please let me know and have a drink with me in the mountains.'

IN MEMORIAM

Johnny would probably have greatly enjoyed a drink in the mountains with Dr Schmidt. Perhaps he did so. But he did not have long to enjoy the peace he had so valiantly fought for. Johnny died suddenly in early November 1960 at the age of 66. He had been hailing a cab near Hyde Park when he suffered a fatal heart attack. The tributes flooded in. Sir Campbell Stuart wrote that Johnny had given Britain 'a service which in physical devotion has rarely been equalled', that he was 'endowed by a constitution that allowed him to swim the Hellespont' and 'unusual personal charm'. Wings Day pointed out that in RAF prison camps Johnny was always the oldest man (though he seems to have forgotten Pop Green).

In this youthful and ebullient company Johnny was a tower of strength. On one side he identified himself with all escaping activities and did the most daring things—such as jumping out of a fast-moving train in broad daylight in view of a lot of trigger-happy guards. On the other he used his great gifts of a powerful personality, charm of manner, charitableness and kindness to bring those around him a balanced way of thought and action.

Wally Floody, the principal engineer of the Sagan

tunnels 'Tom', 'Dick' and 'Harry', praised his 'magnificent outlook and bearing'. Referring to The Ends of the Earth Club, he said Anglo-American friendship and cooperation was the cause he strove for most in his life. 'There never was a more loving or giving man. He was unique . . .'

Johnny was cremated in Sussex and his remains placed in a quiet plot of St Andrew's Church, Ferring. They are there today alongside those of his beloved wife, Minerva. His memorial service was held on 11 November 1960, at the church of St Michael's in London's elegant Chester Square. Some of the most eminent people of post-war Britain were among the congregation, including Lord Longford (or Frank Pakenham, as he was then) and Enoch Powell, as well as Group Captain Douglas Bader, the celebrated fighter pilot hero of the Second World War. Others, less well known, included Wings Day, Sydney Dowse, Jimmy James and Jack Churchill. The one notable absence was Flora, Johnny's mother. Why has never been explained. Perhaps she could not bear the pain.

Presiding over the proceedings was Murdo Ewan Macdonald, the former padre of Stalag Luft III, who read a lesson from *Pilgrim's Progress*. Giving the address was Johnny's old Gallipoli commander, the redoubtable Lieutenant General Bernard Freyberg, VC, GCHG, KCB, KBE, DSO & Three Bars. Freyberg said:

Johnny was built on heroic scale both in physique and character. Tall and splendid looking, he had a selflessness, a simplicity and a generosity of nature that made him loved by all who had the good fortune to call him their

366

friend . . . So on this day we say 'goodbye' to a fighting soldier with great sorrow, but with pride and thanksgiving, for it is through the example and inspiration of such men that the British tradition endures.

Freyberg then quoted the touching sonnet of Maurice Baring:

Because of you we will be glad and gay.
Remembering you, we will be brave and
   strong;
And hail the advent of each dangerous day,
And meet the last adventure with a song.
Whatever new paths, new heights to climb
   you find,
Or gallop through the un-footed asphodel,
We know you know we shall not lag behind,
Nor halt to waste a moment on a fear;
And you will speed us onward with a cheer,
And wave beyond the stars that all is well.

THE GREAT ESCAPERS

Because Johnny died in 1960, he missed the furore created by the subsequent Hollywood film that immortalised one of the greatest adventures of his life. John Sturges' *The Great Escape* came out in 1963, three years after Johnny's sudden and unexpected death. The movie, starring Steve McQueen, Richard Attenborough and a host of Hollywood stars, was based on the 1950 book of the same name written by Paul Brickhill. An Australian writer who had been a Spitfire pilot with the RAF, Brickhill had been in Stalag Luft III. (He had been offered a chance to take part in the escape but when he was taken down the tunnel for the first time, declined, finding the experience unbearably claustrophobic.) The film of his book was a huge box-office hit and quickly achieved classic status. It remains one of the most popular movies of all time. Even today, almost half a century after its premiere, *The Great Escape* continues to attract an enormous audience in television repeats and DVD rentals. It sparked worldwide interest in the real story, which, eventually, the main protagonists were astute enough to capitalise on with a flurry of their own books and memoirs.

In today's world, even the most fleeting brush with death or danger is instantly turned into a mass media event, the central characters transformed overnight into television celebrities. But for the men and women who survived the deprivations of the Second World War, it took some time to realise that their stories were worth telling. The first that Jimmy James knew of the film was when he saw the publicity surrounding its premiere. 'I was in that caper,' he commented without fanfare to his wife, Madge. He had never mentioned his role in it to her during more than a decade of marriage. 'Jimmy didn't talk about the war for a long time,' Madge told this author before she died. 'There were a lot of painful memories.' Sydney Dowse was also not aware of the film until it came out, and he too greeted it with indifference bordering on boredom.

The world had to wait until 1970 for Wings Day's eponymous account of his wartime escapades. It was told in his biography, *Wings Day: The Man Who Led the RAF's Epic Battle in German Captivity*, written by former RAF Squadron Leader Sydney Smith, who had been a prisoner with Day. Smith told his tale in the sort of chummy, hero-worshipping, public-schoolboy style that was a familiar genre of the time. Wings was not entirely happy with it, and at one time considered withdrawing his cooperation from Smith, but was persuaded by his publishers not to do so. The book went on to earn him a modest amount of money to supplement his RAF pension and his other less-than-satisfactory sources of income in post-war austerity Britain. And it brought its subject a modicum of fame. Wings was a subject of the *This is Your Life* series, presented by Irish television star Eamonn Andrews, and he appeared on other programmes to be reunited with old comrades and even his German captor Hermann Glemnitz.

It was more than 12 years before Jimmy James came out with his own story. His slim wartime memoir, *Moonless Night*, eventually became a cult classic in its own right, though it earned him comparatively little money by today's standards. (Over dinner one evening a few years before he died, Jimmy told this author that he had made 'about £25,000' from the original book and its subsequent reprinted editions over the years. Perhaps, in modern money, the equivalent of £50,000 or so—hardly the sort of pay cheque that would prompt, say, *Bravo Two Zero* author Andy McNab to get out of bed.)

In the intervening years, a clutch of other books have been written by veterans of the Great Escape. Their publishers invariably insist that the authors were the original inspiration for Steve McQueen's fictitious Hilts character in the movie. The louche, 'goon-baiting' American, who ended the film being chased on a motorcycle by half the Wehrmacht, didn't exist in real life, of course. There were no Americans in the actual escape, though scores of them had taken part in building the tunnels before their removal to a neighbouring compound put paid to their hopes of escape in them. Johnny was American born, but his character did not resemble Hilts in the slightest. (The character nearest to Johnny in the movie was probably Cavendish, the relentlessly optimistic Englishman who acted as choir conductor to drown out the sound of digging—as Johnny had done.)

In fact, there was an American in Stalag Luft III whose character very much resembled Hilts. He was William Ash, a Texan who in his youth bore a distinct resemblance to Steve McQueen, and cast a debonair figure as he flew Spitfires for the Royal Canadian Air Force. After being shot down

371

and taken prisoner, Bill became an inveterate escapologist (he had been in the famous latrine break-out from Schubin) and was involved in several episodes identical to those portrayed in the movie involving Hilts. But Bill wasn't in the Great Escape: on the night of the break-out he was in the cooler being punished for one of his many misdemeanours. Bill, a convinced Marxist, was awarded the MBE for his escape activities and published his own account, *Under the Wire*, with Brendan Foley in 2005. He is alive and well and living in London. If anyone is the 'real' Steve McQueen character, it is the indomitable figure of William Ash.

Until now, Johnny's story has never been told. Paul Brickhill had hoped to write Johnny's biography, and was engaged in research on his formidable subject when he died in 1991. The *Superman* (1978) film actor, Christopher Reeve, had hoped to make a big screen 'bio-pic' of Johnny. Reeve's interest in Johnny was piqued when he starred as him in a 1988 NBC television series entitled *The Great Escape II: The Untold Story*. The series revolved around the post-war investigation into the murders of the 50 escapers, and Reeve was cast as Major Dodge, the larger-than-life character who led the investigation. But the somewhat lamentable effort might have been better titled *The Great Escape II: The Untrue Story*, so wayward was it with the facts. (There is further discussion of this NBC series in Appendix II.) Johnny had nothing to do with the post-war investigation other than supplying witness testimony, and the dramatic shoot-out that came towards the end of the series owes more to Hollywood's febrile imagination than real life.

Christopher Reeve was hopelessly embarrassed by the end result and wrote an apologetic letter to Johnny's family. He vowed to make his own film about Johnny's life and was helped in his research by a near-neighbour in Virginia, Phyllis Dodge, whose own efforts to write a book about her distinguished namesake occupied the last years of her life. But, as we know, Reeve became a quadriplegic after a riding accident in 1995 and passed away in 2004. His film remained unmade. Phyllis's efforts had also come to nothing when she passed away shortly afterwards. In the circumstances it is fair to say that Johnny seemed jinxed.

But if Johnny, thanks to these multiple strokes of misfortune, was not immediately able to join his old friends in the media 'hall of fame' that grew in the 1970s to celebrate their achievements, he was never far from their thoughts. Every one of their books mentions the charismatic figure of Major Johnny Dodge, and no interview with a 'Great Escaper' would be complete without a reference to this formidable character who seemed to have touched all their lives. The Great Escapers remained, after the war, one great big fraternity of men who were bound by their common experience and stayed in touch with one another to the end of their lives. There were many reunions and get-togethers. Not just the escapers who had actually emerged unscathed from the break-out of March 1944, but the families of the 50 who were murdered, and the hundreds of other men who had taken part in the tunnelling and many other clandestine operations that made the great feat possible. 'They are like a family,' Wings Day's daughter, June, once said to this author, amazed at the affection they continued to display towards her father long after his death.

Those closest to Johnny—mainly those who escaped with him in March 1944 and afterwards endured captivity in the special camp attached to Sachsenhausen—were his 'family'. Wings Day ended up living abroad, and Jimmy James led a peripatetic existence moving restlessly from one region of Britain to another while serving in a number of diplomatic posts in Europe and Africa. Only Sydney Dowse remained living nearby (in some splendour) in London. Nevertheless, Minerva and Johnny's homes—a house in Chester Row and a lavish flat in Kingston House overlooking Hyde Park—were magnets for the Great Escapers whenever they were in town. He was the rock in their lives, a benign uncle-figure who was the one constant in their ever-changing fortunes.

Wings Day might have led the RAF's epic battle against the Germans from behind the wire, but he found that the great battles of life were by no means restricted to wartime. Peacetime for Wings presented almost as many obstacles to him as had the high command of the Third Reich. In the last weeks of the war, Wings was one of dozens of VIP *Prominenten* hostages whom the SS intended to use as bargaining chips with the approaching Allies. They were moved by the SS from concentration camps throughout Germany towards the long-hoped-for 'Southern Redoubt' around the Führer's Berchtesgaden alpine retreat. Dowse, James and the two Churchills from Sachsenhausen were part of one particularly remarkable convoy of distinguished prisoners whom the SS escorted

374

across the Brenner Pass into the borderlands of the Austrian/Italian Tirol. Thankfully, the Third Reich's glorious last stand never happened. Instead Hitler and his henchmen disappeared with a whimper. And the orders the SS had from Himmler to 'liquidate' their VIP prisoners were never carried out. Wings made it to freedom in one last escape attempt, this time in the company of an Italian resistance fighter called Anton Ducia. He had finally escaped the jaws of the Nazi beast.

But his return some days later to a newly constructed Blackbushe Airport near Camberley, Hampshire, was an anti-climactic affair. His first act was to head for the nearest telephone box and call his wife, Doris. When he got through to her, reports Sydney Smith in his biography, 'Their greetings were cold and brief and held no future promise.' The marriage was, to all intents and purposes, over. Doris had further bad news for her luckless husband—his beloved mother had died in November 1944. 'Wings hung up as a great wave of desolation engulfed him.' During his imprisonment at Sachsenhausen, Wings—like the other Great Escapers—had become a 'non person', not allowed by the SS to send or receive mail. In the absence of any word from him, Wings was convinced that his mother had given up on her own fragile life because she presumed her son was dead.

The immense pressure that Wings had been under during his years of confinement began to take their toll. He succumbed to the dubious joys that drink promises, and disgraced himself somewhat as a result. Once, according to his daughter June, while on a tour of the United States (possibly to promote his book, it is unclear—as no doubt Wings was), an American Army Air Force officer telephoned England to demand that 'somebody come over here and take this bum off our hands'. Worse still, his misjudgement landed him in legal difficulties. In Sydney Smith's book, Wings had implied that the Irish soldiers who had been imprisoned with him in the special compound at Sachsenhausen were as good as traitors. When one of them took exception to this suggestion, Wings was on the receiving end of a solicitor's letter. Unfortunately he was unable to substantiate his claim despite assuring his publisher that he was in possession of certain proof. Nor could Wings explain why, if the men were traitors, he had wholeheartedly supported their claim for compensation in the 1960s. The affair ended in ignominy for Wings. (In fact, though one Irishman in Sachsenhausen was undoubtedly a traitor, the others were comprehensively cleared of any wrongdoing.)

It would be unfair to take too stern a view of Wings. During his years in captivity he had been a fully active member of various escape committees, constantly struggling to confound, confuse and harass the enemy. He had taken part in several escapes, which were all nerve-wracking experiences, all risking sudden death either through a tunnel collapse or the actions of German guards. He had also combined for most of his time behind the wire the onerous duties of being a commanding officer of thousands of men with being a father-figure to many of the younger officers in his charge. Wings had what amounted to a nervous breakdown as early as 1941 at Stalag Luft I in Barth, when the pressure became too much. It is hardly surprising that after five-and-a-half years of captivity, it all became too much for him. Wings may have suffered, too, from that common complaint among members of the armed forces at all times and across all generations—the sheer inability to cope with the tedium of ordinary life.

Wings might have expected some solace in the form of his second marriage, to Margot, but that too broke down. It was bad enough that the newspapers found out that Margot had walked out on him to live with a younger and more dashingly handsome rival. Worse still, perhaps, was that the younger man was his former junior officer, Sydney Dowse. The betrayal was to be an understandable source of bitterness to Wings for many years afterwards.

Wings lived in England immediately after the war ended, dividing his time between a house in a plush part of Knightsbridge and a home on the Isle of Wight. But eventually he moved to the warmer and more tax-friendly climate of Malta, where he became a central and much-respected figure in the ex-pat community. He died in the island's Blue Sisters Hospital on 11 March 1977, still loved and revered by all those who remembered his steadfast commitment to duty during the war. He ended his life with the George Cross, the Albert Medal and the Distinguished Service Order to his credit. He was a member of the Order of the British Empire, and he was also the holder of the Legion of Merit awarded by the US military. The few comrades that remain from his days of imprisonment in Germany have nothing but kind words for him.

Civilian life smiled more kindly upon Sydney Dowse—appropriately enough for somebody who had been nicknamed 'Laughing Boy' for his irrepressible enthusiasm and easygoing bonhomie. Dowse returned to Britain to take up a post in the Colonial Office, and in the 1950s acted as an equerry at Buckingham Palace, an undemanding assignment given his own expensive tastes and love of elegance. He lived in a grand, white-painted stucco house on Chelsea's Royal Avenue, dividing his time between London and his two homes in Monte Carlo. ('One near the sea for when I want to swim; one nearer the town for dinner time,' he once explained to this author.) One of them at least appears to have been half-owned by Margot, possibly with Wings Day as the other part-owner. It was difficult to tell with the impenetrable maze that surrounded Sydney's financial affairs. There are suggestions that he became unwittingly implicated in an infamous fraudulent insurance scandal.

'Sydney always marries well,' Jimmy James once told this author over dinner at the RAF Club in Piccadilly. The comment was made with a knowing smile, but not without a hint of envy. Dowse married three times and had several girlfriends. He owned fast sports cars and was driven around London in a shiny Rolls Royce. He never had to book for dinner at the Savoy, where the staff knew him well and would instantly show him to one of the best tables. He paid out of his own pocket for a 50th anniversary party of the Great Escape at the RAF Club. He never experienced the joy of fatherhood, however. And he seemed to have a love-hate relationship with some of his former comrades. He held a grudge against Wings Day for no apparent reason, though Wings had actually championed the cause of Sachsenhausen

378

compensation on Sydney's behalf. And it was Sydney who had cuckolded Wings, not the other way around. Similarly with Jimmy James, the man with whom he had built the Sachsenhausen tunnel, Sydney would at times display polite courtesy, and at other times unaccountable coldness. At a reunion staged by the Imperial War Museum in 2004 the two were photographed together by newspapers but the simmering tension between them is clearly perceptible. They could hardly look each other in the eye.

One of Sydney's complaints was that Jimmy had 'cashed in' on the Great Escape. It was certainly true that in the last years of his life Jimmy became the public face of the wartime band of brothers who had taken part in the escapade. He appeared in countless television documentaries, radio programmes and newspaper articles, forever recounting the same experiences he had told of and written about a thousand times before. Jimmy also made a modest income from autograph signing at a bi-annual Autographica convention, where famous names of bygone days gather for the benefit of their fanatical followers. But who could blame him? Jimmy, unlike Johnny and to a lesser extent Wings, had no family money. Unlike Sydney he could not depend upon the largesse of wealthy wives to keep him in the style to which he had become accustomed. In fact he lived terribly modestly, ending his days in a tiny red-brick terrace on a modern housing estate in Ludlow. Jimmy had to depend upon the miserable pensions he derived from his brief service in the RAF, and the years he spent in the Diplomatic Corps after the war.

Besides, there was a serious point to Jimmy's

excursions into the public arena, the vast majority of which were fuelled by media interest in him rather than any lust for self-publicity. Jimmy passionately believed that totalitarianism in any form must be opposed wherever it reared its ugly head; and, in turn, liberty must be celebrated—not least by honouring those who risked life and limb in past and ongoing fights for freedom. He was a member of the Freedom Foundation, and a founding member of the committee to commemorate the horrors of Sachsenhausen. He was also a regular guest at many RAF get-togethers, particularly at his old squadron's base at Marham, Norfolk, where he was an inspirational speaker and role model to a younger generation of servicemen and women.

Jimmy had a fulfilling career after the war, though his post-war life was also not without sadness. He met his wife-to-be at a dance in the British Sector of Berlin immediately after the war. Madge was a beautiful Irish nurse. Jimmy adored her. They fell in love immediately and never fell out of love. They married in 1946. He left the RAF in 1958, by which time he had become a squadron leader. Unlike Johnny, who had not managed to learn more than a smattering of German during his endless hours in captivity, Jimmy had diligently studied several languages and emerged from the war proficient in French, German and Russian. His linguistic skills proved valuable. He was appointed the general-secretary of the Foreign and Commonwealth Office-sponsored Great Britain–USSR Association, and subsequently enjoyed a career in the diplomatic service, which he joined in 1964. He held posts in Africa, Western and Eastern

Europe and London. Jimmy retired in 1975 and devoted the rest of his life to commemorating the wartime deeds of his former comrades. He served as the British representative on the International Sachsenhausen Committee.

Madge and Jimmy had one child, a son named Patrick. Sadly, Patrick died in 1970, a tragedy that was to haunt Madge and Jimmy for the remainder of their lives. Jimmy died in January 2008 at the age of 92. His funeral in Ludlow was one of the biggest events the sleepy Shropshire market town had ever witnessed. In Saint Peter's Roman Catholic Church, his coffin was draped in the Union Flag. His medals and Royal Air Force cap graced the top alongside a crucifix symbolising his deep faith. As the RAF honour guard accompanied Jimmy to the cemetery on his last earthly journey, the famous theme music of the film was played and crowds lining the route clapped and cheered. At his graveside, a bugler played the Last Post. And in a final farewell, four Tornado GR9s from his old squadron roared above in a 'missing man' formation.

Sydney Dowse died a few months later. The final few years of his life had brought mixed blessings. He appears to have been suffering from Alzheimer's disease, and a nurse was enlisted to take care of him at his large house in Chelsea. Unfortunately, all was not well with the nurse's credentials and she was removed from her post after irregularities of a financial nature emerged. But Sydney was lucky to have a doting lover in the form of his latest girlfriend, who divided her time between Sydney in Chelsea and her husband at his enormous country estate in Hampshire. When she realised that Sydney had effectively been fleeced, she bought a large modern house for him near the village she lived in with her husband, and paid for a Polish couple to take care of him. Sydney moved in and spent his last years in the company of his lover.

When she showed him Jimmy's obituary in *The Times*, Sydney burst into tears. 'But you hated Jimmy,' she chastised, reminding him of the many unkind words he had had to say about his former escaping partner. 'Yes,' he replied, nodding tearfully, 'but I loved him too.'

Sydney Dowse died on 10 April 2008. He is buried in a sleepy Hampshire graveyard near the ancient manor house of his last lover's husband. The plot beside Sydney's is reserved for her . . . and the one next to hers is where her husband will be buried.

Per Ardua ad Astra.

Appendix I

LORD FREYBERG'S ADDRESS AT JOHNNY'S MEMORIAL SERVICE

This is the full text of Lord Freyberg's address at the Memorial Service for Colonel J.B. Dodge, D.S.O., D.S.C., M.C. on 11 November 1960.

I first got to know Colonel Johnny Dodge when he and I joined the Naval Division in the early days of August 1914. We were then under the command of the Admiralty and were ordered to go overseas, to serve as part of the Expeditionary Force, for Winston Churchill was eager to put up a special effort to defend Antwerp against the first German onslaught in August 1914. In those days it was first come first served, and we got away to a flying start.

When we came back a month later after the fighting at Antwerp, those of us who did adequately had already gained a certain experience, and I considered myself fortunate in being given command of a Company in the Hood Battalion.

I look back on this appointment with the greatest satisfaction as I found myself commanding a remarkable collection of young men who were serving as my Hood Battalion platoon commanders. They were mostly friends of Winston Churchill—Arthur Asquith, son of the Prime Minister; Charles Lister, diplomat; Patrick Shaw-Stuart, banker; F.S. Kelly and Denis Browne, talented musicians and composers; Johnny Dodge and Rupert Brooke. They were a distinguished group who, had they lived, would have risen to great heights in their respective spheres of life.

Johnny Dodge was one of those who dug Rupert Brooke's grave on the island of Skyros on the 23rd April, 1915, on the eve of the ill-fated Gallipoli Landing, and one of the few of my Hood Battalion Company who survived the First World War. During the actual landing Johnny and his Platoon were detached from the Naval Division and were put on board the *River Clyde*, the Trojan Horse surprise ship, and they were actually one of the first units to land at Cape Helles. When Johnny saw that all was not going according to plan, he led his Platoon into the fighting with the utmost gallantry until he was badly wounded and he had to be sent home to recover. There is no doubt that during the landing operations in Gallipoli, and especially on the beaches, Johnny showed the greatest skill and courage, worthy of the highest praise. After the Gallipoli Campaign Johnny transferred from the Naval Division to the Army and served in continuous campaigns including the battles on the Western Front. Ultimately he was taken prisoner fighting against the Communists on the Russian Front.

On the outbreak of the Second World War he joined up and rose to command an Infantry Battalion, which he did with great skill and determination. He was serving on the front near Calais that was surrounded during the battle for Dunkirk and when the whole front collapsed he was again captured. Characteristically he did not accept captivity passively but made a series of attempts to escape.

Johnny was built on heroic scale both in physique

384

and character. Tall and splendid looking, he had a selflessness, a simplicity and a generosity of nature that made him loved by all who had the good fortune to call him their friend. Twelve years and more have gone by since victory was won, but these years have not been years of joy and triumph, but have been years of bickering all over the world. Johnny made his contribution to the cause of peace in many ways—notably by his untiring work for The Ends of the Earth Club and his loyal support of Old Comrades and Ex-Service activities, where his presence always brought a special measure of happiness.

* * *

Johnny has been taken from his family and his friends with cruel suddenness, and though this may be a merciful parting for those who go, for those who are left to face the shock of such swift bereavement and then the sorrow of loneliness and longing, our hearts do indeed go out in sympathy and understanding. To his wife, who had already endured the long and anxious years when he was a prisoner, to his sons and their young families to whom he was such a guide and inspiration, and to his aged mother, our thoughts and our prayers are offered that they may be strengthened by his courage and comforted by their host of happy memories.

So on this day we say 'goodbye' to a fighting soldier with great sorrow, but with pride and thanksgiving, for it is through the example and inspiration of such men that the British tradition endures.

385

When I lose a soldier friend, I think of the golden words of Maurice Baring, written in memory of his life-long poet friend, Julian Greenfell, killed in Ypres in 1916. He wrote a lovely sonnet, part of which I would like to repeat to you.

Because of you we will be glad and gay.
Remembering you, we will be brave and
     strong;
And hail the advent of each dangerous day,
And meet the last adventure with a song.
Whatever new paths, new heights to climb
     you find,
Or gallop through the un-footed asphodel,
We know you know we shall not lag behind,
Nor halt to waste a moment on a fear;
And you will speed us onward with a cheer,
And wave beyond the stars that all is well.

Lieutenant Governor's Office,
Windsor Castle.

CHRISTOPHER REEVE AND *THE GREAT ESCAPE II: THE UNTOLD STORY*

The Great Escape II: The Untold Story might very well have been called 'The Great Escape II: The Untrue Story'. The 1988 NBC four-hour television mini-series was billed as the story of Major John Dodge the 'Allied officer and P.o.W. who returns to Nazi Germany to find the killers of fifty fellow prisoners'. Johnny, in fact, had little to do with the post-war RAF investigation into the murders of the 50, beyond supplying as much information as he possibly could to the investigating authorities. He certainly did not return to Germany in search of the murderers, and the absurd shoot-out scene that takes place in the television series is pure fiction. It appears that Christopher Reeve, the star of the series, despite his initial enthusiasm for the project—prompted by his passion for the story of Johnny's life—wanted little to do with the production once it came out.

The film owes its origins to Phyllis Dodge's book, *The Phelps–Dodge Connection*. The family history book was sent for review to the Princeton office of Barbara/Margaret Johnson, the editor of the town's weekly *Town Topics* newspaper. She happened to be the mother of the *Superman* actor and sent him the copy. 'It was a real bonanza for me,' said Reeve. 'And she sent it to me, you know, saying, "You're playing John Dodge, aren't you?"' Having been fascinated by *The Great Escape* as a boy growing up in Princeton, watching the film at least 15 times and reading the book until the cover came off, Reeve's curiosity was piqued by the largely untold story of one of the principal participants in the real-life drama. It turned out he lived only ten miles away from Phyllis Dodge, whose home was in Pownal, Vermont on the Massachusetts border. They met and Reeve spent hours going through Johnny's letters home from his days in Stalag Luft III, and other camps.

Reeve subsequently met Johnny's elder son, Tony, in London and his impression of the man was confirmed.

He was an incredible man, intelligent, fearless . . . According to Tony he never had anger or hatred for anyone, not even the Germans. To me he was like a nineteenth-century man in the twentieth century. I was impressed with his generosity of spirit. He turned his back on a life of privilege and put himself in dangerous situations.

Superficially, at least, Reeve bore a passing resemblance to Johnny. Tall and handsome, he was an accomplished flier, skier, horseman and pianist. Eventually the film was made and included in its cast Ian McShane (as Roger Bushell, Big X), Judd Hirsch and Donald Pleasance, who in the original *The Great Escape*, of course, played a prisoner forger but in *The Great Escape II* is a villainous Gestapo official among those responsible for the killing of the 50.

Unsurprisingly, the 'sequel' to this classic true story received dire reviews. 'There are moments . . .

when I thought I was watching *Hogan's Heroes*. So incredible is this story, it's hard to believe it actually happened . . . Christopher Reeve is totally colourless as Major John Dodge.' The *New York Times* said, 'Among all the required suspensions of disbelief in *The Great Escape II: The Untold Story* . . . no doubt the most demanding is to accept as Sir Winston Churchill's cousin . . . The film was inspired by a true story, which in television means that the facts can be adjusted for the sake of dramatic licence.'

Writing to Jane Aitken, Tony Dodge's ex-wife, Phyllis Dodge said the film was 'about as near the truth as Pownal is to Toronto!' According to Jimmy James, Paul Brickhill had his name taken off the credits. Brickhill himself appears to confirm this in an apologetic letter to Tony Dodge in which he wrote: 'I fear they may use my name . . . Johnny would have been mortified . . . it is unforgiveable.' After seeing the film on television, Phyllis B. Dodge wrote to Reeve diplomatically praising the 'good job' he did but lamenting the 'incredible' plot and saying, 'I winced when Johnnie [*sic*] called Churchill "Winnie".' Privately with the Dodge family, Reeve was at pains to distance himself from the project. But the late actor can hardly escape blame. He made several statements in the pre-publicity for the series which cast doubt on his judgement. Identifying Dodge as the officer who led the escape, he said, 'But because he made the decision to go when he did, he carried the burden of guilt with him for a lifetime.' It is doubtful whether Johnny would ever have claimed that he had 'led' the escape, and he certainly didn't carry a burden of guilt with him about the dreadful murders. In the same New York newspaper interview, Reeve explained why it had been decided to recast Johnny in the role of the avenging RAF investigator [Wing Commander Bowes]. 'To switch mid-way to another character would destroy the film's flow.'

Appendix III

THE REAL GREAT ESCAPE

It would be a mistake to think that the 'Great Escape' came as any great surprise to the Germans. About 100 tunnels had been constructed in Stalag Luft I at Barth, and a similar number would be built at Sagan's Stalag Luft III before the end of the war. Tunnels were routinely dug out of many of the other camps housing Allied prisoners, army and air force. By 1944 when the Great Escape took place, it was not unusual for the tunnels to be of a similar intricate construction to that of Tom, Dick and Harry; and for the escapers to be equipped with well-designed bogus documents and disguises. Some 50 NCOs were involved in such an escape only weeks before the break-out from Sagan. This escape, along with a mass escape by French officers, has received very little publicity. Undoubtedly, the single factor that marked the Great Escape for special attention was the murder of the 50, a kind of reprisal that did not take place in any other instance.

At Stalag Luft III in the months before the break-out, Colonel von Lindeiner had received many reports from his security staff, which indicated something bigger and more complex than usual was afoot. He was especially concerned about this because he knew that the problem of escaping Allied prisoners was beginning to aggravate the Nazi high command, which was angry at the huge number of personnel and resources being diverted from valuable war work in order to track the escapers down.

Von Lindeiner tried always to respect the Geneva Convention but was aware that Berlin's attitude towards escaping officers was becoming more ruthless and to a certain extent cavalier. There had been some ugly incidents in other camps. Even Dulag Luft was no longer the oasis of civility that it had been in the days of Major Theo Rumpel when Johnny had first been taken prisoner. In one instance at the Frankfurt transit camp, an SS officer had ordered two Luftwaffe guards to shoot an Allied airman in their care. When they refused he took out his gun and shot the man on the spot. The episode provoked the new commandant of Dulag Luft to travel to Berlin and protest. But his protest fell on deaf ears.

In early 1944, the German authorities issued two orders that had ominous portents for future Allied escapers. The first, Stüfe Romisch III, came from the headquarters of the OKW, the Oberkommando der Wehrmacht (Supreme Command of the Armed Forces). It stated that future escapers who were recaptured, with the exception of the British and Americans, were to be handed over to the Gestapo rather than the appropriate German military authorities. The British and Americans were to be held in military or police jails, while the authorities decided whether or not to hand them over to the Gestapo.

The prisoners became aware of this order when one Allied officer found himself alone and unguarded in von Lindeiner's office and to his surprise realised the safe was open. When curiosity got the better of him he found the document lying

392

there in front of him. Whether von Lindeiner deliberately left the safe open will never be known, but it would certainly be characteristic of him to do so. The second order was even less subtle. Aktion Kugel, the Bullet Decree, was secretly issued by Gestapo chief Heinrich Müller. It decreed that all recaptured officers, again except Britons and Americans, were to be taken to Mauthausen Concentration Camp and executed before their names were even entered on the camp register. They would simply disappear.

Von Lindeiner was not only worried about the reactions of the SS and the Gestapo, two organisations that were widely feared throughout the Reich. The camp commandant was also concerned about the feeling among the general civilian population towards Allied airmen. For many months the mood had been turning ugly against the 'terror fliers' who were reducing Germany's cities to ashes, killing thousands of innocent women and children.

The Nazi propaganda minister, Joseph Goebbels, had asked: 'Who is in the right? The murderers who expect humane treatment after their cowardly attacks? Or the victims of those foul and cowardly attacks who seek their revenge? We owe it to our people, which is defending itself with so much honesty and courage, that it not be allowed to become human game to be hunted down by the enemy.'

There had been cases of lynch mobs setting upon downed aircrews who were only saved at the last moment by the Home Guard or Hitler Youth that generally arrived on the scene as soon as a plane hit the ground. Von Lindeiner wondered what sort of reception escaped airmen would receive if they were caught by angry Germans and there was nobody there to step in and save them.

When von Lindeiner heard that the prisoners were planning a mass break-out he decided to summon senior officers from every compound to warn them of the dangers. Von Lindeiner said the war could not possibly go on for more than another year and it was folly to take such risks in the circumstances. He wasn't the only one worried. Many of the German staff were genuinely fond of their Allied prisoners and passed on their concerns to them. It wasn't through self-interest alone that Hauptmann Hans Pieber privately warned the Allied officers to avoid a mass break-out. He told them the Gestapo were looking for any excuse to take matters into their own hands. But most of the prisoners, in their isolated existence, knew nothing of the change in mood outside the camp.

The German warnings of courts martial the previous year had not been taken seriously, and certainly few Allied prisoners believed the Germans would shoot them in cold blood. One English officer displayed a commendably gentlemanly view of the enemy when he insisted they would never be so 'unsporting'. Some of the prisoners believed that the rumours they were hearing from the camp staff were part of an orchestrated campaign to dissuade them from staging an escape which could only reflect badly on von Lindeiner.

The Luftwaffe, as von Lindeiner repeatedly warned the Allied officers, could only guarantee their safety and proper treatment while the prisoners were in its hands. Once outside the wire, there was a bewildering array of different criminal and quasi-military bodies that the airmen could fall into the hands of. Few of them could be trusted to take as indulgent a view of Allied airmen as Hermann Göring did. The most feared organisation was Heinrich Himmler's Reichssicherheitshauptamt, the RSHA or Central Security Headquarters. The RSHA's responsibilities ranged from regular police traffic patrols to extermination in the concentration camps. There were many wings of the RSHA including the Kripo (the Criminal Police) headed by General Artur Nebe and the Gestapo (which the former was often confused with) headed by Gruppenführer Heinrich Müller. And there was one particular department concerned purely with preventing escapes from prisoner-of-war camps. The man from the department responsible for Stalag Luft III was an SS Major called Erich Brunner.

In February of 1944, von Lindeiner asked Brunner to come to the camp. During a short meeting with him, he is believed to have expressed fears that a mass escape was imminent. Curiously, despite this explicit warning, Brunner failed to reinstall seismograph equipment that had been removed from the camp for maintenance work. (It was an oversight that led to speculation after the war that the Nazi authorities were hoping there would indeed be an escape, and that they would use it as an opportunity to make an example of the escapers.)

Most prisoners displayed what in retrospect appeared to be a naive confidence in the strictures of the Geneva Convention. 'The Geneva Convention makes it quite clear that it recognises an officer's duty to escape, and that escaped prisoners of war are a protected species so long as they don't break the law of the land they are in,' Jimmy James once remonstrated with a fellow prisoner. 'If apprehended we should give up in a peaceful fashion and we will be conveyed back to our prisoner-of-war camp.'

Appendix IV

EDITED EXTRACTS FROM JOHNNY'S LETTERS HOME WHILE IN CAPTIVITY

I present these letters, some of which have been used in the preceding text because, seen in their raw state, they afford a refreshing glimpse of Johnny's life as a prisoner of war. It was a fairly comfortable existence, I would contend, quite different from the image that is conjured up in the many films about Second World War prison camps. The letters also give a comparatively unedited insight into Johnny's character and mentality. His love of his fellow man and child-like lack of guile; his fairness towards the enemy; his balanced approach towards life; his ever-inquiring sensibilities and boundless optimism for the future—these are the characteristics that prompted so many people to like him, even when they violently disagreed with his views of life.

The letters have been edited to avoid excessive mundane detail or repetition.

29 June 1940
To Flora
This takes you + Minerva + David + Tony my love. You are all constantly in my thoughts, + how I wish we were all together, singing, talking, working, eating, reading . . . On the 12th June I was wounded in both feet + on the 13th June I was captured by the Germans. Yesterday after

bussing + marching 250 miles, I thought for a short time I should soon be with you again, but it was not to be. Today I am in Germany after being recaptured, in a camp occupied mostly by R.A.F. prisoners. I don't know much as they have very kindly put me to bed in a room to myself in a house for sick prisoner officers, after bandaging my feet which are bruised, swollen + blistered . . . before I was captured on the 13th I tried to swim to a British ship 3 miles out to sea and tell it where our troops were, but when I got half way to it, it moved away. I reached shore again 4 hours later, 3 miles away from my clothes and shoes, with Germans in between, so I lost everything. Walking along the seashore that night, barefooted on the rocks with the tide out, wounded + hurt my feet badly. . . . Yesterday morning, I jumped overboard from the small steamer we were on, in the hopes of getting home to you all sooner, but after swimming a 1 + ½ hrs, about 2 miles, I was soon retaken after reaching shore. [Source—local newspaper]

Barth, Stalag Luft I
1 January 1942
To Minerva
The Red X is doing splendid work for us P.O.W. + we appreciate it very much. Their food parcels make all the difference + their Xmas ones were excellent + we are grateful.

I am i/c of debates + we have some very interesting ones fortnightly + general knowledge games as well. I am also arranging lectures on different subjects of common

398

interest Wednesday evenings at 9.

Madge produced 3 one act plays by Noel Coward last Friday afternoon + they were a great success. Next week we are producing a pantomime.

Our band is very good, especially the leader South African Lt. Wilkins, a fine trumpeter, + the pianist, a Canadian Fl. Lt. Corbett from Ottawa.

Xmas evening we had some beers and sang songs. A Xmas present of books for the camp from King + Queen was very much appreciated.

Stalag Luft I
Undated, 1941/42
To Minerva
Thanks for your letters of Oct 24th + Nov 5th + Tony's beautifully written one . . . Have you sold the car? Has Florida been rented?

We all here are very grateful for everything the Red X is doing for us. We realise that at present we are no use + therefore appreciate all the more anything Madelain B [Madelaine Balfour, Head of Air Mail Despatch room, Joint War Organisation of the British Red Cross Society] + her friends at the Red X have + are doing.

Have been reading 1st + 2nd Kings in O.T. which is fascinating. Also Macaulay's . . . Historical Essays especially one on 'Gladstone on Church + State.'

Stalag Luft I
1 February 1942
To Minerva

I do hope Peter is alright again now + am delighted he is going into the U.S. Army on account of the tradition of his name. Give him my love + best wishes.

He asks to be remembered to 'my old friends in Mile End . . . + our friends at Gillingham'. There is a nice chap from there, name Poulter, an observer here, who used to audit the Borough accounts.

Have been enjoying Ford's 'Life + Work'. I think that many of his ideas on business are very sound especially 'Service comes before profit'.

Stalag Luft I
28 February 1942
To Minerva
My love to Peter. So glad he is well + wish him the Best of Luck. My love to Tony. He must have enjoyed the tobogganing. I play ice hockey daily. Our Army team, which I captain, played the Navy the other day. We were beaten 4-3. We play again tomorrow.

Read 32nd Chapter 2nd Chronicles. Am appreciating O.T. as never before.

Have been reading Buchan with delight, 'Midwinter + the Dancing Floor'.

I am delighted with what Clemy's husband has done in Washington + also with our representative there.

Stalag Luft I
22 March 1942
To Minerva
W/Cmd Day with 1/3rd of the compound have been moved to another camp + the rest of us

join them next month.

The Red X food parcels are splendid + the work they do for P's of War generally. They send excellent parcels from Argentina + Canada as well as U.K. My love to Balfours + tell her how much we appreciate all Red X are doing for us.

The Sergeants gave us an excellent concert last week + our officers orchestra played beautifully last month.

W/Comdr Day the S.B.O. has written the Red X asking for an authoritative course of general study with examinations for preparing p's of w to play their part in the world after the war. This is particularly wanted by the young ones who are uncertain as to their future careers + therefore lack a guide as to how to employ the time available for reading + studying. The examinations would provide the necessary incentive if the results were placed on their record which otherwise would be blank. Ask Baxter to support the idea.

Read Macaulay's Essay on Addison. I know you will enjoy it as I did.

I hope David will carry on as he is + not go away to school for at least another year or so.

Stalag Luft I
31 March 1942
To Flora
The Red X parcels arriving now are beautifully packed—sugar, cheese etc + the contents are excellent. They send some food parcels direct from Canada + the Argentine + U.S.A. and the same applies to them. 300 Pyjamas (Ajax) came

401

from [indecipherable] to the S.B. officers here on the 6th + were much appreciated. Presumably your 200 were among them. Many thanks to you and your friends from us all. On the 9th 12 parcels of cigarettes + food arrived from Jack Greenway + 2 more parcels from him today. Please thank him very much for these + for the parcels he has also sent my friends here. A parcel of sardines + nuts + raisins came today from Mrs. Ian Campbell of the Portuguese Red X, presumably arranged by Olive + Bertie. Please thank them too.

Sorry to hear about . . . Lady Hamilton. Please give Sir Ian my sympathy + love. I am proud to have had the privilege of serving under him.

I am so pleased at David's progress, + hope that he will remain with you + not go to school for at least another year or two.

Am enjoying Macaulay's essay on Lord Byron. 2 nights a week we listen for an hour to classical gramophone records sent to us by the Red X + it is a joy.

The other day I saw the 1st bullfinch this year + early this am the sound of the birds reminded me of Ferring in Spring.

My comrades come from the flower of the youth of the empire + are delightful companions. I hope I may be of some use to them.

Easter Monday, 1942
To Minerva
Am reading John in the O.T. + find it comforting. Have also enjoyed Richard III, read act 4, scene III + act V, scene V.

At times like these we learn how much we can do without, which before we mistook for necessities. This afternoon we had an amusing game of cricket with a bed board made into a bat + a tennis ball. It is wise not to depend upon material things for our happiness.

After the war there will be more love and unselfishness + less envy + hatred. More cooperation, respect + toleration of others.

Stalag Luft III
23 April 1942
To Flora
Thank you for sending me 'The Dragon Book'. I like what Huc said about the basis of society. [Évariste Régis Huc, or Abbé Huc, (1813–1860) was a French missionary traveller, famous for his accounts of China, Tartary and Tibet.] 'The idea of the family is the grand principle which serves as the basis of Chinese society. Filial piety, the constant subject of dissertation for moralists + philosophers, + continually recommended in the proclamations of the emperors + the speeches of mandarins, has been the fundamental root of all other virtues.'

We are gradually settling into this new camp, which is much larger + therefore we need fewer circuits to walk any distance. My room-mate + I take our meals with 6 others in their room. Among the 8 are 2 South Africans, 1 Canadian, Hardy de Forest [actually, Hardie deforest], 1 New Zealander, 1 Anglo-Indian. I bathe by pouring basins of water over my head in the wash-house. The water is good, soft + cold + the air is good too. I feel very well + have

403

enjoyed digging up tree stumps for a sportsfield.

We all here admire Clemy's husband + are glad he is where he is as we have complete confidence in him. Each and every one of us say 'God bless him'. I feel . . . this will teach men + nations the necessity of more unselfishness + more cooperation between nations + all sections of any community, if the whole is to be strong, healthy + happy . . . Life here teaches one to appreciate + be grateful for blessings which one too often ignores + takes for granted. Many of my comrades here are thinking of farming overseas after the war + I hope they will be encouraged to do so.

Stalag Luft III
26 April 1942
To 'My Precious Son' [Probably David]
To-day I picked up a volume of Hans Andersen's Fairy Tales which I expect you will have read or will do before long. His stories have taught millions yet he had very little school life + was very poor. Have been walking barefoot around the compound a distance of over ½ mile + throwing the medicine ball + volley-tennis stripped to the waist in the sun. Nearly every form of sports is being carried out here—cricket, fencing, boxing, tennis, quoits, 'Judo', throwing the discus + javelin + long + high jump. At 8am there is a physical exercise class. Have been digging up the roots for sports fields. Hope the Doggies, chickens + goats are well. Love, Daddy.

Stalag Luft III
10 May 1942
To Flora

2 pairs of pyjamas containing each 7 pairs [*sic*] arrived from you last week + were much appreciated. Am loving Pope's Iliad [the *Iliad* of Homer, translated by Alexander Pope] and extracts from Thomas of Kempis, especially Chapter LVIII, Book 3 'on searching into mysteries.'

Have been playing the mandolin with a Canadian who plays the guitar—de Forest—, + we have been singing the old songs we sang together at Ferring. I wish I had some gramophone records of you playing the guitar.

There are an extraordinary fine lot of young men from all parts of the Empire + the States here now + I enjoy their companionship.

So glad you have some ducks + goats as well as the chickens. Your cow + milk book, plus the one you wrote on chickens should be printed for every young person to read who goes overseas or leaves school after the war. Included in it should be some of your maxims + hints re domestic science. We must all get back to a simpler + less artificial life + the closer we are to nature + the earth the happier + more independent we shall be.

The older I am, the more I appreciate what a wonderful Mother you have been + are to me. Thank God for you.

Stalag Luft III
12 June 1942
To Minerva

As Buchan says, 'It is quite right that youth should be hostile to tradition + hot for new things, but if a fellow has any real stuff in him, he will come to see that the only freedom is that which comes from the willing + reasoned acceptance of discipline, + the only true originality that which springs from the re-birth of historical tradition in a man's soul.' Do read his essay 'The Interpreter's House'. I think Belloc is right when he says 'Truth lies in Proportion.' 'Religion is the main determining element in the foundation of any civilisation.'

From the principles of reason + insight + struggle + application a community develops, not a promiscuous herd, like a flock of sheep following a bell-wether, but with an order of its own in which each member has a special place to fill according to his gifts + ability. The ideal society is built up on achievements, on the principles of reason + insight, + can demand a contribution from each member, but protects each single member belonging to it.

Stalag Luft III
14 June 1942
To Flora
Thank you . . . for your 2 clothes parcels, containing battle-dress, leather for repairing shoes . . . + with pyjamas (2 pr) socks (4 pr) pants + vests (2 pr) pullover 5 Hankies etc. You have sent me everything I ever needed. A parcel with 1 large bath towel 1 pr wool-lined leather mits from Uncle Poultney + vest + pants arrived a fortnight ago.

My best wishes to Mrs. Neville Cham. I always

admired them both so much + he will be appreciated more + more along with his predecessor as time passes. We have a drawing of Clemy's husband hung over the door of our mess. He is trusted + beloved by everyone here.

Am running ½ mile barefoot and swimming in the fire reservoir each morning before breakfasting at 7.30. Have not been so well for ages. Hope to see you by Xmas.

Stalag Luft III
23 June 1942
To Minerva
Have enjoyed reading Samuel's 'Belief + Action' + 'Shorty Bill' by McNeile. Bax would like them I think especially chapter 7, parts 1 of the latter + chapters 7 to 13 incl. + 15 of the former. Do read Books 22 + 24 of Pope's Iliad. Peter would enjoy the whole of it. The discussions we have had are on subjects similar to those touched upon in the chapters referred to in Samuel's book, which is why Bax would be interested.

I generally walk from 8.30 to 10 when I go to bed. This with my ½ mile run barefooted, followed by either a swim or a cold shower before 7.30 breakfast, is doing me a world of good.

'Earth's crammed with heaven, And every common bush afire with god; But only he who sees takes off his shoes.' Eliz. Browning. 'To know what we know, + know what we do not know, that is wisdom.' Confucius.

Stalag Luft III
21 July 1942
To Flora
Eton has the reputation now of having a good system of teaching + individual attention + produces a high percentage of leaders in all spheres of activities. Westminster too, has its good points + I am sure whatever you decide will be right.

Have enjoyed Proverbs especially the first chapters + Ecclesiastes. I hope the war will soon be over and we can work for the restoration of well-divided property, upon which economic freedom + therefore the dignity + permanence of the family depend. Peace + progress is impossible where class warfare ideas exist. I hope the boys will be imbued with your idea that everyone should primarily consider how he can be of use + serve others, as the only way of being happy. In other words, think first of what he can give the community + afterwards about what he may get out of it.

Please thank Uncle Poultney for his p.c. + his daughter Dorothy for hers + Olive and Bertie for their food parcels from Lisbon + 2 boxes of cigars which I gave to W/Cmdr Day who only smokes them + has been an inspiration + example of what an officer and gentleman should be. As you have often said, 'Being in tune with the infinite is our only source of strength.' The more I read + see, the more certain I am of 'Divine Will + Purpose' in everything that happens.

Our band gave us a very good concert last week + we are having some very good Rugby football games. The Canadians are learning the

English game. It's a splendid one.

26 July 1942
Stalag Luft III
To Minerva
Congratulate Peter on what he is doing. You have every reason to be proud of him. Give him my love + best wishes.

Long for the day when peace will reign once more. When it comes, everyone will, I hope think rationally + understand that the members of every community are knit together by destiny + either perish or stand united. I hope the boys realise that daily bread cannot be had permanently except by struggle. It is an eternal truth that 'struggle is the father of all things.' Where something has to be accomplished + success achieved, action must be based on insight + reason, the knowledge that men must stand together.

Had a 2 hrs walk last week with 4 others outside. Lovely change.

Stalag Luft III
31 July 1942
To My Precious Tony
Has your mother read you the Fairy Tales of Hans Andersen or Grimm + the stories of Jack the Giant Killer in Jack + the Beanstalk? If not, ask her to get you the books as a present from me + read them to you.

Stalag Luft III
31 July 1942
To Minerva

Had a 2 hour walk outside, the other day, through lovely woods + had a beautiful view of a river flowing slowly along a rich valley. It seemed as peaceful + reminded me of the Thames.

So glad David enjoys his school. He will learn there the necessity for working + pulling together with others for his own benefit + the team's. Efficiency is the test as to whether or not the best means are being employed for any desirable end. Inefficiency has to make way for efficiency. It is a law of nature . . . Read Ecclesiastes occasionally to Tony.

Stalag Luft III
23 August 1942
To Minerva
'English principles of toleration, respect for personal liberty, doctrine that all power is a trust for the public good, were making rapid progress in 1753. A great change in the whole social system was at hand. A wise man would have censured their errors, but he would have remembered that, as Milton has said, error is but opinion in the making.'

Thank you . . . for the 400 cigs from Milner's, Walter Rosen for the 400 cigs + Tony Fraser for thousand Pall Malls + Tom Carr for his cigs all of which were much appreciated.

Stalag Luft III
28 August 1942
To Flora
Thank you for your lovely July letters, with its news of you + David visiting Eton + Stowe; the

birds, fruits + vegetables in your garden. Also for the useful clothing parcel which came in useful for some new boys. The socks I particularly needed. My size is 46. Please send some McLean's toothpaste in future parcels.

When I came to sick quarters, I found a small photo of Clemy's husband over my bed. You can imagine how pleased I was. Am enjoying Shakespeare's Henry IV. We all here are distressed to hear of Kent's death + feel the deepest sympathy for his mother + brother.

Stalag Luft III
30 August 1942
To Minerva
There were too many people at home after the last war who did not realise how comparatively well off they were + were urged on to ask more from + give less to the community by misleaders like Morrison + Bevin. They did their best to disarm us mentally as well as physically. They preached class consciousness + class war. It seems strange to see them where they are today, conscientious objectors as they + so many of their friends have been. Perhaps they have reformed some of their ideas + aims. If so, good. If not, they should be put into prison, if they won't fight. It is largely due to the foolishness of men of their way of thinking in Russia, France + elsewhere that war broke out + we were so ill-equipped to meet it. In future we shall have to regard National Service more as an honour + sacrifice than as they would make it out to be, a means of getting more out of the community for less work.

411

May peace come soon. We have as much to learn from the Germans as they have from us.

Stalag Luft III
31 August 1942
To Tony
Thanks for your letter. Your handwriting + spelling has improved. Practice will make perfect. I should like you to read a short passage of Shakespeare's Henry V, Act III, Scene I. King 'Once more into the breach etc' + Act IV Scene III King 'What's he that wishes so?' Perhaps you will learn by heart one of these. It will improve your memory + power of concentration. I hope the animals are all well. Especially the 'doggies'. Give Grandmother a Kiss from me on her birthday Oct 18th.

Stalag Luft III
9 September 1942
To Flora
I am glad that you have taken back 'Florida' + hope you can make use of it. Lance can arrange in my absence any necessary legal details that may be required. Everything there including furniture etc., is yours. Thank you + Lionel so much for the use of it + the happiness we all have had out of it . . . Returned from sick quarters last week. The week's change did me good + I am quite well again. Am enjoying Henry VI + Aristotle's Politics.

412

? September 1942
To Minerva
You will remember I offered 'Florida' and
everything in it to Mother some time ago. I am
so pleased she has accepted it + am sure she
will put it to good use, which is the purpose of
everything. I am most grateful for all the
happiness + use it has been to us in the past.

Oflag XXI B
4 November 1942
To Minerva
Had hoped to be back home with you + the
children + Mother for Christmas by jumping off
the train last Friday, on the way to this new
camp Oflag 21B, but my plan failed owing to a
guard who saw me + stopped the train. My
freedom only lasted 10 minutes. 96 of us live in
a large room . . . I am glad to see new scenery +
faces. A change is good for everyone. You may
be able to do something for U.S.A. p's thru
friends like E of E Club. Lt Col Clark at Stalag
Luft 3 is charming.

Oflag XXI B
4 November 1942
To My Precious Son
I had hoped to be back home with you before
Christmas by jumping off the train that brought
us here last Friday, but unfortunately a guard
saw me + I was only free for about 10 minutes.
Next year we shall all be together again for
Christmas, I hope.

Oflag XXI B
8 November 1942
To Flora
I miss you more than I can say. Some of the happiest times I have as a prisoner is when I think of you + the happy times we have had together. Whenever I read anything good in the Bible, Shakespeare, Pope or elsewhere, it reminds me of you + what you have often said. Am doing 10 days in the cooler for my unauthorised leave of absence from the train + have brought Pope's poems + Plato's Republic to keep me company.

Oflag XXI B
12 November 1942
To Minerva
It froze last night and snowed a little. The country reminds me of Canada. I am doing 10 days in the cooler for my unauthorised departure from the train. Each a.m. + afternoon I get an hour's walk. Lights go out at 9 pm. I feel like a monk in a cell. Yesterday I put my shirt on wrong side out, observed 2 minutes silence, read Plato's Republic + after reading the papers in the evening sang myself happily to sleep.

Oflag XXI B
16 November 1942
To Tony
I hope you will learn to play some musical instrument like the piano, flute or guitar. Training in music will introduce rhythm and harmony into your soul + have a socialising

influence in which the whole life of man stands in need.

Oflag XXI B
29 November 1942
To Flora
The brown rubber-soled shoes you sent me last year fitted me perfectly + have been a great comfort to me . . . Snow is covering the ground + it reminds me so of 'The Island'. The Swiss Mission visited us the other day + one member was a friend of Bigelow's. Have organised an international relations group here to extend our knowledge of one another's countries. Most of the world's troubles + misunderstandings, I feel certain, come from ignorance + anything we can do to remove this will help to promote peace, prosperity + happiness among nations after the war.

Oflag XXI B
November/December 1942: Exact date not legible
To Minerva
I dreamt I was home the other night + saw Mother + David so vividly. It was a joy.

Oflag XXI B
8 December 1942
To Flora
Have enjoyed some sleighing in the compound which is on a slope. There is an able young man named Paget here whose grandfather was governor of the Fiji Islands. The natives there asked for a separate church because they said

415

'the whites smelt'. We have prepared a skating ring on the football ground + and [*sic*] hope to get some hockey . . . I wish every prison camp could have a copy of your 'Casting out fear' + 'Cow + milk + chicken books.' The agricultural section of our International Society are very popular.

Oflag XXI B
Christmas Eve, 1942
To Flora
It makes me happy to think of you + Minerva + the children being together to-night over Christmas. The other night I dreamt that you and Lionel + I were together. We had just moved in to a new house in London. The children will have fun together over the holidays with you. I can see your lovely sitting room with the big open fire, the paintings on the wall + the sun streaming in the windows. The birds + chickens in the garden, we made so much of ourselves + the puppies. Yesterday we had a nice Xmas festival of 9 lessons + carols. An officer from each part of the camp read the lessons + the choir sang well. To-day we had a very amusing Pantomime produced by ourselves. Band, conjuring, hilly-billy songs included. Dick Whittington + his cat were splendid . . . There is a lot of talent here.

Oflag XXI B
Christmas Eve, 1942
To Minerva
So glad to think of you + the children being at Ferring with Mother to-night + over Xmas. I am with you all in spirits [*sic*]. I am very well.

Sorry, some of the things I have written you sound queer. Perhaps I have not taken enough time to express my ideas properly in the few words at my disposal + give you a wrong impression of what I mean. One or two of my letters were written while I was sick with a temperature last summer, which perhaps accounts for what I wrote about men in high places, who had been conscientious objectors + pacifists. Of course everyone can change their minds + we must be ready to forgive + be tolerant. The people will be happy when genuine philosophers are elected into power in every part of the State; men who will despise all existing honours as mean + worthless, caring only for the right + the honours to be gained from that, + above all for justice as the one indispensible thing in whose service + maintenance they will reorganise the State.

Oflag XXI B
5 January 1943
To Flora
I am sure that David has knowledge + appreciation of a lot of worthwhile things that many other boys of his age haven't got. I think every boy before leaving school should be able to milk a cow + harness + drive a team of horses. He should also know how to make butter + cheese + keep milk clean. With this knowledge, he could make himself a useful citizen anywhere in the Empire. 'The happy life should be 3 parts practical.' 'A man will love his country the better for (owning) a pig.'

Oflag XXI B
6 February 1943
To Flora
Thanks for your letter which came Jan 20th +
the lovely clothes parcel + cricket things +
football + games. They are all much
appreciated by the camp. W/Cdr Hyde + I play
Backgammon every day after lunch at 12 tea at
4 + supper at 7.30. One of your sweaters I have
given to a Maori who recently gave us an
exhibition of a Maori dance of welcome. 2
Americans have each been given 1 pr. of your
pyjamas. David Crawley + others have had
some of your underclothes. W/Cdr Hull, a
South African has your lovely light brown
blanket + W/Cdr Kyle + others some of your
towels. Lt/Cdr Buckley has your chess men . . .
Have been skating recently and sliding down
the toboggan run on homemade sleighs. All
great fun. The mild weather has interfered with
our winter sports a good deal . . . Am wearing
your lovely blue sweater from Harrods.

Oflag XXI B
7 March 1943
To Minerva
So glad Peter has joined the Air Corps . . .
Thank Tony for his nice letter. I am so glad he is
learning carpentry + likes history . . . Thank
David for his well-written letter of Nov 15. I am
so glad he is getting on so well at school + likes
it. Have just finished Green Mansions by
Hudson, which I enjoyed enormously. Reading
about other people's trials + sufferings such as
are described in it + Garibaldi's Defence of the

418

Roman Republic makes one's own seem trivial.

Oflag XXI B
8 March 1943
To My Precious Son
A Canadian—Campbell gave us a talk the other day on the Eskimos in Northern Canada where he lived for 5 years working with the Hudson Bay Co. Eskimos never cook their food + live on raw meat + fish. They do not suffer from scurvy although they never have fresh vegetables or fruits. They are great hunters + trappers + fishermen.

Oflag XXI B
23 March 1943
To Flora
The news of your visits to London + old friends makes me feel as if I had been there with you. Many thanks for the books from Hatchard's + games from Harrods . . . S/Ldr Barrett our bird expert saw or heard today 34 different species of migrant birds, including Robins, Thrushes, Wrens, Black Red Starts, Black Headed Gulls, White Wag Tails, Larks, Wood Larks, Green Finches, Chafinches, Gold Finches, Linnets, Great, Blue, Marsh + Cole Tits, Curlew, Wigeon, Mallard, Golden Crested Wren, Heron, Peevits, House + Tree Sparrows, Starlings, Great Spotted Woodpecker, Common Buzzard + Pigeon. Your music always soothed me + your singing. Aristotle says music has the power of purifying the soul.

Oflag XXI B
6 April 1943
To Flora
I have always had the greatest admiration for Mrs Neville Chamber + her husband, we all here have. Give her my best wishes . . . The British Red X doing splendidly. Their food parcels are excellent + much preferred by everyone including the Americans here to the American Red X food parcels.

Stalag Luft III
29 April 1943
To Minerva
2 weeks ago we returned to the camp we were in last summer but are in a new compound which is an improvement + a change is good . . . I am now sharing a double room with Capt. Green, charming, an air gunner who was a machine gunner in the last war . . . Capt. Macdonald from Portree, Skye, is also a great help + a wonderful character. He is a fighting padre.

Stalag Luft III
30 April 1943
To Flora
Spending the winter in a new camp with its change of scenery, soil, trees + ground, together with many different faces + a different atmosphere was very pleasant. Now to be back among old friends again in comparatively comfortable conditions, is also a nice change. Your lovely clothes parcel sent on Jan 23rd came today with just the things I wanted. In it was ½ lb. of delicious chocolate . . . I have been

busy since arriving here organising an international union to provide the men with entertainment, useful information + general knowledge with a view to giving them something worthwhile to think about. We are doing this by means of general interest talks, common interest discussion groups, debates + an 'Any Questions?' on B.B.C. lines. I long for the day when we all have learnt our lesson + there is peace again. Every situation in which we find ourselves is meant to teach + develop us. My love to Clemy + her husband. How happy he must feel.

To Flora [Separate letter on same date]
Have been doing some brick laying + work as a general labourer helping to build a theatre + general social centre. It has been great fun doing it + has reminded me of the building Lionel + I have done together in Canada + at Ferring. I often think of him + feel he is with us. What fun we used to have at Ferring and on The Island in Canada with Lucy before the last war . . . There are growing numbers of Americans here + I am glad to be able to do here a little of the kind of work Minerva is doing for them at home. If they can get into the houses of representative people + make friends it will do more good than anything else . . . I love hearing from you about the singing of the black birds + thrushes. I always associate them with your lovely house + garden. The birds, the doggies, the chickens, the cows, the garden + the fields.

Stalag Luft III
28 May 1943
To Minerva

I hope the Negroes are behaving themselves in Wales + are being treated properly. They require knowing, like everyone else. The number of Americans here together with representatives from all parts of the Empire enables me to carry on here the work you are doing so well at home . . . Community singing + poetry Sunday evenings, rounded off the programme which is based on the teachings of J.C., not K.M.

Stalag Luft III
30 May 1943
To Flora

I am delighted about David's boxing + poetry recitation + general progress at school. I have started community singing Sunday evenings accompanied by guitar, violins, accordions, etc + interspersed with Shakespeare + other poetry. The music from each nation is beautiful + all produce harmony . . . I am sorry my name has been so much in the papers + only wish I had done something to deserve publicity. I suppose Rogers [Claude Rogers, Chairman of the Gillingham Conservative and Unionist Association] has done what he has, to help the cause we stand for. It's a pity any personal publicity is necessary for a man in public life. It makes me very happy to hear that David has been helpful + is sensible + reliable + can still be so much himself.

Stalag Luft III
20 June 1943
To Minerva
The father of one of our batmen use [*sic*] to suffer before the war from diabetes + could hardly walk 100 yards with help. Since the war he has had to live on vegetables + fruits without meat or sugar + can now walk 10–15 miles daily. He is 72 + lives in the Channel Islands . . . My belief is that 'without Christianity, we live in a state of chaos, wherein we lose not only our peace of mind, but also the gifts of distinguishing things + appreciating them at their true value. Nothing attracts us, nor does anything suit our taste. We know not what to do nor what to decide upon. By Christianity, I mean the truth, which bridges the gulf between rich + poor, social ranks, nations + races.

Stalag Luft III
27 June 1943
To Flora
From my window I could look down a lovely path through a pine wood. It reminds me of Freudenstadt. A woman on a bicycle, with a small child sitting behind, occasionally passes by + reminds me of the world outside . . . Am reading Buchan's Cromwell. It points out how issues in the strife of the early 17th century in England lay at the root of all democracy—the right to personal liberty, the denial of any power to dispense with the law which normally protected a subject's life + property, the hostility to special tribunals which usurped the duties of common courts of justice. A settled

423

law + the equality of all men before it were claims which survived the wreckage, for behind them was the spirit of England.

Stalag Luft III
29 July 1943
To Flora
Have finished reading right through the Bible since becoming a Kriegie + find its fascination grows with knowledge of it.

Stalag Luft III
21 August 1943
To Minerva
Give Tony my love + congratulate him from me for winning the 80 yards run + doing so well in geography + history. The war has taught Kriegies geography as most of us have maps of the world pinned up in our rooms.

Stalag Luft III
29 August 1943
To (Either David or Tony)
Congratulations on reciting Julius Caesar so well . . . The boys have been playing cricket + water sports lately + we have had some good races, high jumping, throwing the discus + putting the shot. How are you getting on with Botany? Knowledge is power.

Stalag Luft III
29 August 1943
To Flora
'It is only about learning about nature + her laws + by applying our knowledge to the end

that we are better equipped to obey + take advantage of those laws that we can actually make ourselves masters of life + winners in the great battle. All living organisms have three powers inherent in them: power to fight for their self-preservation, power to re-create themselves + power to vary. Throughout all nature the most cunning + sometimes intricate machinery is provided by the individual itself, or by nature for the individual, through which it can protect itself from its enemies + take advantage of the help of its friends. Nature does not heed or give thought to the individual, but she seems to be intent on the whole organisation—the species shall go on.'

Stalag Luft III
28 September 1943
To Flora
I long to see you again + the animals + garden. So pleased David is such a good shot + that you are putting him down for Eton.

Thanks for the uniform + 2 clothing parcels. Also the Benson + Hedges cigarettes. Thank Miss Roberts for hers and Mrs Morton for the lovely socks + Mrs Dawes, Montreal, for cigarettes, books + puzzle. Our orchestra of 26 gave an excellent classical concert recently. Roy Wilkins a South African is conductor. The Theatre Guild produced 'George + Margueret' [*sic*] last week, which was great fun.

Stalag Luft III
28 September 1943
To Minerva

The Americans have been put into a separate compound + we miss them very much. Group Captain Wilson, an Australian, has arrived + taken over the job of S.B.O. Major Mountford, + Major Ross DSO paratroops have arrived. Very wise and able fellows. 'By the mere force of increased contact, the war will teach us to think more favourably of each other + to discard that foolish contempt in which nations formerly indulged. The better one country is acquainted with another, the more it will find to respect + to imitate.'

Stalag Luft III
30 September 1943
To David
Congratulations on shooting that rabbit from the roof. I once shot a pigeon in Burma with a .22. What fun you must have had with Aura harvesting, driving a tractor + riding. You will soon learn how to look after a farm on your own.

Stalag Luft III
29 October 1943
To Flora
Thank Olive + Bertie for a parcel of delicious nuts, raisins + prunes . . . Thanks for another clothing parcel which came three days ago, with 2 shirts, tooth brush, socks, pullover, chocolate, all of which I needed . . . 5 books have arrived including the Cherry Orchard + Eminent Victorians.

Stalag Luft III
29 October 1943
To Minerva
. . . best wishes for a Merry Christmas + happy
new year, which I hope + pray will see an end to
hostilities + a peace dictated by truth + justice.
Have enjoyed reading Pope Pious XIII's [*sic*]
Encyclical written in 1893 + believe Bax would
like it too.

Stalag Luft III
30 October 1943
To David
A very Merry Christmas to you + best wishes
for a happy new year. I wonder if you ever
exercise on the horizontal bar + the parallel
bars. They are good for developing balance,
coordination + confidence + I should like to
see expert instructors in every school. Some of
the men here are splendid with them. Take care
of the family, till my return next year. Keep up
your shooting + riding.

Stalag Luft III
14 November 1943
To Flora
'Speaking generally, the landed gentry are
enduring witnesses of past worth + good work
done + until they forfeit our esteem they
deserve to be respected + honoured. High place
is lost as easily that when a family has been of
long continuance we may be sure that it has
survived by exceptional merit. Nature rapidly
finds out when the wrong sort have stolen into
promotion. When a Knave makes a fortune his

427

son spends it—one generation sees an end to him. Even among the best there is quick succession. Warriors, lawyers, politicians, press perpetually to the front . . . material is for ever being replaced. Each family thus raised is for ever on its trial. Those who survive remain as links between the present + the past, + carry on unbroken the continuity of our national existence.' Frocade. Thanks to you + Mrs Roberts for the books + your parcel. The Red X is doing wonderful work. Casson gave us a splendid production of Macbeth. Best wishes for 1944.

Stalag Luft III
28 November 1943
To Flora
The Theatre Club put on 3 very good 1 act plays the other night + a few days before that, an amusing variety show was produced. Last summer a number of model sail boats were made + sailed on the fire pool. Now model aeroplanes are being flown. They have been made most ingeniously + fly beautifully. The other day I saw 2 little girls walking along the road with a goat, which behaved first like a dog, + it reminded me of the goats you have kept. I am sure boys + girls can do important auxiliary work suited to their years + having a definite value for the young people themselves as it builds them up physically + enlarges their outlook. I am so glad David has done farm work.

Stalag Luft III
28 November 1943
To Minerva
Winant's son is in an adjoining compound . . .
My love to your mother and mine. I appreciate
more + more, the importance of the home +
family life + wish we had at least 5 children. We
need bigger + better families.

Stalag Luft III
29 November 1943
To Flora
So glad to hear of David's self-confidence. It
comes from self-discipline, self-reliance + self-
government . . . I am so proud of all you have
been doing to help people, the Red X, Toc H,
etc. I am a member of the local branch of Toc H
+ think it serves a most useful purpose. Much
appreciated Lance's letter + am convinced his
idea is right, that reciprocal aid is the basis of
the solution of both international + social
problems. 'Those who, in the past, took up the
notion that nation or class is naturally hostile to
nation or class, + that the wealthy + the
working men are intended by nature to live in
mutual conflict, made a great mistake. So
irrational + so false is this view, that the direct
contrary is the truth. Just as the symmetry of the
human frame is the result of the suitable
arrangement of the different parts of the body,
so in the society of nations or in a State, it is
ordained by nature that all nations + both
classes should dwell in harmony + agreement so
as to maintain the balance of the body politic.
Each needs the other: nation cannot do without

nation; capital cannot do without labour, nor labour without capital. Mutual agreement results in the beauty of good order.'

Stalag Luft III
30 December 1943
To Minerva
When peace comes, I hope the Empire Training Scheme of the RAF can be utilised as the basis for an Empire Settlement Scheme. The RAF could hand over some of their surplus land + buildings for use as Imperial Development Colleges. The young men must be trained for at least 6 months before being taken on by approved farmers in the Dominions. All the orphanages and Boys' Homes in England could with advantage be moved to the Dominions, where the facilities for their training + their opportunities are better. Perhaps Bax could get the ball rolling.

Stalag Luft III
29 January 1944
To Flora
Gave a talk yesterday for the E.S.U. on Chamberlain whom I admire very much. The political life of man finds an analogy in the organism of the animal or plant + change is a slow process in the one as in the other. The State is a natural product, which stands, as Burke said, 'in a just correspondence + symmetry with the order of the world.' Not decades but centuries must be allowed for each stage of its development.

Stalag Luft III
26 February 1944
To Flora

Please thank Olive + Bertie for the delicious parcels of nuts, raisins + sardines they sent me + others here via Miss Lester for Xmas. Please ask her not to send us anymore, as the Red X give us all we need. In 1940 her parcels were a great help. She asked me to send her a few names of friends then, which I did, thinking she might pass on to friends in the U.S.A. who might want to adopt a 'Kriegie', which has been done in some cases. I am sorry to hear that they are hard up + that we have been a burden on them. I dare say, some of my friends sent her other names, which enlarged my original list of about 6 in 1940. None of my friends here need parcels either. It was sweet of you to send her the present and I am glad Charlie sent £50, although under the circumstances I think it should have gone to you. So glad David is better and won 1st prize in declamation + 4th in shooting. We are holding a 'Kriegie parliament' soon + I have been asked to form a government. It should be fun . . . Saw a wonderful variety show here recently produced by the theatre club. Most amusing . . . Cold shower every morning + exercises am + pm have kept us splendidly all winter. Have given up eating meat. Your blue sweater + brown blankets have been a blessing + I use them + all the other things you sent me.

Stalag Luft III
27 February 1944
To Minerva
Srgt. Gilmour has been secretary of our
International Union ever since it started + is
mainly responsible for any use it may have been
to the camp in arranging talks + debates. He
holds classes weekly on social problems in
connection with the Education Programme +
does other communal work besides, with the
result that, much to my regret, it is impossible
for him to find time to continue as secretary.
However, I am glad to say he is remaining on
our committee so we shall have the benefit of
his valuable advice. Had he not been taken
prisoner, he almost certainly would have been
appointed to commissioned rank long ago, + I
feel he is a man well fitted to hold a commission.
He is anxious to become a political agent after
the war + has written the chief agent at
Conservative H.Q., asking to take the exams
here as is done for other professions. He would
make a most excellent agent + I would be glad
if you would write to our mutual friend at
Central Office + tell him what I have written, as
I want to help Gilmour achieve his ambition.

Stalag Luft III
24 March 1944
To Minerva
There is a delightful officer here, named Fl/Lt
Ferry, from Western Australia, who runs the
Australian group of the International Union.
His brother is a Sergeant in England + I would
be glad if you could help to give him a good

time. My room mate is a very fine fellow named Green (Fl/Lt) who was in the Machine Gun Corps in the last war. Have enjoyed reading J.S. Mills' essay on 'Liberty' + am sure Beverly likes it. 'The individual is not accountable to society for his actions, in as far as these concern the interests of no person but himself. For such actions as are prejudicial to the interests of others, the individual is accountable + may be subjected either to social or legal punishment, if society is of the opinion that one or the other is requisite for its protection. It is their remarkable diversity of character + culture, not any superior excellence in them, which has made the European family of nations an improving, instead of a stationary portion of human kind. The unlikeness of a person to another is generally the first thing which draws the attention of either to the imperfection of his own type, + the superiority of another, or the possibility, by combining the advantages of both, of producing something better than either.'

Stalag Luft III
24 March 1944
To Flora
It has been snowing the last few days and there is still snow on the ground which has reminded me of Spring on The Island in Canada. Have given up smoking for Lent + feel much better for it. Many of us smoke much too much + I did for one. I am surprised that with all the wealth in America, Olive should collect money in England for the extra food she has sent a few R.A.F. officers who were taken prisoner in 1940.

None of us need this food she has been so kind as to send for Xmas, as the Red X supply us with all we need. Please thank her and ask her to discontinue sending more . . . The South Africans here are a remarkably fine lot . . . They gave an interesting talk on their country for our International Union last week . . . Have been taking a cold shower every morning this winter + walk 3 hours a day + feel very well.

[The dates of these last two letters are confusing as they imply they were written on the night of the Great Escape when it would have been thought Johnny would have other things on his mind. But perhaps they were written in the long hours during which the men waited in Hut 104 to go down the tunnel. They were the last letters that Johnny wrote home, as after his escape and recapture he was thrown into Sachsenhausen concentration camp with instructions that nobody in the outside world should know his whereabouts.

The next Johnny's mother-in-law, Mrs John Arrington, heard from Johnny was when she received a cable in 1945 stating, 'Home safely. This family happy. Our love, Johnny Dodge.']

NOTES

Christopher Reeve quote, the (New York) *Daily News*, TV Week section, 6–12 November 1988.

Jimmy James quote, Letter to Phyllis B. Dodge, 23 January 1989.

Preface
The quote is from Lord Freyberg's address at Johnny's memorial service on 11 November 1960, from a photocopy of the original address courtesy of the Alice Berkeley Collection, London.

Chapter 1 Wookyi-Tipi
The bulk of the material that appears in this chapter is taken from Phyllis B. Dodge's 'Notes on a Prospective Biography of John Bigelow Dodge'; her 'John Bigelow Dodge, 1894–1960, A Précis of his Life'; and her published book, *Tales of the Phelps-Dodge Family* (Alice Berkeley Collection, London). The information on Lucy Dodge and Caramoor came from *Opera News*, the date of which, nor the author, I'm sorry to say, cannot be ascertained due to the manner in which the article was filed. The section about the history of British decline and American ascendancy came from an amusing and well-researched article in *Vanity Fair* magazine (No. 593, January 2010) by Charles Spencer. The excerpts from letters between Johnny and Flora come from Jane Aitken's private collection (Jane Aitken Collection, Toronto).

Chapter 2 Age Quod Agis
The bulk of the material that appears in this chapter is taken from Phyllis B. Dodge's card index, and her published book *Tales of the Phelps-Dodge Family* (Alice Berkeley Collection, London). The excerpt about St Mark's came from John Franklin Carter's memoir, *The Rectory Family*, pp. 242–244. There were several references to stories from the *New York Times*, of 7 July 1908; 12 December 1908; 8 April 1913; 9 April 1913; 19 April 1913; 16 July 1914; 6 August 1914. The excerpts from letters written to Flora from Johnny and Lucy are from Jane Aitken's private collection (Jane Aitken Collection, Toronto). The suggestion that Lionel might have been responsible for Lucy fleeing London, and that Flora had private detectives put on him, was related to the author in a private conversation by a member of the Dodge family.

Chapter 3 Esprit de Corps
The bulk of the historical background to the Royal Naval Division comes from Douglas Jerrold's *The Royal Naval Division*, and Leonard Sellers' *The Hood Battalion*. Much of the information relating to Rupert Brooke comes from Nigel Jones' *Rupert Brooke: Life, Death and Myth*. Charles F. Horne's *Records of the Great War*, National Alumni, 1923, supplied other valuable information about the conflict. Three letters from Jane Aitken's private collection are used: Letter from Churchill to Flora dated 8 September 1914; Letter from JBD to Flora, dated 19 September 1914; Letter from JBD to Flora, dated 19 September 1914 (Jane Aitken Collection, Toronto).

Chapter 4 Debacle
The bulk of the historical background to the debacle of Antwerp Royal came from Douglas Jerrold's *The Royal Naval Division*, and Leonard Sellers' *The Hood Battalion*. Some of the information relating to Rupert Brooke comes from Nigel Jones' *Rupert Brooke: Life, Death and Myth*.

Chapter 5 The Soldier
Once more, Douglas Jerrold's *The Royal Naval Division*, and Leonard Sellers' *The Hood Battalion* provide much of the historical background to this chapter. Once more some of the information relating to Rupert Brooke comes from Nigel Jones' *Rupert Brooke: Life, Death and Myth*. The letters from Johnny and Flora are part of the Jane Aitken Collection, Toronto.

Chapter 6 Mediterranean Adventure
The historical background to Chapter 6 comes from a combination of James W. Fry and Thomas McMillan's *History of the Royal Naval Division*; Leonard Sellers' *The Hood Battalion*; and Douglas Jerrold's *The Royal Naval Division*. Nigel Jones' *Rupert Brooke: Life, Death and Myth* is the source for material on the poet. Information about Johnny comes from Phyllis B. Dodge's 'John Bigelow Dodge, 1894–1960, A Précis of his Life'; *Tales of the Phelps-Dodge Family* (p. 219); and 'Notes on a Prospective Biography of John Bigelow Dodge' (Alice Berkeley Collection, London).

Chapter 7 A Corner of a Foreign Field
The historical background to A Corner of a Foreign Field comes from a combination of James

437

W. Fry and Thomas McMillan's *History of the Royal Naval Division*; Leonard Sellers' *The Hood Battalion*; and Douglas Jerrold's *The Royal Naval Division*. The description of the run-up to Gallipoli is extracted from Johnny Dodge's own account 'Opening Attack on Dardanelles' (Jane Aitken Collection, Toronto). The report of Rupert Brooke's death is from *The Times* of 26 April 1915. And the chapter relied on sections of Phyllis Dodge's 'John Bigelow Dodge, 1894–1960, A Précis of his Life' (Alice Berkeley Collection, London).

Chapter 8 Gallipoli
The historical background to Gallipoli comes from a combination of James W. Fry and Thomas McMillan's *History of the Royal Naval Division*; Leonard Sellers' *The Hood Battalion*; and Douglas Jerrold's *The Royal Naval Division*. The description of Johnny's role in the Gallipoli landings is extracted from Johnny Dodge's own account 'Opening Attack on Dardanelles' (Jane Aitken Collection, Toronto).

Chapter 9 The Western Front
The letters from Johnny to Flora in The Western Front are part of the Jane Aitken Collection, Toronto. And the chapter relied on sections of Phyllis Dodge's 'John Bigelow Dodge, 1894–1960, A Précis of his Life' (Alice Berkeley Collection, London).

Chapter 10 Death Revisited
Death Revisited is entirely derived from Flora's own account of her trip to Belgium and France,

which she made with Lionel, 'Account of trip to continent starting March 4' (Jane Aitken Collection, Toronto).

Chapter 11 To the Ends of the Earth
Once more, Phyllis B. Dodge's 'John Bigelow Dodge, 1894–1960, A Précis of his Life' proved the basic building block for this chapter.

Various editions of the *New York Times* (31 March 1904, 7 September 1906) charted the origins of The Ends of the Earth Club. And *Mark Twain Speaking*, University of Iowa Press, 1996, Fatout, Paul (Ed.), supplied details of the great author's criticisms of the club. Anthony Cave Brown's *The Secret Servant: The Life of Stewart Menzies, Churchill's Spymaster*; Michael Joseph, London, 1988 provided a valuable insight into the sort of Anglo-American spy rings that developed in the immediate aftermath of the First World War.

The outline description of Johnny's trade activities in the Far and Near East was derived from a now defunct magazine called *World's Work* of June 1922 (Jane Aitken Collection, Toronto). This is supplemented by an unpublished and untitled document which is in Jane Aitken's archive in Toronto and which gives a much expanded version of his activities in this region, including many absorbing episodes he obviously thought were wise to omit in the publicly published document. There is a third document in Jane's archive, an infuriatingly incomplete and muddled folio of 30 or so out-of-sequence pages that cover his travels through China, Mongolia, Japan and Russia, including a 1,700-mile trek on horseback, before his arrival in Persia (via India and the North-West Frontier). This was written, it appears, some five years after the fact and parts of it were intended to be the basis for a book, but where the remaining pages are is a mystery.

Chapter 12 *A Great Game*
For Chapter 12 I leant heavily on Johnny's account of June 1922 in *World's Work* (Jane Aitken Collection, Toronto) and the 'third', incomplete document in Jane's archive mentioned above.

Chapter 13 *Of Bandits and Brigands*
The narrative of this chapter follows closely that of Johnny's own account in his unpublished and untitled journal which I have named 'Travels in Persia and the Caucasus' (Jane Aitken Collection, Toronto). Also *World's Work* of June 1922 (Jane Aitken Collection, Toronto). There is also some detail from Phyllis B. Dodge's 'John Bigelow Dodge, 1894–1960, A Précis of his Life' (Alice Berkeley Collection, London).

Chapter 14 *Trading with the Enemy*
The narrative of this chapter follows closely that of Johnny's own account in the now defunct *World's Work* of June 1922 (Jane Aitken Collection, Toronto), and his private untitled and unpublished journal, which I have named 'Travels in Persia and the Caucasus' (Jane Aitken Collection, Toronto). The second source contains many details that were left out of the first, no doubt because they were politically sensitive; it clearly implies Johnny was on something more than a trade mission. There is also some detail from Phyllis B. Dodge's 'John Bigelow Dodge, 1894–1960, A Précis of his Life' (Alice

Berkeley Collection, London).

Chapter 15 Prisoner of the Cheka
Once more, Johnny's private journal 'Travels in Persia and the Caucasus' (Jane Aitken Collection, Toronto) provides most of the narrative and detail for this chapter. It is supplemented by the article he wrote for (the now defunct) *World's Work* in June 1922 (Jane Aitken Collection, Toronto). Dennis Ogden's scholarly article, 'Britain and Soviet Georgia 1921–1922', *Journal of Contemporary History*, Vol. 23 (1988), pp. 245–258, proved to be enormously helpful on the historical background. As ever I am indebted to Phyllis B. Dodge's 'John Bigelow Dodge, 1894–1960, A Précis of his Life' (Alice Berkeley Collection, London).

Chapter 16 Appointment with Death
This chapter is almost entirely dependent on Johnny's private journal 'Travels in Persia and the Caucasus' (Jane Aitken Collection, Toronto); for the crucial parts only two people can have known what was said. The explicit suggestion that Johnny was serving the government in an anti-Bolshevik capacity was made by his old friend Bernard Freyberg in his address at Johnny's memorial service, June 1960. Freyberg said, 'After the Gallipoli Campaign Johnny transferred from the Naval Division to the Army and served in continuous campaigns including the battles on the Western Front. Ultimately he was taken prisoner fighting against the Communists on the Russian Front.' Lord Freyberg's Address at Memorial Service to Colonel J.B. Dodge, D.S.O., D.S.C., M.C., 11 November 1960 (Alice Berkeley

Collection, London).

Either this was a genuine mistake, Freyberg's memory clouded by time, or, more likely, it was a faux pas made by a blunt, no-nonsense individual, which finally revealed the truth about Johnny's espionage activities.

Chapter 17 From Far East to East End
Phyllis B. Dodge's 'John Bigelow Dodge, 1894–1960, A Précis of his Life' was the basis for much of the outline information in this chapter (Alice Berkeley Collection, London). It was supplemented by contemporaneous newspaper cuttings in Jane Aitken's Toronto archive (Jane Aitken Collection, Toronto) and general historical research.

Chapter 18 Minerva
This chapter leans heavily on excerpts (given with the author's permission) from Johnny's stepson Peter Sherman's unpublished 'Memoirs of Another Time, 1922–56'. I am grateful to Peter for allowing me to use these parts of his memoir; indeed, in a fit of generosity he gave me permission to use all of the book, but I would not be so presumptuous. Once more Phyllis B. Dodge's 'John Bigelow Dodge, 1894–1960, A Précis of his Life' (Alice Berkeley Collection, London) came in useful. And I use one excerpt from the *New York Times* of 2 August 1929. I am indebted to Maldwin Drummond, OBE, for details of Johnny's yachts, the *Windstream* and the *Rose of Sharon*.

Chapter 19 A Final Note
I referred to Phyllis B. Dodge's 'John Bigelow Dodge, 1894–1960, A Précis of his Life' (Alice

Berkeley Collection, London) for this chapter along with Peter Sherman's 'Memoirs of Another Time, 1922–56' (unpublished memoir by Peter Sherman). The bulk of Johnny's description of his efforts to escape from the advancing German armies; his subsequent capture, re-escape and recapture come from his intelligence debriefing immediately after his return to England. (Dodge, John Bigelow; intelligence debriefing post repatriation to England, April 1945; courtesy Alice Berkeley Collection, London.)

Chapter 20 Prisoner of War
Much of the information for this chapter was derived from Johnny's post-war debriefing at the hands of MI9. (Dodge, John Bigelow, intelligence debriefing post repatriation to England, April 1945; courtesy Alice Berkeley Collection, London.) The remainder was taken from his letters home, mainly to Flora and Minerva, which form such a valuable part of Jane Aitken's archive in Toronto. The reference to Minerva 'entertaining' American officers in England while Johnny was away is not a casual item of gossip. The quotation cited was made by a close relative and the author discovered that most members of the family interviewed were aware that Minerva, not unsurprisingly, had embarked upon several war dalliances (including one with Bernard Rickatson-Hatt, the editor-in-chief of Reuters). According to family folklore, Johnny had only one affair while married to Minerva, with an unnamed German aristocrat. (The obvious thought occurred to me that this woman could have been the 'elegant widow' of the SS Major Johnny stayed with in Berlin after his

release from Sachsenhausen, but I have not the slightest bit of evidence to substantiate the idea.) Some family members hold that slight deviation against him despite Minerva's many extra-marital liaisons.

Chapter 21 Oh, What a Lovely War!
Chapter 21 relied to a large extent on excerpts from Sydney Smith's biography of Wings Day, *Wings Day: The Man Who Led the RAF's Epic Battle in German Captivity*, Collins, London, 1968. Wings Day's daughter June Bowerman provided the quotes regarding her father's and Johnny's friendship with Theo Rumpel during an informal chat with the author in the delightful garden of her Kent home in May 2008. Aidan Crawley's 'official' version of RAF escapes from Germany, *Escape from Germany, 1939–45: Methods of Escape Used by RAF Airmen During the Second World War* (The Stationery Office, London, 2001) was invaluable, as was, as usual, Phyllis B. Dodge's 'John Bigelow Dodge, 1894–1960, A Précis of his Life'. Johnny's letters home from Dulag Luft, mainly to Flora and Minerva, lend the narrative a great deal of colour (Jane Aitken Collection, Toronto).

Chapter 22 With Major Rumpel's Compliments . . .
For this chapter I am indebted to Sydney Smith's *Wings Day: The Man Who Led the RAF's Epic Battle in German Captivity*, Collins, London, 1968; the *Chatham, Rochester & Gillingham News*, Friday, 9 May 1941 and the *Kent Messenger and Observer*, Saturday, 17 May 1941.

Chapter 23 Baltic Interlude
For this chapter I consulted and used Sydney Smith's biography of Wings Day: *Wings Day: The Man Who Led the RAF's Epic Battle in German Captivity*, Collins, London, 1968. Jimmy James' memoir of captivity (James, Bertrand Arthur, *Moonless Night*, Leo Cooper, 2001) was invaluable. I quoted from a letter of 29 December 1988 from Leonard Hall to Phyllis Dodge, and the *Daily Mail* of Saturday, 25 August 1941.

Chapter 24 Göring's 'Escape Proof' Camp
Jimmy James' memoir of captivity (James, Bertrand Arthur, *Moonless Night*, Leo Cooper, 2001) was most useful for this chapter. I quote a brief reminiscence from the late Albert Patton Clark, the Senior American Officer in Stalag Luft III, whom I interviewed at the United States Air Force Academy, Colorado Springs, for a television documentary for the US Learning Channel.

Also, a quote from Alan Bryett interviewed in 2009 for the *Sunday Times Magazine*. Much use was made of Johnny's letters home from Stalag Luft III mainly, once more, to his mother, Flora, and his wife, Minerva (Jane Aitken Collection, Toronto).

Chapter 25 Polish Interlude
For this curious little episode, I depended upon several secondary sources including William Ash's *Under the Wire* written with Brendan Foley, the wartime memoir of a Spitfire pilot, legendary escape artist and 'cooler king' (Transworld Publishers, 2005) and Robert Kee's *A Crowd is Not Company* (Sphere Books Ltd., London, 1989). Jimmy James' memoir of captivity (James, Bertrand

445

Arthur, *Moonless Night*, Leo Cooper, 2001) was, as ever, useful, as was Sydney Smith's biography of Wings Day, *Wings Day: The Man Who Led the RAF's Epic Battle in German Captivity*, Collins, London, 1968. The first-hand material came from Johnny's letters home, courtesy of Jane Aitken (Jane Aitken Collection, Toronto).

Chapter 26 Tom, Dick and Harry
First-hand material for this chapter came from Johnny's letters home, courtesy of Jane Aitken (Jane Aitken Collection, Toronto). I also depended upon the same secondary sources noted above: William Ash's *Under the Wire*, Jimmy James' *Moonless Night* and Sydney Smith's *Wings Day: The Man Who Led the RAF's Epic Battle in German Captivity*, as well as Arthur Durand's *Stalag Luft III: The Secret Story* (Louisiana State University Press, 1988).

Chapter 27 Last Letters Home
Once more, first-hand material for this chapter came from Johnny's letters home, courtesy of Jane Aitken (Jane Aitken Collection, Toronto). I also depended upon the same secondary sources noted above, namely, William Ash's *Under the Wire*, Jimmy James' *Moonless Night* and Sydney Smith's *Wings Day*, and Arthur Durand's *Stalag Luft III: The Secret Story*.

Chapter 28 Per Ardua ad Astra
Much of the first-hand material for Chapter 28 was obtained from interviews with Albert Patton Clark at the United States Air Force Academy, Colorado Springs, in 2000, and over several years with BA

446

'Jimmy'. In addition Jimmy James' own memoir of captivity and escape was invaluable (James, Bertrand Arthur, *Moonless Night*, Leo Cooper, 2001). Sydney Smith's biography of Wings Day, *Wings Day: The Man Who Led the RAF's Epic Battle in German Captivity*, Collins, London, 1968 was equally useful. I used Phyllis B. Dodge's 'John Bigelow Dodge, 1894–1960, A Précis of his Life'. Johnny's last letters home were provided by Jane Aitken (Jane Aitken Collection, Toronto). Much of the information for this chapter was derived from Johnny's post-escape debriefing, at the hands of MI9. (Dodge, John Bigelow; intelligence debriefing post repatriation to England, April 1945; courtesy Alice Berkeley Collection, London).

Chapter 29 Death Postponed
Much of the information for this chapter was derived from Johnny's post-escape intelligence debriefing, at the hands of MI9. (Dodge, John Bigelow, intelligence debriefing post repatriation to England, April 1945; courtesy Alice Berkeley Collection, London.) Jimmy James' own memoir of captivity and escape was invaluable (James, Bertrand Arthur, *Moonless Night*, Leo Cooper, 2001). Sydney Smith's biography of Wings Day, *Wings Day: The Man Who Led the RAF's Epic Battle in German Captivity*, Collins, London, 1968 was equally useful. I used Phyllis B. Dodge's 'John Bigelow Dodge 1894–1960, A Précis of his Life'. I also consulted and used many excerpts from Peter Churchill's notes for his unpublished narrative, 'Escape from the SS' (Jane Aitken Collection, Toronto). The details of Wings Day's meeting with Anton Kaindl come from his own account in the

Royal Air Force Museum, Hendon.

Chapter 30 The Sachsenhausen Tunnel
The same sources as for Chapter 29 were used for this chapter. The details of the RAF memorial service for the murdered 50 were derived from the *Evening Standard*, London, of Tuesday, 20 June 1944.

Chapter 31 Escape from the SS
A small amount of the information for this chapter was derived from Johnny's post-escape intelligence debriefing, at the hands of MI9. (Dodge, John Bigelow, intelligence debriefing post repatriation to England, April 1945; courtesy Alice Berkeley Collection, London.) Jimmy James' own memoir of captivity and escape was invaluable (James, Bertrand Arthur, *Moonless Night*, Leo Cooper, 2001). Sydney Smith's biography of Wings Day, *Wings Day: The Man Who Led the RAF's Epic Battle in German Captivity*, Collins, London, 1968 was equally useful. I used Phyllis B. Dodge's 'John Bigelow Dodge, 1894–1960, A Précis of his Life'. I also consulted and used many excerpts from Peter Churchill's notes for his unpublished narrative, 'Escape from the SS', which I found in the Jane Aitken archive (Jane Aitken Collection, Toronto).

Chapter 32 Mission to Downing Street
A small amount of the information for this chapter was derived from Johnny's post-escape intelligence debriefing, at the hands of MI9. (Dodge, John Bigelow, intelligence debriefing post repatriation to England, April 1945; courtesy Alice Berkeley Collection, London.) For Hans Wilhem Thost's

version of events I consulted a translation in Jane Aitken's Toronto archive of the 1952 serialisation that Thost wrote for *Der Mittag* newspaper (*Der Mittag*, 1952, and Jane Aitken Collection, Toronto). Jimmy James' own memoir of captivity and escape was invaluable (James, Bertrand Arthur, *Moonless Night*, Leo Cooper, 2001). Sydney Smith's biography of Wings Day, *Wings Day: The Man Who Led the RAF's Epic Battle in German Captivity*, Collins, London, 1968 was equally useful. I used Phyllis B. Dodge's 'John Bigelow Dodge, 1894–1960, A Précis of his Life'. For information about Thost in pre-war England I consulted James and Patience Barnes's *Nazis in Pre-War London, 1930–39: The Fate and Role of German Party Members and British Sympathisers* (Sussex Academic Press, 2005).

Chapter 33 Berlin Days
The aftermath of the escape from Sachsenhausen is covered in all the relevant books, most notably Jimmy James' *Moonless Night* and Sydney Smith's *Wings Day*, and I have drawn upon that material. The new material is derived from Johnny's post-repatriation MI9 debriefing, and Hans Thost's own description of his adventures with Johnny as reproduced in 1952 in the now defunct Düsseldorf daily *Der Mittag*, a translation of which is contained in Jane Aitken's archive (Jane Aitken Collection, Toronto). Fortunately, as mentioned in the text, Johnny's recollections closely coincide with those of Thost. Thost would not have had access to Johnny's MI9 debrief so it is out of the question that he would have deliberately tailored his own version of events to match that of Johnny. If anything, Thost's

narrative does Johnny a disservice as it implies it was he who raised the possibility of returning to England, not Thost. This suggestion, as I have noted, had already been put to Sydney Dowse and he had turned it down as potentially treasonous.

Chapter 34 Travels with Dr Thost
The material in this chapter derives almost entirely from Johnny's post-repatriation MI9 debriefing, and Hans Thost's own description in *Der Mittag*, 1952, of his adventures with Johnny. The profusion of letters contained in Jane Aitken's collection from Germans, including Thost, to Johnny after the war seems to corroborate at the very least the general essence of both men's accounts.

Chapter 35 Home
The information for this chapter was derived from Election Poster (Jane Aitken Collection, Toronto). The *Daily Telegraph*, 20 July 1945 (Jane Aitken Collection, Toronto). *South Eastern Gazette*, 31 July 1945 (Jane Aitken Collection, Toronto). Letter: Leonard Hall to Phyllis Dodge, 29 December 1988 (Jane Aitken Collection, Toronto). Letter: Squadron Leader Gardham, Air Ministry to JBD, 7 October 1946 (Jane Aitken Collection, Toronto).

Letter: JBD to Squadron Leader Gardham, Air Ministry, October 1946 (Jane Aitken Collection, Toronto). Beverley Baxter's amusing article about his dinner with Johnny is excerpted from the *Cape Times* of Monday, 14 March 1955.

Chapter 36 Shadows and Fog
I made use of the following letters in Jane Aitken's Toronto archive: Dodge, JB to Flockhart, Squadron

Leader Bruce, letter dated 6 September 1945 (Jane Aitken Collection, Toronto). Dodge, JB to Flockhart, Squadron Leader B, letter dated 10 January 1946 (Jane Aitken Collection, Toronto). Rumpel, Theo to JBD, 21 November 1950 (Jane Aitken Collection, Toronto). Paeffgen, Erika to JBD, 12 November 1946 (Jane Aitken Collection, Toronto). Dörrfus, Heinz to JBD, 23 September 1947 (Jane Aitken Collection, Toronto). Risch, Pierre to JBD, 20 December 1946 (Jane Aitken Collection, Toronto). Schollmerer, Herbert, 27 October 1946 (Jane Aitken Collection, Toronto). Raffel, Hans-Peter, 5 March 1948 (Jane Aitken Collection, Toronto). Waleck, Margarethe Prinzessin zu to JBD, 30 January 1947 (Jane Aitken Collection, Toronto). Ach, Clifford to JBD, 20 July 1946 (Jane Aitken Collection, Toronto). Hedecke, Robert to JBD, 28 April 1947 (Jane Aitken Collection, Toronto). Arendt, Maria to JBD, 4 June 1947 (Jane Aitken Collection, Toronto). Alvensleben, Frau von to JBD, 26 January 1949 (Jane Aitken Collection, Toronto). JBD to British Control Commission February 17, 1949 (Jane Aitken Collection, Toronto). Schaumburg-Lippe, Prinzessin Stephan zu to JBD, 8 July 1947 (Jane Aitken Collection, Toronto). Kemmetex, Frau Kresz to JBD, 11 August 1947 (Jane Aitken Collection, Toronto). Schmidt, Dr Paul, 26 August 1950 (Jane Aitken Collection, Toronto).

The reference to Johnny's 'angelic' view of the world was from Smith, Sydney; *Wings Day: The Man Who Led the RAF's Epic Battle in German Captivity*, Collins, London, 1968, p. 81.

The details of the war crimes trial in which Hans Thost found himself embroiled came from:

Testimony of Dr Hans Wilhelm Thost attached to memo from Capt Wallace Wharton, Office of the Chief of Naval Operations to Capt J.J. Robinson, Navy Division (JAG) War Crimes Office, Sept. 22, 1946, RG153, 8–9, Box 116, NARA.

I used the following letters from Jane Aitken's Toronto archive: British Control Commision to JBD, 26 March 1946 (Jane Aitken Collection, Toronto). Thost, Hans to JBD, 19 February 1947 (Jane Aitken Collection, Toronto). Thost, Hans to JBD, 9 September 1947 (Jane Aitken Collection, Toronto). Thost, Hans to JBD, 30 September 1947 (Jane Aitken Collection, Toronto). JBD to Thost, Hans, 30 September 1947 (Jane Aitken Collection, Toronto). Thost, Hans to JBD, 19 October 1947 (Jane Aitken Collection, Toronto). Thost, Hans to Rickatson-Hatt, 23 November 1947 (Jane Aitken Collection, Toronto). Thost, Hans to JBD, 1 January 1948 (Jane Aitken Collection, Toronto). JBD to War Office, 9 January 1948 (Jane Aitken Collection, Toronto). Thost, Hans to JBD, 10 May 1948 (Jane Aitken Collection, Toronto). Thost, Hans to JBD, 29 August 1948 (Jane Aitken Collection, Toronto). Thost, Hans to JBD, 10 October 1952 (Jane Aitken Collection, Toronto).

Chapter 37 In Memoriam
Information for In Memoriam came from Dodge, Phyllis B, card index (card notations for potential Johnny Dodge biography compiled over several years before her death); Dodge, Phyllis B, Notes (unpublished notes for prospective biography accumulated over several years before her death); and Dodge, Phyllis B, 'John Bigelow Dodge, 1894–1960, A Précis of his Life'. Also, the full text of

Lord Freyberg's address at Johnny's memorial service on 11 November 1960, from a photocopy of the original address courtesy of the Alice Berkeley Collection, London.

Appendix I
Full text of Lord Freyberg's address at Johnny's memorial service on 11 November 1960. Photocopy of original address courtesy of the Alice Berkeley Collection, London.

Appendix II
The information for this Appendix was extracted mostly from the following sources: the *Trenton Times*, 6 November 1988; the *Daily News*, TV Week section, 6–12 November 1988; the *New York Times*, 7 November 1988; Notes, Dodge, Phyllis B., unpublished notes for prospective biography accumulated over several years; Paul Brickhill to Tony Dodge, Letter, 18 October 1988, courtesy Alice Berkeley (Alice Berkeley Collection, London).

Appendix III
The source of this information is the research of secondary and primary sources completed over the years by the author; see notes for preceding chapters.

Appendix IV
Edited extracts from Johnny's letters home while in captivity.

SELECT BIBLIOGRAPHY

Books

Ash, William, with Foley, Brendan, *Under the Wire: The Wartime Memoir of a Spitfire Pilot, Legendary Escape Artist and 'Cooler King'* (The Bantam Press, London, 2005).

Barnes, James J., and Barnes, Patience P., *Nazis in Pre-War London, 1930–39: The Fate and Role of German Party Members and British Sympathisers* (Sussex Academic Press, Eastbourne, 2005).

Brickhill, Paul, *The Great Escape* (Cassell Military Paperbacks, London, 2000).

Carter, John Franklin, *The Rectory Family* (Coward-McCann, New York, 1937).

Cave Brown, Anthony, *The Secret Servant: The Life of Stewart Menzies, Churchill's Spymaster* (Michael Joseph, London, 1988).

Chisholm, Anne, and Davie, Michael, *Beaverbrook: A Life* (Pimlico, London, 1992).

Crawley, Aidan, *Escape from Germany, 1939–45: Methods of Escape Used by RAF Airmen During the Second World War* (The Stationery Office, London, 2001).

Dodge, Phyllis B., *Tales of the Phelps-Dodge Family* (New York Historical Society, Princeton University Press, Princeton, 1987).

Durand, Arthur A., *Stalag Luft III: The Secret Story* (Louisiana State University Press, Baton Rouge, 1988).

Fry, James W., and McMillan, Thomas, *History of the Royal Naval Division* (Hutchinson & Co.,

London, 1919).

Gill, Anton, *The Great Escape* (Review, London, 2002).

Guest, Flora Bigelow, *The Jewelled Ball* (Cambridge Corporation, Montreal, 1908).

Holmes, Richard, *The Western Front* (BBC Books, London, 1999).

James, Bertrand Arthur, *Moonless Night* (Leo Cooper, Barnsley, 2001).

Jerrold, Douglas, *The Royal Naval Division* (Hutchinson & Co., London, 1927).

Jones, Nigel, *Rupert Brooke: Life, Death and Myth* (Richard Cohen Books, London, 1999).

Kee, Robert, *A Crowd Is Not Company* (Sphere Books Ltd., London, 1989).

Meyer, Karl, and Brysac, Shareen, *Tournament of Shadows: The Great Game and the Race for Empire in Asia* (Little, Brown and Company, London, 1999).

Sellers, Leonard, *The Hood Battalion* (Leo Cooper, Barnsley, 1995).

Smith, Sydney, *Wings Day: The Man Who Led the RAF's Epic Battle in German Captivity* (Collins, London, 1968).

Vance, Jonathan F., *A Gallant Company: The Men of the Great Escape* (Pacifica Military History, Pacifica, 2000).

Periodicals

Dodge, Lieutenant Colonel John Bigelow, DSO, DSC, 'Adventuring for Trade: Experiences among brigands and Bolsheviks in Persia and Asiatic Russia during a world journey for the study of commercial congestion and in search of business openings', *World's Work*, June 1922.

Ogden, Dennis, 'Britain and Soviet Georgia, 1921–22', *Journal of Contemporary History*, Vol. 23, 1988, pp. 245–258.

Opera News, Vol. 33, No. 11, 11 January 1969.

Spencer, Charles, 'Enemies of the Estate', *Vanity Fair*, No. 593, January 2010, pp. 134–146.

Unpublished Accounts

Churchill, Peter, 'Escape from the SS'. An unedited document found in the Jane Aitken Archive, Toronto.

Dodge, John Bigelow, Miscellaneous Narrative Relating to a Potential Book on his Travels Through China, India and Communist Russia. A collection of 30 or so typewritten pages, not in chronological order and uncertainly paginated, evidently written by JBD to form the basis of a book. (Jane Aitken Collection, Toronto.)

Dodge, John Bigelow, Opening Attack on Dardanelles. A typewritten account of the action which Johnny witnessed, undated. (Jane Aitken Collection, Toronto.)

Guest, Flora, Account of trip to continent starting 4 March, 1919, Jane Aitken Collection, Toronto.

Documents

Dodge, John Bigelow, MI9 intelligence debriefing report post repatriation to England, April 1945 (Alice Berkeley Archive). (There are several copies of this MI9 report in the National Archives, Kew, in various files including the general file containing MI9 debriefs, and the Imperial War Museum in the papers of Major G. Hamilton-Gay.)

MI5 file on Hans Thost, PRO, KV2/910-14

Research Material

Dodge, Phyllis B., card index (card notations for potential Johnny Dodge biography compiled over several years before her death).

Dodge, Phyllis B., Notes (unpublished notes for prospective biography accumulated over several years before her death).

Dodge, Phyllis B., 'John Bigelow Dodge, 1894–1960, A Précis of his Life' (unpublished précis of JBD's life, 1990).